D0706628

MYTHS
gods
&
fantasy

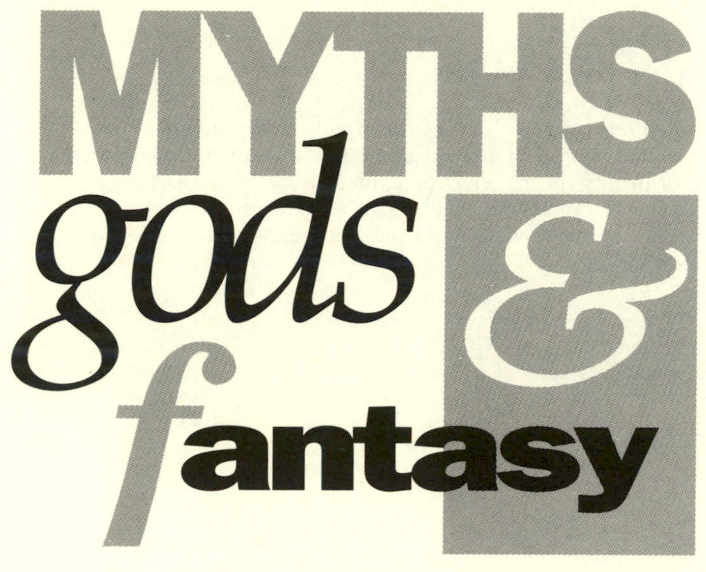

Pamela Allardice

ISBN 0-87436-660-7

98 97 96 95 94 93 92 91 10 9 8 7 6 5 4 3 2 1

First published in Great Britain in 1991
by Prism Press, 2 South Street,
Bridgport, Dorset DT6 3NQ

Published in the United States by
ABC-CLIO, Inc.
130 Cremona Drive, P.O. Box 1911
Santa Barbara, California 93116-1911

This book is printed on acid-free paper ∞
Manufactured in the United States of America

For Nevill

who had the idea in the first place

'. . . as imagination bodies forth

The forms of things unknown, the poet's pen

Turns them to shapes, and gives to airy nothing

A local habitation and a name.'

J.A. VINYCOMB *Fictitious and Symbolic Creatures in Art*

Preface

A dictionary such as this is very much overdue, and Pamela Allardice's *Myths, Gods and Fantasy* will be warmly received. After all, concise compilations of information on mythic and supernatural beings are relevant not only to students of comparative religion and the occult, but also to those seeking meanings for symbolic or esoteric references in literature, poetry, drama and folklore. It is ideal to have at one's fingertips a volume of interesting and entertaining material, succinctly and eloquently summarised.

How else would we know that a *lamas* is a benevolent or protective spirit, that Rakim was a Micronesian god who flew on a cloud and assumed a serpentine form, or that the Zulu god Unkulunku cracked a mighty whip across the sky when angered?

Pamela Allardice is to be congratulated for the excellent research she has undertaken in compiling this invaluable dictionary. With over 500 carefully selected entries, her book is a most welcome addition to the collections produced in earlier times by such noted folklorists as Katherine Briggs and Lewis Spence — works which are no longer easy to come by. It is also worth noting that the sheer range of subject matter covered in *Myths, Gods and Fantasy* is perhaps unparalleled in a compact reference work of this size. It is a book that will be read and re-read as an accessible source of pertinent information.

Nevill Drury

Introduction

Man has always found mystery irksome and, in pursuing his need to understand and catalogue natural phenomena, he has created a rich heritage of folklore, myth and superstition.

In particular, his curiosity about the boundaries of the visible world has given life to a host of marvellous beings of his own imagining which inhabit the edge of darkness. In every era and every land, stories of dazzling beasts, mighty gods and encounters with the spirit world have been passed from one awe-struck generation to another. Many such tales have been preserved in legends and folk-songs, or brought to life in the art, poetry and sculpture of the time.

We may smile at credulous folk of yore who petitioned:

> From ghoulies and ghosties
> And long-legged beasties
> And things that go bump in the night,
> Good Lord, deliver us!

However, few would dispute there is an eerie world close to ours, peopled with spirits who sometimes walk amongst us. An enormous variety of such apparitions exist, from headless queens and wandering monks to spectral dogs, houses and even boats.

The majority of ghostly tales echo some long-ago tragedy which resulted in an unhappy soul forever pacing the mists of time. Such shadows of the past include banshees and traditional shackled skeletons, along with bloodied battle heroes, forsaken women and children untimely dead.

Other accounts of experiences with the spirit world are not so easily explained. Ill-tempered poltergeists wantonly damage a suburban house, then disappear. Some spirits cling stubbornly to their last mortal remains, and object strongly if their resting place is disturbed. Still others seem to manifest as a function of powers vested long ago in sacred artefacts, or certain tracts of land and water.

The spirit world should not be feared, however. As long as we remember to treat its denizens with respect, the odds are in favour of our receiving similar courtesy in return. Unfortunately, this quite simple rule has been most often flouted by mortals prying into the fairy kingdom. While fairies are rarely malicious, nor are they the vapid race or 'painty-winged, wand-waving sugar-and-shake-your-head set of impostors' so despised by Kipling's Puck.

At the height of the fairies' power, in King Arthur's day, the 'Britons spoke with great honour [of] this land fulfilled of fayrie.' Although there are no longer so many idyllic green hiding places for them, Lewis Spence tells us that 'fairy music may often be heard at certain spots and, like the fairies themselves, be of exquisite beauty.'

So many different types of fairy have been recorded. Shakespeare says, in *The Merry Wives of Windsor:*

> fairies black, grey, green and white,
> moonshine revellers and shades of night.

And traditional folklore tells of dryads, elves, goblins, water sprites, leprechauns, spriggans and pixies, to name but a few.

Distinctions within the fairy world are often hazy, with the same species being given a variety of names according to where it is found, and different species blurring to become the same. Not only is the nomenclature variable, so are beliefs in fairy origins. One school of thought has it that fairies were ghosts or dispossessed spirits which were lost between Heaven and Hell. Dryden accordingly wrote of:

> All those airy shapes you now behold
> Were human bodies once . . .
> Not yet prepared for upper light
> Til Doomsday [they] wander in shades of night.

Another idea was that fairies were fallen angels or unbaptised children, though most pre-Christian beliefs saw fairies as elementals, or nature spirits, begotten by the gods who frequented lakes, trees and rocky outcrops.

This predilection for worshipping plants, birds, beasts and the universe itself occurred long before man thought of god in his own image. The environment was a thing of wonder and fabulous tales were contrived to explain the greatest puzzle of all — the creation of the world.

In the beginning, all was possible. Man worshipped horses, maggots, horned gods who lived under the sea and sun kings who oversaw harvest and tribe fertility. Our forefathers told of giants who chiselled the mountains into shape with enormous hammers, birds' eggs which hatched into different races and petulant gods flinging fire at each other across the heavens, thus creating deserts and volcanoes.

Many of the exotic creatures described in these creation myths and folk-tales bear little resemblance to accepted zoological lore. Egypt, in particular, had an extraordinary menagerie of divine animals, only to be matched later by the monsters found in medieval English bestiaries.

Some were frightful to see, notably dragons and other monsters who menaced people and ravaged their homes. To the Greeks, who ascribed to the ideal of an ordered universe, daemonic beings such as lamia, harpies and fire-breathing serpents represented the formidable powers of the irrational. Constant vigilance and struggle were required to keep the balance in favour of their disciplined, scholarly culture.

Other mythical beasts were beautiful and noble, fabulous creatures of heraldry which represented man's finer qualities, such as the unicorn and the phoenix. Certainly, many medieval species represented the simplified moral teachings of the church, demonstrating good vanquishing evil at every opportunity. Envious of flight, man often endowed these creatures with wings, a characteristic later adopted as representing spiritual aspiration. Still other beasts discussed in this book were clearly the result of travellers' tales and referred to actual animals which may now be lost to us.

Perhaps more of these fabulous beasts would still be nearby if they had been given sanctuary or, at the very least, if their powers had been afforded respect. They have now fled into their own world, where mortal hunters cannot find them. There, no doubt, they rub shoulders with the other denizens of the supernatural, who were once believed to be absolutely real. Who are we, in an age of uncertainty, to say they are any less powerful than they once were? The question should not be whether strange kingdoms are with us now, but whether we have eyes to see and ears to hear — Lewis Carroll's Alice has the last word on the matter:

> Alice could not help her lip curling as she began: 'Do you know, I always thought unicorns were fabulous monsters? I never saw one alive before!'
>
> 'Well, now we have seen each other,' said the unicorn, 'if you'll believe in me, I'll believe in you. Is that a bargain?'

A

Abbey Lubbers From the fifteenth century onwards, it was generally believed that monks had become lazy and corrupt, preferring drunken revelry to sober prayers. Such monks were said to be tempted by Abbey Lubbers, the GHOSTS of greedy or drunken friars who haunted monastery cellars. The only way to banish an Abbey Lubber was for the Prior to confront him and demand in full view of the other monks that he leave — in short, to publicly repent. Friar Rush was a well-known Abbey Lubber in England. Banished for his misdeed, the other shocked monks reformed and took to virtuous living when he had gone.

Abrasax A demon-beast first referred to in Persian mythology and described as a cross between a two-legged DRAGON and a serpent, with the head of a cockerel, wielding a whip over his subjects' heads. The name means 'supreme being' and, in Greek notation, the sum of the letters is the mystic number 365. Thus Abrasax was believed to be the Lord of the 365 Virtues, one of which is supposed to prevail on each day of the year. His name gave rise to the magical word Abracadabra, which according to Samonicus was:

> A powerful weapon against ague, flux and toothache when written on parchment and suspended around the neck by [a] linen thread.

Achilles Also known as Achilleus, he was one of the greatest of the Greek kings and enjoyed divine status, being born of a mortal and the sea-nymph Thetis (*see* NEREIDES). The hero of Homer's epic poem *The Iliad*, Achilles was an invincible warrior portrayed as being brave and relentless, albeit with a violent temper. Homer wrote of this 'great wrath of Peleus' son' when

Achilles quarrelled with Agamemnon over the maiden Briseis. As a consequence, his friend Patrolocus was slain, and a furious Achilles rushed across the battlefield to kill the culprit, Hector. Tying the grisly corpse behind his chariot, he galloped three times around the walls of Troy to demonstrate the grim fate of his enemy.

According to a favourite post-Homeric legend, his mother Thetis sought to make Achilles immortal by dipping all his body — save his heel, which she clasped — into the subterranean River Styx. It was a poisoned arrow shot by Paris (or APOLLO disguised as Paris) into this one vulnerable point which killed Achilles. Hence, the strong tendon running from the heel to the calf of the leg is known as the 'Achilles heel'.

Actaeon In Greek mythology, Actaeon was thought to have been sired by Autonoe and her husband, Aristaeus, and raised by the great centaur CHIRON, though popular legend has it that he was the son of PAN. The latter theory is more likely, for this wanton demi-god took great delight in drinking ambrosia and other earthly delights. He also grew to become a fine huntsman. His lecherous gaze was his downfall and, when he chanced upon ARTEMIS and her NYMPHS as they bathed, this ruthless goddess of chastity changed Actaeon into a stag and set his own dogs to tear him to pieces. In his *Merry Wives of Windsor* Shakespeare was later to use the name Actaeon as a simile for cuckold, or fool, thus:

> Go thou, like . . . Actaeon, with Ringwood at thy heel . . . divulge Page himself for a . . . wilful Actaeon.

Adonis The name derives from the Canaanite title *adon* (lord). Adonis was an extremely handsome boy-god, beloved by APHRODITE. He was also a Phoenician god of vegetation, and thought to have been born of the myrrh tree. In the Bible he was called Tammuz and his cult was darkly referred to by Milton as the 'idolatries of alienated Judah'. As PERSEPHONE was also enamoured of him ZEUS decreed that Adonis should spend half his life in the Upper World and the other half in the

Underworld. His death each autumn and re-birth each spring were commemorated at annual festivals of a mystic cult of women, who decked silver statues of the three with purple ribbons and floral garlands. Part of these ceremonies survive in the Greek allusion to 'Adonis gardens', which usually comprise fennel and lettuce planted in terracotta pots, their rapid flowering and withering symbolising the brief life and death of the boy-god. Adonis was killed by a wild boar while hunting with Aphrodite and, according to romantic fable, a blood-red rose sprang from his spilled blood. Shakespeare wrote:

> . . . no flower was nigh, no grass, leaf, herb or weed — but stole his blood and with him to bleed.

Aeolus Aeolus was once the son of POSEIDON, Lord of the Ocean, and a mortal princess. He grew to be a fine seaman, inventing the sail to harness winds and drive his ships, rather than oars. His father rewarded Aeolus for his invention and successful sea-faring adventures by granting him immortality and, as a god, Aeolus came to live on the island of Lipara off the coast of Sicily. There he kept all the winds of the world chained in a cave — Zephyrus the West Wind, Eurus the East Wind, Boreas the North Wind, and Notus the South Wind — releasing them in turn to create different weather patterns. It used to be that sailors could petition Aeolus for favourable winds, and unscrupulous crones sold warm trade winds for sixpence in the Orkney Islands as recently as 1903. This custom harks back to the time when Odysseus requested a bull's hide in which Aeolus had tied all the contrary and dangerous winds. Unfortunately his curious crew opened the bag and the winds were unleashed, destroying the boat. The gods bestowed another gift upon Aeolus — a talent for music. Thus the Aeolian Harp bears his name. It is a box on which fine strings are stretched, and when placed near a breeze the harp 'sings' without human intervention.

Aesculapius A god of healing, whose methods were first recorded in Rome in the third century BC in Rome, during a plague; also known as Asclepius and Asklepios. Although in Homer's *The Iliad* he is described as a mortal who was taught the healing arts by CHIRON, king of the CENTAURS, other sources claim he was the son of the god APOLLO and the NYMPH Coronis. In his capacity as all-healer he was one of the most popular gods of the early Roman Empire. Sacrifices were customarily offered to Aesculapius after recovering from an illness, and many temples were erected in his honour. Socrates' last words were a lament that he 'owed a cock to Aesculapius'.

The Emperor Marcus Aurelius, believing imitation to be the most sincere form of flattery, had his portrait sculpted in the likeness of Aesculapius, as a bearded man bearing a staff around which a serpent is entwined. Ever since, this staff (or caduceus) has been the emblem of the medical profession, and Aesculapius' name was given to the first college of medicine, the Aesclepiadae.

Unfortunately Aesculapius was so successful in curing human ills that ZEUS, fearing he would create a new race of immortals, killed him with a thunderbolt. His two daughters, however, continued their father's great work, Hygeia being the goddess of good health and hygiene, and Panacea an auxiliary goddess who was associated with healing and pain relief.

Aesir The collective name for the first gods in Norse mythology, also known as the Creators of the Cosmos. They included the twelve gods and goddesses worshipped in Scandinavia. The gods were ODIN, THOR, Baldur, Niord, Frey, TYR, Bragi, Heimdall, Vidar, Valli, Ullur and Forseti. The four main goddesses were Frigga, FREYA, Iduna and Saga. The father of them all was the giant, YMIR, who gave birth to them from his armpit as he slept. His son Odin became the chief of the Aesir, who directed the construction of the Cosmos using Ymir's body as raw material — his blood becoming the salty sea, his hair the trees and his flesh the earth. His skull was placed in the heavens, where one eye became the sun and the other the moon. When the god BALDER was slain by the evil LOKI, the Aesir swore revenge and waged war on heaven and earth. They were eventually overthrown by the Frost Giants on the Day of Doom, the Ragnarok. However, they achieved immortality through the final act of Odin. He created the first man and woman in the image of the gods, from two dead trees, and this couple survived the cataclysm.

Afanc A water beast, variously described as a giant beaver or crocodile, said to inhabit the River Conway in Wales. Other witnesses have described the afanc as being like a CENTAUR, and maintain that a colony of them was driven from the water and live in caves in the mountains. Whatever its appearance, the afanc is feared by the locals for its habit of dragging men and beasts to a watery grave. The term 'Llyn yr Afanc' is still used to describe the whirlpools and eddies which signal the beast's presence below the water's surface.

Rather like the UNICORN, the afanc could only be captured through a maiden's treachery, for it would leave the water to lay its head in a virgin's lap. Then hunters could bind it and drag it away with a team of oxen to be killed. The enormous claws from the afanc's hind legs were especially prized trophies, being hung over barn doors as a talisman against theft or illness.

Afrit The Arabian afrit is the ghostly spirit of a murder victim. One is said to rise from each drop of blood shed by that person. The afrits then set about tormenting the aggressor, hoping to bring them to an untimely end also. Afrits are WRAITH-like in appearance, resembling wisps of smoke, though their terrified prey can clearly see their glittering, ruby-red eyes and some who have lived to tell of their ordeal swear these spirits carry pistols. The only way to arrest their grim progress is to drive a new nail into each bloodstain, thus pinning each afrit to the ground.

Ahkiyyinni The name of an Eskimo fisherman, now immortalised in folklore. During his life, Ahkiyyinni loved to dance, and he let the fish swim free while his neighbours criticised him for his levity. When he died, his bones were interred by the water, so his spirit could gaze upon the river he loved. One day a boatload of his neighbours came to Ahkiyyinni's stretch of water and began to strip it of fish. The angered spirit became visible, but the men refused to leave — one even leant out of the boat and mocked him, saying: 'Why not dance now, Ahkiyyinni? Why not dance now?' To this taunt, the spirit ordered its mouldering skeleton to burst from the earth and, beating its shoulder blade like a drum, frightened the fishermen so their boat overturned and they all drowned.

Ahpuch The Mayan god who ruled the silent kingdom of the dead. He was thought to ride the skies during times of pestilence, his terrible black eyes seeking and claiming victims as he went. Ahpuch was usually depicted as a powerfully built man with a hollow skull instead of a head, and his appearance was heralded by inextinguishable fires, comets and strange bird-cries. He could be temporarily appeased by extravagant gifts and was known to enjoy wearing the flayed skins of young warriors; however, he would inevitably return to claim the newly dead.

Albatross These huge sea-birds are called the Cape Sheep for their habit of frequenting the Cape of Good Hope. An albatross is said to sleep in the air, because its flight is a gliding without any apparent motion of its long wings. Its grace and confidence in riding the winds above the roughest seas has led sailors to believe this bird is favoured by the spirits of sea and air. Therefore ill-fortune befalls a sailor who shoots an albatross, and Coleridge's *Ancient Mariner* is based on this superstition. The bird may only be avenged by tying its carcass around the offender's neck and lashing him to the mast. There he must stay as monstrous spirits, such as Life-in-Death, play dice for the souls of the crew:

> Her lips were red, her looks were free
> Her locks were yellow as gold;
> Her skin was white as leprosy
> The nightmare Life-in-Death was she,
> Who thicks man's blood with cold.

Amalthea The eldest daughter of Melisseus, the King of Crete. She appeared as a goat to suckle the infant ZEUS with her milk when he was hiding from his murderous father, CRONUS. In gratitude Zeus broke off one of her horns and gave it to the royal family, promising that the possessor would always find it filled with whatever food or drink was desired. This horn became known as the Cornucopia, or Horn of Plenty. Amalthea was then placed in the heavens, where she appears as the constellation Capricorn.

Ama-terasu The sun-goddess Ama-terasu was the most important deity in Japanese mythology. She was born from the left eye of the first god, IZANAGI, while her brothers Tsuki-Yomi, god of the moon, and Sus-no-o, god of the sea and storms, were born of his right eye and nose, respectively. Frightened by her belligerent brothers, Ama-terasu hid herself in a cave and blocked the entrance with a stone, thus plunging the earth into blackness. The other gods enticed her to come out by festooning the entrance with jewelled mirrors and torches, then staging a dancing play. Ama-terasu, intrigued by the lights, and the sounds of laughter and jest, emerged from her cave. So as to avoid a recurrence, the deities arranged for Tsuki-Yomi and Sus-no-o to have their beards clipped and their finger and toe-nails removed, curtailing their powers to wreak havoc on earth again.

Ama-terasu is thought to have sent the youngest of her eight nephews, Ninigi, to earth to rule as the first Emperor of Japan. Her gifts to him included the sword Kusanagi, which has a blade made from the tail of an eight-headed snake, and still forms part of the Imperial Family's emblem.

Amazons According to Greek mythology, a race of women who were originally the offspring of ARTEMIS and her lover, ARES. Some said they lived in South America, and the Spaniards recorded instances of women joining their menfolk in attacking the Conquistadores; however, more evidence points to their living by the Turkish Black Sea.

A warlike matriarchy, the Amazons worshipped the moon. They provided for their continuance by meeting once a year with a neighbouring tribe, the Gargareans. Any boy children born of such unions were killed, while girls had their right breast removed at puberty, so as not to impede drawing a bow-string in battle — *a* (without), and *mazos* (a breast). Despite this deformity, Amazon women were tall, lithe and exceptionally beautiful, as well as being formidable warriors.

In Homer's *The Iliad* the Amazons fought BELLEROPHON and Priam, though they were finally bested by HERCULES, whose ninth labour was to seize the golden girdle worn by the Amazon Queen, Hippolyta.

Amphisbaena Referred to by Dante as 'amfisibena', this was a snake with a head at both ends. The poet Nicander describes it thus:

> . . . slow in motion, two-headed, always dull of eye. From either end protrudes a blunt chin; each is far from the other.

They were known to be aggressive and poisonous, and said to have fed on corpses of soldiers from Cato's army who fell when marching through Libya. Prophetesses and women of high rank wore gold bracelets carved in the likenesses of an amphisbaena to signify their power. More recently, this snake was believed by Milton to be one of the forms assumed by Satan's helpers in Hell:

> Dreadful was the din
> Of hissing through the hall, thick swarming now
> With complicated monsters, heads and tails,
> Scorpion and Asp, and Amphisbaena dire. . .
>
> *Paradise Lost*

Amun Variously referred to as Amen, Amon and Ammon, this was the Egyptian sky god, usually depicted with a human body and a ram's head with two large horns, or plumes, and bearing a disc to represent the sun. Amun had a famous oracle at the Temple of Siwa in Libya, and the acid derived from the dung of his sacred camels tethered there was first named 'ammonia' and used in divination.

Rather than fight him for supremacy, Amun was later incorporated with his rival, the sun god RA, as Amon-Ra, and was well-loved as the most generous and munificent deity and the Creator of the Universe. Alexander the Great claimed to be a descendant of Zeus-Amon, in much the same way as the Pharaohs claimed to be the progeny of Amon-Ra.

Ananta Also known as Sesha, or the Endless, this is the prodigious, thousand-headed serpent of Hindu mythology. VISHNU, the god of life, sleeps on Ananta's back as it floats in a sea of milk which represents all manifestations of the primeval essence.

Ananta's periods of quiescence only occur between the Cycles of Creation, during the Night of Brahma when the Lord of Creation sleeps. Every hundred years, BRAHMA is re-born on a lotus stem growing from Vishnu's navel, and climbs upon the mighty GARUDA bird to fly the skies. At the close of another hundred years (of which each day exceeds 43 million of our mortal years), Ananta vomits fire which destroys all creation. The mighty snake-god was famed for creating the elixir of immortality, amrita, which it did by churning the ocean into a frenzy with its tail.

Angakok An Eskimo magician or SHAMAN. He or she is possessed by the spirit of the tribe's totem animal — such as a walrus or deer — and has the power to communicate with all other spirits. The angakok's prime responsibility is to safeguard the tribe from pestilence and bad weather; this is achieved by conversing with ancestral GHOSTS and making the appropriate propitiations to them to assuage any anger they may have for their descendants. Should the angakok be unsuccessful, he is banished for a period of time and his igloo packed with ice and sealed. Then he is told to visit the sea-goddess who dwells beneath the waves, and only to return when he has received her advice.

Angiak In Eskimo lore, this was a 'child of the living dead'. During harsh times, an unwanted baby was taken out into the snow by the tribal elders and left to die of exposure. Unless the tribe moved on to another hunting ground, they could expect to be haunted by the small, miserable GHOST. It would return to suckle at its mother's breast each night, thus strengthening itself to wreak revenge on the elders. The only way to avoid creating an angiak was to forego naming the poor mite before it was killed, for only by acquiring a name did a human being gain a spirit.

Ankou Also known as 'the graveyard watcher', the ankou guards cemeteries throughout Europe. In olden times, whenever a new graveyard was established it was customary to bury some poor soul alive in an unmarked grave in the northernmost corner. This ghostly guardian would then frighten grave-robbers and witches away from the newer graves. Stepping over such a plot would result in a 'shiver down the spine'.

In Brittany the ankou is not confined to its churchyard, being often seen travelling in a carriage, drawn by a pale grey mare, at twilight. His head is cowled and neither the wheels of the carriage nor the horse's hooves make any sound. An observer will shrink from the sight, for it is a sure death omen.

Antaeus In Greek mythology, the son of POSEIDON and the Earth Mother, GAEA. He became a gigantic wrestler whose strength was invincible — as long as he could touch the earth:

> As once Antaeus, on the Libyan strand
> More fierce recovered when he touched the sand.
>
> HOOLE *Ariosto*

Antaeus lived in a house built from the skulls of his victims and forced all who passed by to wrestle with him. It was HERCULES who eventually killed him, holding him aloft so he could not draw strength from his mother the earth, as described by Erasmus Darwin in his *Economy of Vegetation* (1791):

He lifts proud Antaeus from his mother's plains
And with strong grasp the struggling giant strains;
Back falls his panting head and clammy hair,
Writhe his weak limbs and flits his life in air.

Antelope A creature of myth and heraldry which differs from its modern cousin in possessing a head like a tiger, two serrated horns and tufts of soft fur growing down its spine and on its thighs. Its nature, too, was markedly different from the gently grazing creature of today; in *The Faerie Queene*, Spenser describes them as ferocious brutes to be subdued by the lusty Sir Satyrane:

Wild beasts in iron yokes he would compel;
. . . the antelope and wolf, both fierce and fell . . .

Anubis The jackal-headed god of the dead in ancient Egypt. Son of Set, the god of evil, and Nepthys, the goddess of the Underworld, he was charged with guarding cemeteries and escorting the souls of the dead to stand before OSIRIS, the judge of the afterlife.

Also known as Lord of the Cave Mouth, Anubis came to be identified with HERMES of Greece, and they were both thought to weigh the heart and soul of new arrivals on special scales which indicated whether they were worthy of immortality. If they were not deemed so, they were summarily eaten by the monster Ammit, a creature with the body of a lion, head of a hippopotamus and fierce jaws like a crocodile's.

Anubis was also the patron of the holy ritual of embalming, and thought to be responsible for the transfiguration of the mummified deity in the afterlife. One of his early achievements was to bring the slain Osiris back to life.

Aphrodite The Greek goddess of beauty, fertility and love, Aphrodite differed from her Roman counterpart, Venus, by patronising all ties of affection which bind men together, as well as sexual congress. She was so named because she sprang from the sea foam, or *aphos*. Her lusty behaviour may be explained by the nature of her birth, for, the posthumous daughter of CRONUS, she was born of her father's castrated phallus. Also known as Dione, Erasmus Darwin described the goddess thus in his *Economy of Vegetation* (1791):

> So young Dione, nursed beneath the waves,
> And rocked by Nereids in their coral caves . . .
> Lisped her sweet tones and tried her tender smiles . . .

Aphrodite was awarded the golden apple inscribed 'For the Fairest' by Paris, and her reward for this compliment was to give him the love of Helen of Troy — thus precipitating the Trojan War. She possessed a magic girdle which made her irresistible to gods and men, and much-disliked by the rest of the goddesses. The unfaithful wife of the ugly HEPHAESTUS, Aphrodite was the lover of ARES, god of war, and the beautiful ADONIS. Amongst her many children was the mischievous EROS and his twin, Anteros, who was the god of unrequited love. Aphrodite's sacred symbol was the dove, a device featuring on many of her temples, which were also centres for ritual prostitution.

Apis Also known as Hap or Hapi, this was the sacred bull of Ptah in Egyptian mythology. Originally a symbol of fertility, it came to be regarded as the god OSIRIS incarnate, recognisable by its black hide, a knot like a beetle under its tongue, a white triangular mark on its forehead, and the figure of a half-moon on its left side. The beast was believed to be a holy oracle and to foretell the future. Each honorary bull was not suffered to live more than twenty-five years, when it was ceremonially drowned in the Nile and mummified. The madness of the great Cambyses was said to have resulted from his killing of a sacred bull.

Apollo Twin brother of ARTEMIS, the virgin Greek goddess of the hunt, Apollo was one of the greatest of the Olympian gods, with a variety of functions. A model of manly beauty, he was the god of sun and light, an attribute referred to by Shakespeare in *A Winter's Tale*:

> Apollo's angry and the heavens themselves
> Do strike at my injustice.

He was also a patron of the intellect and the arts, a great healer, prophet and musician, being credited with the invention of both the flute and the lyre. Shepherds worshipped Apollo, for he was believed to keep wolves away from livestock. At birth, the god is reported as having said:

> Dear to me shall be the lyre and the bow and in oracles I shall reveal to men the inexorable will of Zeus.

His most celebrated shrine is at Delphi, where he slew the dragon PYTHON only a few days after his birth.

Apollo is often symbolised in art by a laurel tree, in memory of his lover Daphne, whom he turned into a laurel. Amongst his many lovers were the mortal Cassandra, whom he cursed with a gift for making prophecies which no-one would believe; Coronis, who bore his son AESCULAPIUS, and the unfortunate Cumaean Sibyl. The latter angered Apollo when she asked him to let her live as many years as she could hold grains of sand in her palm. He retaliated by allowing this but denying her eternal youth, so she grew painfully aged and longed for death.

Apple Tree Man According to Somerset folklore, towards the end of the apple season the spirit of the oldest tree in any apple orchard assumes the shape of an old man with gnarled, twig-like fingers. The last apple of each crop should be left under this tree as a gift for him when the harvest is complete.

Ares The son of ZEUS and HERA, Ares was the Greek god of war. He was generally disliked, having inherited his mother's temper and his father's relish for a quarrel. Like many bullies, Ares was a coward and fled to Zeus for protection when he was wounded. In fact, his cry on that occasion was said to equal the roar of 10,000 lions in pain. The only immortals who enjoyed his company were his sister, Eris the goddess of discord, and the lovely APHRODITE, who bore him three children, including Phobus (fear) and Deimus (terror). This affair also produced one of the greatest scandals on Mount Olympus, when Aphrodite's cuckolded husband HEPHAESTUS surprised the couple together and trapped them in a fine bronze net, so the other gods could laugh at the bawdy spectacle.

Some sources claim that the formidable AMAZONS were Ares' daughters. The Romans adopted Ares and re-named him MARS, making him the Protector of Rome as well as the god of war. March, the first month of the Roman year, was named for him.

Argos Also known as Argus, this was a giant of Greek mythology. With over one hundred eyes scattered over his body he was entrusted by HERA to watch over Io, one of ZEUS' many mistresses who had been transformed into a white heifer to avoid Hera's wrath. Argos was the ideal guardian for, as his eyes only slept in shifts, he was constantly watchful. The beast was finally tricked by HERMES, who lulled it to sleep with sweet music before killing it and liberating Io to be reunited with Zeus. So incensed was Hera that she killed Hermes and transplanted Argos' eyes into the tail of her peacock. There, to this day, they appear as ever-open orbs which miss nothing.

Ariadne Originally a Cretan goddess of vegetation, Ariadne was the daughter of Minos and her name means 'she who shines in splendour'. She fell in love with Theseus, the warrior who came to her father's palace to slay the MINOTAUR. When Theseus entered the Labyrinth, Ariadne gave him a ball of magic twine to help him find his way out again. The ungrateful Theseus abandoned Ariadne as she slept on the beach at Naxos, and Byron described her plight:

> . . . leaning upon her sad knee
> this Adriatic Ariadne.

Ariadne later wed the god of wine, DIONYSIUS. On her marriage, ZEUS gave her a marvellous crown of diamonds, which she set as a constellation in the heavens (Corona Borealis) to show her whereabouts to her first love, the recalcitrant Theseus.

Ariel The enchanting 'airy spirit' created by Shakespeare in his play *The Tempest*. Coleridge described him thus:

> In air he lives, from air he derives his being, in air he acts; and all his colours and properties seem to have been obtained from the rainbow and the skies.

Ariel inhabited the Island of Prospero and led a band of nature-spirits. He was imprisoned by the witch Sycorax and her retarded son Caliban in the trunk of a tree as a punishment when he refused to join her coven. When he was released by Prospero, Ariel became his loyal servant, though he also proceeded to tease and terrify his pursuers, first appearing as a HARPY, then causing an enormous tempest, then taking on the powers of flame:

> I flames amazement; sometimes I'd divide
> And burn in many places; on the top-mast,
> The yards and bowsprit would I flame distinctly
> Then meet and join . . .

Artemis The daughter of ZEUS and the twin sister of APOLLO, Artemis was the Greek goddess of the hunt and also emblematic of chastity. As soon as she was born, she demanded a golden bow and quiver of arrows from her father and is always depicted as accompanied by game, such as lions, deer and birds. She appeared with her attendant NYMPHS at the time of the full moon and exerted enormous influence over agriculture and the fertility of all animals, including man. Artemis was particularly associated with childbirth (having assisted her mother with the delivery of Apollo a few minutes after her own birth) and with the protection of newly born baby animals. One of the reasons why she sent a fierce wind to plague Agamemnon was that he had killed a pregnant hare.

Wild blood-sacrifices often attended worship of Artemis. Homer tells us that blood was taken from the throats of male victims by female dancers dressed in bear skins, and used in fertility rituals. Artemis' wrath was terrible. Despite her association with fertility, she forswore sex following the demise of her true love, ORION, and forbade her nymphs the same pleasure. When one of them, Callisto, was willingly seduced by Zeus, Artemis turned her into a she-bear and hunted her with spears.

Ashur Also known as Assur and Asshur, this was the name given to the god of war in ancient Assyria. He was eventually promoted to the rank of national god, and controller of fertility. His epithets Great Mountain and Father of the Gods indicate the esteem with which he was regarded. In art, he was portrayed as a winged disc enclosing a stretched bow ready to shoot an arrow. Ashur's consort was ISHTAR — in an ill-tempered moment the god likened her warlike temperament to his own and cursed her with a beard which grew to her breasts rapidly each time it was cut.

Asparas These fairies are known to the Hindus as sky-dancers who bless man kindly at the important staging posts of life. They will often be seen at weddings and appear to those dying on a battlefield as beautiful courtesans, offering delight rather than fear in the world to come. Asparas are believed to live in fig trees, a fruit widely regarded as a fertility symbol. Rarely, they use their seductive charms to exhaust mortal scholars and scientists, thus ensuring men do not venture into areas of knowledge which the spirit world deems unfit for human eyes — the scholars will become mad as a result.

Asrai Small and delicate water fairies who live at the bottom of deep lakes. They are very beautiful, with long green hair and webbed feet, and are many centuries old. Extremely shy, asrai will only come to the surface to gaze at the moon once every hundred years and they melt away in a pool of water once captured, or exposed to sunlight.

Astarte The goddess of the moon in Syrian and Phoenician mythology, Astarte controlled love and fecundity. In the Bible, she was called the Queen of Heaven by Jeremiah, and she was also known as the Lady of the Mountain for her temple was built atop Mount Saphon. Milton in *Paradise Lost* refers to:

> . . . moon'd Ashtaroth
> Heaven's Queen and mother both . . .

She was often depicted naked and standing in a crescent moon or wearing one as a head-dress. Her cult was marked by many excesses, notably temple prostitution, and she was strongly likened to both APHRODITE and Venus in her sexual predilections.

In spite of constant references to Astarte as a 'gentle maiden', she was also temperamental. With the epithet Mistress of Horses and Chariots she waded in the blood of human victims as the Philistine goddess of war, lustily slaying all enemies with a silver battle-axe and shocking others with her garb, which featured a freshly severed bull's head atop her own.

Ate The Greek goddess of disaster, Ate personified blind folly and infatuation, dealing out all the sudden impulses which often lead men to ruin. One of ZEUS' many offspring, she usually managed to avoid the gods' wrath for, being fleet of foot, she would out-run them before they could chastise her. However, when she caused a great quarrel between Agamemnon and ACHILLES, Ate took refuge amongst men and proceeded to wreak havoc with their lives, a talent wryly referred to by Shakespeare in *Julius Caesar*:

> With Ate by his side come hot from hell
> . . . cry 'havoc!' and let slip the dogs of war.

Athach A general name used in Scotland to describe monsters who haunt lonely lochs or valleys in the Highlands. Most usually they are giant creatures, including the one-legged and one-eyed FACHAN and the Rag, a female wanton who seduces lone shepherds and then claws them to pieces.

Athene A warlike virgin, Athene was the tutelary protectress of Athens and the goddess of wisdom. She sprang fully formed, and dressed in battle regalia, from the forehead of ZEUS. Also known as the Owl-Eyed One, both the owl and the olive tree are sacred to her. A warrior goddess, Athene was charged with carrying the terrible aegis — the head of the Medusa — upon her shield when she led troops into battle. She despised violence for its own sake, as practised by ARES, and preferred the boldness of wisdom. Athene was also the patroness of craftsmen, having invented the plough and the loom.

A well-known fable involves Athene being challenged by the mortal weaver, Arachne, to create a most beautiful tapestry. Angered by the girl's superb work, Athene changed her into a spider, cursing her and her descendants to weave endlessly forever more.

Atlas Son of the Titan Iapetus and Clymene, Atlas waged war against ZEUS and lost. As punishment he was sentenced to carry the weight of heaven on his mighty shoulders. He was doubly unlucky, for he received a chance to shed his burden when HERCULES, wanting Atlas to fetch him the Golden Apples of HESPERIDES, temporarily assumed the weight. Relishing his freedom, Atlas refused to return until Hercules tricked him, asking him to hold the world for just a moment while he fashioned a pad for his shoulders.

Atlas was later turned to stone by PERSEUS, who showed him the head of a gorgon, and he became the range of Atlas mountains in Africa, poetically referred to by James Thomson in *Autumn* thus:

> But Atlas, propping heaven, as poets feign
> His subterranean wonders spread . . .

The first map of the world was called an 'atlas' by the publisher Mercator, who used as a frontispiece an illustration of the god bearing the world on his back.

Aughisky An Irish fairy beast, usually taking the form of a long-haired young horse who frequents salt-water lochs and streams. The aughisky preys on cattle, herding them into the water to drown and then eat them. They are most savage just before Christmas when the lochs freeze over, emerging to gallop by the water's edge. If a man can capture an aughisky, saddle and bridle it and turn it inland, he will possess a fine, strong horse; if, however, the creature is allowed scent or sight of sea water, the rider is lost, for it will gallop wildly deep beneath the waves, there to devour its rider, leaving only the liver to float to shore several days later.

Awona-wilona The Pueblo Indians of New Mexico worshipped this hermaphroditic deity. Half-man, half-woman, the god's name may be translated as 'all container', an apt reference to its four wombs from which sprang the sun, sea, earth and sky. Having given birth to the elements of the universe, Awona-wilona set about producing the animals, birds, insects and reptiles to inhabit the earth. The god's consummate act was to create Poshaiyangko, the wisest of men, who taught the first creatures how to adapt to their new world outside the four wombs and to live in harmony with each other. This was not an easy task, and the first men cowered with terror when they saw the sun rise. Those who did not wish to learn the ways of Poshaiyangko were struck down, only to crawl forth as cripples or idiots, and descended to earth on fine silver filaments.

B

Baal It was among the Phoenicians that the great god Baal originated. Literally meaning 'lord', he was the god of storms and rain, and also of fecundity. Baal battled the spirits of the seas and trees for supremacy, emerging as their master and controller of the tides, seasons and resultant crops. At one time, he even dominated Mot, the surly god of death, and banished him to exile in the desert. Baal was typically depicted wearing a conical cap, decorated with a red band and bull's horns. He was said to mate with cows when strengthening himself for battle. Trapped by drought, he was eventually bested by Mot, who ripped the weakened god to pieces with a sharp knife and scattered pieces of his body 'with a winnowing fan' before scorching and grinding the remains to a powder.

Baal's name was latterly adopted as a title of honour, both by other gods and mortal kings and leaders, such as Hanni-bal.

Ba-Bird One of the forms assumed by OSIRIS, the Egyptian god of creation who was exiled to the Underworld by HORUS the falcon. Although his body never left the dark realm, the ba-bird's soul wandered daily amongst men and was often seen perched on the steps of the temple near the busy market-place, the better to observe mankind's activities. Its feathers were turquoise and tipped with crimson, and towards sunset each day its beaked profile became that of Osiris, looking towards the Nile.

Bad Lord The rowdy GHOST of a certain English nobleman, Lord Lonsdale. A notorious drinker and womaniser, he flogged his workers and extorted high taxes. Not content with being a thoroughly unpleasant fellow in life, he attempted to bully

Death in the life to come, first sitting bolt upright in his coffin in the church service, screaming and terrifying the minister. His ghost became known as the Bad Lord, it being a noxious POLTERGEIST who irritates the family's descendants more as time goes by — roaring in the cellars, splintering furniture and frightening maidservants.

Badb A fearsome giantess, the Irish goddess of war. Battlefields were called the Lands of Badb, and her appearance was anxiously sought to determine omens. Sometimes she took the form of a crow, sitting quietly by as the soldiers went into the fray. More often, Badb was seen striding to a river on her great legs to wash clothes. Woe betide any man who recognised one of these garments as his own, for it meant he would not survive the day. Badb's cry was also to be feared as a death omen, it having been she who taught the BANSHEES to keen and wail.

Baka An awesome GHOUL, native to the voodoo island of Haiti. After death, members of a certain tribe return to earth as bakas, skeleton-like spirits who maim victims before attempting to eat their flesh. They have been known to tire of tormenting their poor victims, often leaving them by the roadside, mortally wounded but still alive.

Balder The son of ODIN and Frigga (*see* AESIR), Balder was the embodiment of all graces and virtues and, as such, was loved by Aesir and adored by mortals. His name meant courageous, or bold. Perhaps a personification of the sun, Balder was described in the *Edda* (a play about Scandinavian mythology) as being handsome, brave and of 'shining' appearance. His flesh was thought inviolable, but Balder was killed by the blind war-god Hoder at the instigation of the eternal trouble-maker LOKI, by a mere sprig of mistletoe. The whole world mourned him and the Aesir petitioned HEL, the goddess of the Underworld, to allow him to return. The goddess agreed, on condition that all living things wept in unison to prove their grief. This duly occurred, with one exception — an evil old crone named Thaukt (who some say was Loki in disguise) who refused to weep for the god. As a result, Balder was only allowed to return for a certain period of time, only to disappear and return again. This pattern is repeated in the route of the sun's progress in the northern hemisphere today.

Balor An ancient Celtic myth explained the puzzle of creation through the story of Balor. This was a wicked demon who lived beneath a primordial swamp, in which seethed evil beings and spirits. Balor's eyes were poisonous and he had succeeded in destroying all warmth and living things by staring at them. However, one day as he dozed, the god of Spring (Lugh) flung a bright stone named Tathlum, which had escaped Balor's evil gaze, through his eye socket and succeeded in blinding him. Thus it is explained why the sun reigns supreme for six months of the year, followed by deadly winter until such time as the god of Spring blinds him again.

Banshee Also known as the 'bean si', this word is derived from the Celtic 'Bean Seidh' (Woman of the Fairies). To see a banshee, said the Irish, meant to foresee one's own death. It is nearly always female and her voice is usually heard wailing near the family's ancestral home just prior to a person's death. Many tales have been recorded of descendants of Irish families who have died far across the seas, just as a banshee has been heard to wail outside their birthplace in Ireland. The banshee's lamentations are in a language no-one can understand, and her cry is an appalling blend of a wild goose's screech, the screams of an abandoned child and the howl of a wolf.

The banshee sometimes appears as a horrific woman with straggling black hair, one nostril, protruding front teeth, and eyes red from weeping. Other traditions claim she is a pale and beautiful young woman wearing a grey cloak and green gown, or a HAG in a winding sheet, though most often she is attired in loose white drapery, 'putting forward her mournful wail' with the coming of dusk.

The Scots have a form of banshee, known as the Bean-Nighe

or Little Washer by the Ford. This sad harbinger of death is the GHOST of a woman who died in childbirth, eternally washing grave-clothes of those who are about to die. Anyone brave enough to approach her and suckle one of her wizened breasts will gain a wish, though they are more likely to be struck down in terror. According to Lady Wilde:

> . . . flying past in the moonlight, crying bitterly . . . this spirit is mournful beyond all other sounds on earth and betokens certain death . . . whenever it is heard in the silence of the night.
>
> *Ancient Legends, Mystic Charms and Superstitions of Ireland*

When several banshee keen together, it means the death of some very great or holy person is imminent.

Baobhan Sith An evil spirit found in the Highlands of Scotland. It is rather like a BANSHEE, with wails like those of a woman and which pierce the countryside for miles around. However, Baobhan Sith is far more dangerous, taking the form of a succubus and drinking the blood of young men who are abroad at night. The spirit appears first as a raven or a crow, then as a beautiful maid in a green dress and plaid sash. Wary men should attempt a glimpse of such a girl's feet, should she appear by their fireside, for if they take the form of hooves it is wiser to flee.

Barguest A species of BOGEY-BEAST or mischievous HOBGOBLIN which has horns, claws, pointed fangs and blood-red eyes. They are particularly disposed to frighten or harm a wicked child; a well-behaved one is less at risk. Most common in the north of England, they pass along streets at night, making horrid shrieks and scaring folk from their slumbers.

Barnacle Geese For centuries, European people ate the Solan goose on Fridays, believing it to be more fish than bird. The filaments on the underside of barnacles were found to resemble the bird's feathers, so it was assumed the goose emerged half-grown from the barnacles clustered on floating logs. Gerard, the sixteenth-century herbalist, speaks of:

> broken pieces of old ships on which is found certain spume or froth, which in time breedeth into shells, and the fish which is hatched therefrom is in shape and habit like a bird . . .
>
> *The Herball* (1597)

Basilisk This native of the Libyan deserts derives its name from the Greek *basileus* (king), for it is the deadliest and most formidable of serpents. Also known as the COCKATRICE, it has a cock's comb on its head and it is born from an egg laid by a rooster and hatched by a snake. Although its body was serpentine it moved, not by slithering along the ground, but by rearing the forward half of its body along in a coil. Pliny said, 'all other serpents do flee from it and are afraid'. One baleful glance from its enormous eyes could kill, as would its touch, while its breath would kill even birds which flew far overhead. Beaumont speaks of the 'basilisk's death-dealing eye' in *The Woman Hater*, and in Christian art it was the absolute symbol of evil and sin:

> . . . like a boar
> Plunging his tusk in mastiff's gore,
> Or basilisk, when roused, whose breath
> Teeth, sting and eyeballs are all death.
>
> KING *The Art of Love*

This monster may only be killed by sighting its own horrid reflection, though weasels have been known to best it in battle. Other protective measures include rue — no basilisk can come near a patch of this herb — and a cock's crow, at the sound of which a basilisk will perish.

Bast Also known as Bastet, this was the daughter of ISIS and the supreme fertility goddess of Egypt. She controlled the sun's rays and adopted the cat or lion as her emblem. In art, she is often depicted with a cat's head while carrying a shield and rattle, to frighten away thunder-storms, and a basket to carry grain.

The patroness of musicians and dancers, marvellous festivals were held in Bast's honour. Cats and cat statues were worshipped, and mummified cats were buried with much ceremony in the goddess' sanctuary at Bubastis. The classical author and traveller, Herodotus (*c.*480-*c.*425BC), was much astonished by the devotion shown to Bast's chosen animals, and wrote:

> When a fire breaks out, very strange things happen to the cats. The Egyptians gather in a line, thinking more of the cats than of putting out the flames, but the cats dart through or leap over the men and spring into the fire. Then there is a great mourning . . . dwellers in a house where a cat has died . . . shave their eyebrows . . .

During the festivals of Bast, hunting lions, a favourite sport at other times, was a crime punishable by death.

Bayard An enchanted horse of medieval folklore which was incredibly swift. Originally stolen by a wizard from a DRAGON's cave, the Emperor Charlemagne gave it to the four sons of Aymon. If only one son mounted, the horse was an ordinary size; but, as all four mounted, the beast's body elongated to accommodate them all. Even today, the name is used to describe any valuable horse or other animal. Bayard sometimes appears as a cloud, scudding across the sky on Midsummer's Day.

Bean-Nighe *see* BANSHEE

Behemoth A Hebrew monster described as The Lord of the Mammals. So enormous was it that the behemoth was believed to drink whole rivers and consume one-thousand mountains a day. God realised that this creature could not exist alongside the giant fish, LEVIATHAN, else the world would be entirely destroyed. He therefore decreed that before either could reproduce they must fight to the death, with the flesh from the loser being fed to deserving men. At this edict, the leviathan disappeared to the depths of the oceans, while the behemoth lay down to sleep, the mighty folds of his body becoming the

Himalayan mountains. Rather more realistically, perhaps, the behemoth has been latterly identified as either the hippopotamus or rhinoceros. The poet James Thomson described it thus:

> Behold!
> In plaited mail,
> Behemoth rears his head . . .

Bellerophon The grandson of ATLAS, Bellerophon was a beautiful if rather arrogant youth. Being handsome, he had enjoyed only good fortune and fine adventures in his life, not the least of which included slaying the CHIMERA and defeating the AMAZONS. HERA gave him a golden bridle with which he tamed the splendid horse, PEGASUS. He then decided to ride his winged steed to the top of Mount Olympus and take his place with the throng of gods and goddesses. ZEUS was, however, unimpressed by Bellerophon's temerity and sent a gadfly to sting Pegasus on the rump. As the horse buckled, Bellerophon was unseated and fell to earth. Although he did not die, his handsome face was shattered and he was condemned to wander the world in poverty, begging for alms.

Bergmonck According to many legends, caches of treasure are usually guarded from meddlesome mortals by a spirit or god. In Germany, this spirit often takes the form of a 'bergmonck' or huge, pale monk who wards off travellers venturing too close to a mine rich with lodes of gold. He is thought to be the GHOST of a good friar who hid golden candlesticks and chalices from marauding heathen tribes during the religious wars.

Bicorn Surely a creature of some wry medieval imagination, the bicorn was a hybrid of a panther and a cow. It was said to dine exclusively on the bodies of hen-pecked husbands. The two-horned creature's plump and well-fed appearance was attributed to the fact that its prey was so plentiful.

Big Ears The name of the green-eyed demon cat of Scotland which would materialise as part of the occult ceremony called Taghairn. A gruesome ritual undertaken by the sorcerer-in-charge was to roast cats on spits until Big Ears was goaded into appearing. Grudgingly, he would grant all requests so as to cease the torture inflicted on his friends. Even today, tourists may see the claw-marks on a stone where Big Ears was said to have appeared the last time this ceremony was performed.

Black Annis Described by Milton as a 'blew, meager hag', Black Annis was a hideous, cannibalistic spirit with a blue face, a single, piercing eye and iron claws. She was thought to haunt the Dane Hills of Leicestershire in England, and to live in a cave she had dug out of the rock with her own hands. It was her habit to hide behind a nearby oak tree until dark, leap out and catch children in the vicinity, and then devour them. Only the grinding of her teeth alerted her prey, though other reports said Black Annis gave away her whereabouts with a trail of bones.

Black Annis was sometimes associated with the Celtic goddess, Danu, who was responsible for calling up storms. Other tales claim she was the GHOST of a monstrous and savage cat that once prowled the area. The latter gave rise to the custom of 'baiting Black Annis', with a dead cat soaked in aniseed, every Easter in an attempt to make her show herself so the priest could exorcise this malevolent spirit. As recently as the Second World War, Ruth Tongue quoted a child as saying:

> When Black Annis howled, you could hear her five miles away and then even the poor people in their huts fastened skins across the window and put witch-herbs above it to keep her away safe.
>
> *Forgotten Folk Tales of the English Counties*

Black Baroness A well-known German GHOST, the Black Baroness is the spirit of Marianna, wife of the Grand Duke Ferdinand. She appears only to male descendants of the family who slaughtered her own long ago, dumping their bodies in Lake Darmstadt. Although her black garments and veil are a sure omen of death, the Black Baroness's charming laugh and exquisitely beautiful face ensure she always traps her victim. Her favourite method is to seduce the fellow at a ball, then lead him to the garden between dances — the gardener will later find the body which appears, strangely, to have been immersed in lake-water for many weeks.

Black Dogs Also known as Black Hounds, these dangerous animals are about the size of a pony, and menace the Devonshire roads of south-western England at dusk. They have fiery red eyes and some say they are the Devil's own pets, roaming the countryside with him each evening in search of the newly dead. Their howl will make the blood run cold, their footfalls make no sound and they leave a spoor like black gunpowder on the ground. Folklorists attribute various behaviours to Black Dogs; most usually, those who have the misfortune of seeing one will die in the coming year. However, some have been known to guide travellers and one, known as the Church Grim, was buried in a graveyard to deter thieves and evil GHOSTS.

Black Dogs themselves may be the unhappy ghosts of humans, dead untimely, who are doomed to haunt their old homes. They may be laid to rest by ringing a bell which has been blessed in church when they are sighted, then burying the bell in one stretch of water and the clapper in another. The Black Dog will only be able to resume its hauntings if the two items are re-united.

Invariably jet-black and headless (though sometimes having the heads of human beings) Black Dogs have been reported for centuries as loping along lanes by ancient churchyards. Two of the most famous Black Dogs in the British Isles include Moddy Dhu and Black Shuck. Moddy Dhu was the PHANTOM dog of the Isle of Man, and the sight of it caused immediate death. Black Shuck, or Old Shuck, was so named from the Anglo-Saxon *scucca* (demon). His appearance warned of a death in the family, and, as this old poem suggests, the beast usually manifested itself standing in a graveyard, howling:

Grisly ghosts have leave to play
And dead men's souls with courage brave
Skip from out each several grave
And walk around when the Black Shuck comes.

A fearsome Black Dog from Lancashire in northern England is Skriker, who has large feet and huge, green saucer-shaped eyes which hypnotise its victim. Another is Padfoot, a creature with long, smooth hair who will creep unheard alongside a traveller, then suddenly rattle a chain, much to that person's consternation.

Blue Cap An industrious GHOST thought to haunt Scottish mines. He expected to be offered wages that would have been paid to any other miner; on receipt of them, he would undertake tasks with great speed and strength. His name was derived from his habit of wearing a blue hood of coarsely woven cloth which masked his face.

If any foolish mine-owner tried to cheat Blue Cap of his rightful wages, the ghost would assume the form of a blue flame and scorch the inside of the mine-shaft, weakening the pylons which supported the roof. This recriminatory behaviour was typical of the nature of Scottish soldiers, who would not countenance any breach of fair play, as Sir Walter Scott testified:

England shall many a day
Tell of the bloody fray
When the blue bonnets came over the border . . .

Blue Hag of the Highlands *see* CAILLEACH BHEUR

Blue Men Also known as Minch Men or Blue Men of the Minch, these are evil-natured, blue-skinned mermen (*see* MERMAID), often considered to be fallen angels. They possess enormous strength and enjoy tormenting sailors. Their favourite sport entails swimming the straits in northern Scotland to better waylay and wreck passing freighters. Fortunately, their mischief can be thwarted by the ship's captain if he is adept with rhyming banter and riddles, for the Blue Men love to be entertained and leave a ship with good grace if they are bested in a game of wits.

Boa This beast was a cross between an enormous DRAGON and a snake, having great purple and green scales, a forked tail and long fangs. According to Pliny, the name was derived from *bos* (cow), and referred to the supposition that boas slithered between farms, sucking whole herds of cattle dry before eating them. Edward Topsell described this phenomenon in his seventeenth-century *Histories of Serpents*, the boa being:

> . . . a kind of dragone which Italy doth breed
> Men say, and upon the milk of cows doth feed . . .

Bogadjimbri Northern Australian Aborigines attribute all things in creation to twin boy gods named Bogadjimbri. Born of Dilga, the Earth Mother, they fashioned the first genitals from the magic fungus for the hitherto sexless and infertile humans who had aimlessly wandered the earth. They also taught man the rite of circumcision and the secret languages of birds and animals so that he was able to trap or befriend them, and showed him how to divine water.

The brothers Bogadjimbri grew like giant trees until they reached the sky; there, one day, their youthful laughter annoyed the wild cat, Ngariman, who slashed at the pair with its powerful claws and killed them. This so enraged their mother Dilga that she drowned all the Cat-people in a river of milk and re-incarnated her sons, one as a giant water-snake, the other as a placid white cloud.

Bogey-beast A mischievous HOBGOBLIN who preys on disobedient children and keeps them away from harm; hence water bogies frighten children from pools, garden bogies deter them from trampling flower-beds. A well-known Yorkshire bogey-beast is Awd Goggie, who haunts woods and orchards, protecting the fruit and nuts from being damaged or stolen. Similarly the Gooseberry Wife, found on the Isle of Wight, assumes the form of a large, hairy caterpillar who guards the gooseberry crop. Also known as a boogeyman or bogeyman, one can only have an effect if its victim pays heed to it. Thus, the best antidote is to whistle and concentrate on thinking of something completely different.

Boggart Boggarts are particularly mischievous BROWNIES who are mostly found in Lancashire in the north of England. Unlike most denizens of Fairyland, they tend to travel alone. With their ragged appearance, long yellow teeth and simple intelligence, they rank quite low on the social register. They delight in playing tricks on mortals, though they will cease to give trouble if politely requested to do so. If they have been upset or ill-treated, however, they can become very unpleasant and will creep into a bedroom at night, place a clammy hand on the unsuspecting victim's face, then snatch all the blankets away.

Bogie Bogie is a general term for a mischievous or evil-natured GOBLIN. They were once thought to be very dangerous indeed and believed to steal infants for the Devil to torment in Hell. The Scots say they can only be driven away by holding up an open Bible in their face. All have the ability to change shape at will, most assuming icy fingers and yellow eyes that glow in the dark. Sometimes they take the shape of a huge black dog, lurking by lonely roads or in tree trunks. They are most malicious when they prey on liars, murderers and thieves, for they hate to see injustice. Spenser in *The Faerie Queene* referred to:

> a ghastly bogye, which doth them greatly affear.

A favourite method of torment sees the bogie leap on its victim's back as they travel alone at night on a country road, clasping hard hands over the person's eyes so they cannot see. In the case of a thief, he will find he has been relieved of his own purse when he finally manages to jettison his passenger. In a more mellow mood, the bogie will simply play practical jokes. For example, the Hedley Kow from Northumberland in England will assume the form of a beautiful girl and beckon a gullible lad her way, only to disappear. Similarly, farmers in the area will struggle fruitlessly with bales of hay, only to hear raucous laughter when they tumble over as the weight is suddenly lifted.

Boneless A shapeless GHOST who was said to frighten travellers and naughty children. It could possibly have been an animal, for witnesses have described it as being 'woolly' and having a stale smell, rather like a sheep. Ruth Tongue quotes an Oxford person describing Boneless as:

> A shapeless summat as slides behind and alongside in the dark night. Many's have died of fright through his following on. They can't never tell about him, except he's a big shadow and shapeless.
>
> *Forgotten Folk Tales of the English Counties*

Boobrie The comical appearance of the Scottish boobrie belies its bloodthirsty nature. Rather like a gigantic duck, it has webbed feet which leave prints the length of a house, and a loud honking cry. Eye-witnesses claim it dives beneath the surface of Loch Argyll, and its footprints may be seen on the muddy shore each dawn. The scourge of shepherds and farmers, the boobrie is greedy and will gobble up a whole flock of sheep in just one night.

Boogey *see* BUGABOO

Booka *see* BWCA

Brag A mischievous kind of GOBLIN from the north of England and Scotland, with the ability to change its shape. Most often it resembles a horse, though sometimes it looks like a calf with a white flag around its neck, or an ass. In a particularly perverse mood it may assume the shape of a naked man flapping a white sheet, or a chanting girl, or a giant, singing white cat. The brag lives in rivers or lakes and the object of all his eccentric ploys is to lure an unwary passer-by into the water for amusement.

Brahma The Creator of the World in Indian mythology, his four faces contemplate the four far corners of the world he has made. He is depicted seated on a swan, or goose. In his four hands he holds a sceptre, a string of beads, a bow and a book of scripture. Brahma was thought to have sprung from a golden egg floating in primeval waters, or 'brahman'. Along with VISHNU the Preserver, and SHIVA the Destroyer, he constituted the Vedic Triad.

As supreme god of the Devas, Brahma was responsible for the giant god-serpent, ANANTA, churning the ocean so it produced the milk of immortality for the gods to drink each day. He also created the first man, Purusha, from the navel of Vishnu. Brahma was, by and large, faithful to his beautiful consort, Sarasvati; however, an incestuous lapse with his daughter Vak resulted in the creation of mis-shapen godlings named Asuras, whom he ultimately had to destroy.

The Brahmin priests are the highest caste in the system of Hinduism and they worship Brahma as the founder of their religious system. Camoens wrote in the *Lusiad* that:

> Whate'er in India holds the sacred name
> Of piety or lore, the Brahmins claim:
> In wildest rituals, vain and painful, lost,
> Brahma, their founder, as a god they boast.

Brahmadaitya A benign Indian GHOST, thought to be the spirit of a gentle Brahmin priest. Like BRAHMA, the divine Creator of the Universe, these ghostly acolytes feature four faces and four hands. Thus they may observe the whole earth and guard their master against SHIVA. Brahmadaitya are kind to humans, though should one be foolish enough to chop down the palm tree where this spirit lives, the offender's neck will be snapped, like a twig.

Bran A fabled god-giant of Irish myth, Bran was a prince and younger brother of King Lyr. Story-tellers gave him the title The Blessed, in reference to his many artistic talents, for Bran was a gifted harpist and poet. He was also considered blessed by the gods for the extraordinary good fortune he experienced on his travels. A brave adventurer amidst both mortal and fairy worlds, Bran was best remembered for his voyage to the Island of Joy, a delightful place where sorrow, sickness and death were unknown. On his return, Bran penned many lovely ballads describing his experiences, and taught his countrymen how to create sweet music and beautiful lyrics.

Bran was also a zealous patriot and served his country well as a warrior. When he was finally slain in battle, he asked that his severed head be buried facing the ocean so that no foreign armies could set foot in Ireland without him knowing it.

Brollachan A Scottish type of BROWNIE. Gentle natured and helpful around the house, this fairy is very dark with long, strong arms and a shapeless body covered in hair. It rarely speaks, though if frightened it may bleat like a goat. Some occasionally have goats' shanks and hooves as well.

Brown Men Also known as Brown Men of the Moors or Muirs, these DWARVES have red hair, brown skin and twinkling brown eyes. They are loved as the protectors of all beasts and birds. Brown Men only eat nuts, berries and apples, and use their bows and arrows to chase hunters away from innocent game. Anyone who kills or traps an animal after being warned away by a Brown Man will become very dizzy and lose all sense of direction. The angered Brown Man will then push the miscreant into a nearby stream or pool, pelt him with leaves and twigs, and abandon him to contemplate his crime.

Brownie The best-known and most industrious of all HOB-GOBLINS, being found throughout most of Europe and the United Kingdom. Typically, brownies are small and shaggy haired, with a brown, wrinkled face. About the height of a small child and dressed in ragged brown clothes, they are very wiry and strong, despite having no fingers or toes and, in the case of Scottish brownies, no nose. When a brownie adopts a house he happily takes responsibility for many household tasks, which he performs at night. He will cook meals, wash floors, run errands, reap and mow crops and tend animals. He particularly cherishes bees and will sing to them. If there are other servants, he will expose their laziness — in fact, it was once said that brownies were originally created to help relieve men of the burden caused by Adam. Martin wrote:

> It was not long since every family of considerable substance was haunted by a spirit they called Browny, which did several sorts of work and this was the reason why they gave him offerings on what was called Browny's Stone.
>
> *Scotland*

This Browny's Stone was helpful when the householder was brewing beer, for it hastened the fermentation process with its fairy magic.

For their work, brownies are traditionally rewarded with honey-cakes and cream. The most famous brownie was a Swiss house-spirit called Jack O'Bowl, so named from the custom of placing a bowl of fresh, sweet cream outside the cow byre every evening, for, by morning, the bowl would be empty. Such gifts must appear to be left 'by accident'. If the brownies think they are being bribed, they will leave and never return. This happened when a gift of clothes was left for one brownie, who cried:

> What have we here, hempen, hampen!
> Here will I never more tread nor stampen!
>
> TRADITIONAL

Brownies are very temperamental. One whose mowing and threshing of a corn crop was criticised threw the whole harvest over a cliff, saying:

> It's ne'er to be mowed by me again
> I'll scatter it o'er the Raven Stane
> They'll hae some wark ere it's mowed again!
>
> TRADITIONAL

Bucephalus The mighty steed ridden by Alexander the Great, bought from a Thessalian merchant for thirteen talents. The name Bucephalus means 'bull-headed', a reference to the beast's mighty strength. It was also very beautiful, possessing an ivory horn like a unicorn's and a peacock's tail. Alexander was said to be the only mortal Bucephalus would ever respect and the only one who was successful in saddling and mounting him; with all other men, Bucephalus had sensed their greed and weakness and had spurned them. So loyal was he that he rejected his cousins, the UNICORNS, when Alexander's men attacked them for their horns. When he eventually died, Alexander built a city in Bucephalus' honour and died himself shortly afterwards.

Bugaboo Known also as Boogey, this was originally a monstrous GOBLIN introduced in the tales of the Italian romancers, specifically *The Bug Bear*, a play of 1565 about magicians. And in Shakespeare's *Hamlet* 'bugs and goblins' were feared.

The word 'bugaboo' is Indian in origin, describing friendly male and female spirits who guarded children against other, more evil-intentioned entities. The Russians refer to 'buka', the Welsh 'barog' means spiteful, while the Scots usher forward 'boggle-bos', 'bucca-bos', 'bodachs' and 'bugbears' as the solution for misbehaviour in very small children, especially if they refuse to go to sleep when they should. Large, hairy and gruff-voiced, with an ugly, grinning face, these bear-like creatures come down the chimney to the nursery. Unlike the mischievous and often unpleasant BOGIE, however, their appearance belies their nature for they are quite harmless, having neither claws nor teeth. As such, they are part of an extremely ancient tradition for Assyrian mothers who used to scare recalcitrant children with the scarecrow Narses; and a warning widely repeated today is very similar: 'You'd better do as I say, or the boogeyman will get you.'

Bunyip Variously known amongst Aboriginal tribes as Moolgewante, Wowee Wowee and Kine Pratie, bunyips are curious and often bloodthirsty beings. The far-off booming or barking sound heard near swamps and billabongs during rainfall periods is ascribed to the bunyip, and the Aboriginals think it causes rheumatism in those who hear it. Horrific to behold, with a matted crop of weeds for hair and feet turned backwards, the bunyip has a crocodile's tail and the head and torso of either an emu, bandicoot or malevolent man. A relic from the Dreamtime, when giant goannas and kangaroos were to be seen on the horizon, the bunyip captures women and children to eat. They hibernate during the dry season by burrowing deep into the damp sand.

Buttery Spirits There was a strong moral belief in old England that evil spirits only had power over ill-gotten goods, thus explaining why ABBEY LUBBERS could only wreak havoc amongst monks once corrupt behaviour had been evidenced. Similarly, the Buttery Spirits were to be found haunting inns where the proprietor was dishonest or greedy.

An old tale tells of a holy priest who visited his nephew, a scurrilous tavern-keeper. This man used cheap tricks in his work, serving rotten meat and watered-down ale to customers, yet could not understand why he was not making a profit. His uncle pointed out the presence of a gross Buttery Spirit, swilling the rancid contents of the larder, and chastised the tavern-keeper for his wicked ways. When he again came to visit he found a very different situation, with the starving Buttery Spirit stretching out in vain for the wholesome food on the larder shelves. The tavern-keeper had found honesty to be the best policy and, in addition to ceasing to use shoddy ingredients, had marked all dishes and food with crosses.

Bwca A Welsh variety of BROWNIE, also known as Bwciod of Booka. They have dark skin, long noses and wear shabby farmers' smocks. The bwca dislike teetotallers, preferring the warmth and comfort of an inn. If humoured and treated with respect the bwca can be very helpful. He will churn the butter if the kitchen is clean and tidy and a bowl of cream has been set out for him. However, if mistreated the bwca will create havoc in the household by smashing crockery, pinching children, tearing clothes, telling secrets out loud, even tossing babies out of their cradles. Once this occurs, the bwca will not regain his earlier good humour, so the householder will have to enlist the help of a soothsayer to banish the sprite.

An old folktale tells of a bwca who was tricked by a servant girl into drinking urine instead of the customary cream. He promptly left the farm and went to another, where he helped the maid with her spinning, though refused to divulge his name. She pretended to leave the bwca alone one evening, only to creep to his door and eavesdrop on his singing:

> How she would laugh, did she know
> That Gwarwyn-a-throt is my name!
>
> TRADITIONAL

The maid mocked him for his name, and so angry was the sprite that, as he left, fire irons were thrown through walls, dogs howled, doors slammed and all the household fires were extinguished forever.

C

Cailleach Bheur A nature spirit who often appears as a wild boar or an old crone (Cailleach Bheur, meaning 'old woman'). Also known as The Blue Hag of the Highlands, due to the colour of her skin and hair, she personifies the spirit of winter and can freeze the ground with her staff. During this period she herds stray animals to her seashore cave, where she feeds them during the cold months. The Cailleach Bheur fights the oncoming Spring with her staff, but will always lose the battle, hiding beneath a holly bush where green grass never grows, until the seasons change again.

Cairn Maiden The Cairn Maiden was a beautiful, golden-haired girl who appeared at harvest time. She may have originated with the notion of human sacrifice to ensure plentiful crops, for her actions were often bloodthirsty. She would watch the harvesters swinging their scythes through the open corn and, towards the close of day, she would appear in the path of the lad who looked strongest and most virile. On and on she would lure him, enticing him to cut every sheaf left in the meadow, until midnight came and he was faint with exhaustion. She would then face him and, saying her own sickle needed sharpening, neatly slice off his head.

Caith Sith The most magical of all fairy cats, found in the Scottish Highlands. It was large and black with a round white patch on its chest. While BIG EARS was a demon cat, Caith Sith was more benevolent, having been known to mind children and bar the doorway to intruders.

Caladrius A noble bird with the neck of a swan and strange green eyes, believed to have the power of foretelling the future. Well-known in medieval Europe, the caladrius was said to herald the death and birth of kings. It would sit at the foot of the sick-bed and, if it gazed at the patient, its eyes would magically absorb the malaise so the man had a renewed chance of life. If, however, the bird looked the other way, death was inevitable.

Camazotz The ancient Mayan Indians worshipped Camazotz, the god of hunting and fate. Usually portrayed as a bat with two curled fangs, Camazotz was also the Lord of the Wind, and controlled thunder, rain and lightning. He jealously guarded the secrets of the future and Afterworld, though he would offer warriors the chance to play dice, gambling for the gift of immortality. If they failed at the game, Camazotz would swiftly behead them, and their spirits appeared as stars in the eastern sky. If the god was feeling generous towards the victim, he would instead be turned into a fruit bat, to serve Camazotz and his court.

Camel-lepard Also known as the Camel Leopardel, or the lybbarde, this beast was believed to be the offspring of a panther or leopard and a camel. It had the neck and head of a camel with two long horns curved backward, and the dappled body of a leopard. Much noted for its courage, the camel-lepard was widely reproduced in early English heraldry to communicate the virtues of diligence and bravery. It is also believed to have been the word used by Romans when they were attempting to describe the giraffe. However, more recent sightings by Archbishop Trench in the sixteenth century suggest it was a beast in its own right:

> It is . . . a creature combining, though with infinitely more grace, yet some of the height and even the proportions of a camel, with the spotted skin of the pard.

Catoplebas A huge, buffalo-like creature, thought by the Greeks to dwell in Ethiopia. Its name in Greek means 'that which looks downwards', a reference to its head being so heavy that it would only loll lazily in the hot sand, waiting for a victim to walk by. Its sluggish habit was not a hindrance, though, for it could kill with a mere glance or whiff of its breath, as it fed on poisonous herbs whose odour was fatal to man. If the catoplebas was especially peckish it would gnaw on its own forelegs.

Cauld Lad Also known as the Cold Lad, a sad little GHOST of a stable-boy who was murdered by his lord. He was locked in a chilly room as punishment for some misdemeanour and there he froze to death. His ghost wandered the Essex farmhouse in eastern England ever after, its teeth chattering and little body trembling. Sometimes he would make himself useful in the kitchen by cleaning and tidying; however, if accidentally locked in any room the Cauld Lad would make a fearful mess, overturning furniture and scrabbling at the lock. If he wandered into a room where an ill person lay, and touched them, saying:

> Cold, cold, forever cold
> You shall be cold forever more

the patient would surely die.

Ceasg As with most water fairies, this Scottish MERMAID combines the qualities of beauty and treachery. She has the head and breasts of a lovely woman and a salmon's tail. Her hair changes from dark green in the water to bright gold when she emerges, and she dresses it with fine jewelled ornaments from her underwater palace. If netted, she will grant her captor three wishes or gifts, though she will turn the spell against the mortal if possible. The Ceasg is known to be dangerous and will swallow a man whole, possibly in memory of a fish-tailed god to whom human sacrifices were made.

Centaur A lusty race giving allegiance only to EROS, god of love, and DIONYSIUS, god of wine. Possessing the head and torso of a man and the body and legs of a potent stallion, centaurs were the offspring of the first king of Thessaly and the cloud Nephele. They are extremely handsome and sensual, and glory in a drunken brawl. Witness their behaviour at the Lapithae wedding feast when the centaur Eurythion tried to rape the bride. His extraordinary behaviour was immortalised in sculpture in the Temple of ZEUS. The guests fell upon the centaurs and drove them out of the country, so they are now a rare sight indeed. Sometimes called 'sagittary':

> The dreadful Sagittary appals our numbers . . .
>
> Shakespeare *Troilus & Cressida*

Centaurs are often depicted in art as warlike creatures, brandishing clubs made from young pine trees, spears or arrows.

Cerberus The grim, three-headed dog of Greek mythology, Cerberus was the guardian of HADES. His three heads represent the past, present and future; his spittle poisons and burns the earth; he has a mane of snakes and a serpent's tail; his eyes are watchful and his ears are constantly pricked, listening for newcomers as he admits the dead and devours the still-living. Cerberus is nonetheless fallible, for HERCULES managed to overpower him in his Twelfth Labour with his bare hands while Orpheus lulled him to sleep with soft music. The Greeks would attempt to placate Cerberus by placing gifts of honey and cake in the coffins of the newly dead.

Cernunnos An ancient Celtic god who features on coins and pottery ware, possibly because his association with fertility was thought to bring a plenitude of wealth or food. Cernunnos is portrayed as an interesting amalgam of various cultures, his one-shouldered tunic being reminiscent of a Roman toga and his cross-legged position being rather like that of Buddha. Cernunnos is most often described as The Horned One, for his head is adorned with reindeer antlers. Festivals held in his honour were attended by priests carrying reindeer pelts, and devotees of his cult would drink a beverage of the powdered 'velvet' from the tips of the antlers, said to produce visions and act as an aphrodisiac.

Chagrin A strong belief in the supernatural characterises communities of Romany gypsies. A particularly evil GHOST is the chagrin, also known as the 'cogrino' or 'nargirin', who assumes the shape of a large yellow hedgehog. Chagrin is an omen of death and a messenger of the devil, 'o'Beugh'. It delights in startling the horses which pull gypsy caravans; to protect them, therefore, horses wore bridles hung with small, holed stones, the breast-bones of blue-jays and kingfishers, and four-leaf clovers.

Changeling Fairies greatly value human babies as a means of introducing new blood to their dwindling race, so have been known to steal them and leave a useless object behind. This may be a sickly, peevish fairy child, an aged fairy no longer of value, or even a piece of wood carved to resemble the stolen child. Characterised by a swollen head, unearthly howling and a nasty temper, these misfits were, oddly, known as Children of the Quiet Folk. Shakespeare, in *Henry IV*, probably echoed the sentiments of many parents of changelings when he wrote:

> Oh, that it could be proved
> That some night-tripping fairy had exchanged
> In cradle-clothes, our children as they lay
> And called mine Percy, his Plantagenet!
> Then would I have his Harry, and he mine.

Changelings were sometimes said to have been afflicted with 'elf-shot', that is, shot with an elfin arrow and afflicted with an unknown disease. Tangled hair was another indication of fairy interference, for one of Queen Mab's favourite amusements was to tie people's hair in knots, or 'elf-locks', as Shakespeare averred in *Romeo and Juliet*:

> This is that very Mab
> That plats the manes of horses in the night
> And bakes the elf-locks in foul, sluttish hairs.

Often, ill or retarded babies were thought to be changelings and were miserably tortured in an attempt to force them to revert to fairy form. One method was to trick the changeling into revealing its great age; another was to burn the changeling on a hot shovel and throw it on the fire. The fairy would then fly up the chimney and the human baby would be found at the door. As a precaution, since cold iron is repulsive to fairies, scissors or nails could be suspended over the crib to keep the baby safe.

Chimera The chimera was born of the half-serpent, half-woman ECHIDNA and the giant TYPHON. Homer described it as a monster with the body of a goat, tail of a DRAGON and head of a lion, belching flames. Virgil commented similarly in *The Aenid*:

> Amid the troops, and like the leading god,
> High o'er the rest in arms the graceful Turnus rode —
> A triple pile of plumes his crest adorned,
> On which with belching flames Chimera burned:
> The more the kindled combat rises higher,
> The more with fury burns the blazing fire.

Some sources claim the chimera was an allegory of a mountain in ancient Lycia, with a volcano on top, the middle affording pasture for goats and the foothills being infested with snakes. Chimera was said to have been eventually slain by BELLEROPHON, riding the flying horse PEGASUS, who was able to fly through the air and dodge the monster's blasts of flame. In latter times, Philip II of Spain adopted the heraldic device of Bellerophon attacking the chimera, saying it represented the heretical England which he, also, intended to destroy.

Chiron Also known as Cheiron, this was a CENTAUR whose sober and studious character was very different from the rest of his race. Famous for his wisdom and knowledge of medicine, Chiron educated many Greek heroes and scholars, including Homer, AESCULAPIUS and Heracles. He was also a great friend of ACHILLES, whom he taught music and hunting; according to ancient myth, Chiron taught Achilles to run so swiftly by setting him to chase wild deer and eat their raw flesh. When Chiron died, JUPITER placed him amongst the stars where this fabled beast, holding an arrow upon bended bow, is now known as the zodiacal sign of Sagittarius.

Chiveface An unusual, cow-like creature found exclusively in Britain, although its name is derived from the French *chive-vache* (sorry-cow). It was said to prey solely on virtuous and obedient women and, because its food was so scarce, the chiveface was always hungry and appeared to be only skin and bone. Chaucer, in *The Merchant's Tale*, had this to say:

> O noble wyves, ful of heigh prudence
> Let noon humilitie your tonges nayle:
> Ne lat no clerk have cause or diligence
> To write of you a story of such mervayle
> As of Griseldes, pacient and kynde
> Lest chichi-vache you swolwe in hir entraile.

Circe The powerful Queen of the Aegean, Circe assumed otherworldly status through her extraordinary abilities as an enchantress. The hawk was sacred to her, and was used to depict her symbolically in art. The daughter of a sea-NYMPH and HELIOS the sun god, Circe was a powerful sorceress who despised men and would poison and trick them whenever she could. For instance, when Odysseus and his men landed on her island, she transformed them into pigs, an exploit referred to by Milton in *Comus* thus:

> Who knows not Circe
> The daughter of the Sun, whose charmed cup
> Whoever tasted lost his upright shape
> And downward fell into a grovelling swine?

Odysseus was able to escape her wiles by virtue of a magic herb, moly, given him by HERMES. He further conquered her by ensuring she fell in love with him, and she bore him three sons.

Cluricaun Also known as clurican, these merry folk are closely related to the Irish LEPRECHAUN. They usually appear as wrinkled old men, and have knowledge of leather purses of gold coins, usually hidden in the roots of trees or in ruined castles. It is no surprise they all have bright red noses, for their two great loves are tobacco and whisky; they rarely appear without a pipe and are known to raid cellars, particularly favouring home-made ale. When uproariously drunk, they will ride sheep by moonlight, throwing their hats in the air and whooping with glee as they drive the confused flock in circles.

Coatlique The earth mother-goddess of the Aztecs. Of rather grim appearance, she wore a tunic of writhing snakes. Her head was made up of two snakeheads and her sagging breasts bore witness to her eternal fertility. On her back hung thirteen leather thongs, studded with emerald snails, which signified the planets in the sky.

Coatlique was thought to feed upon corpses buried within the soil, and wore a necklace of the skulls. She was, however, a generous goddess, and would give freely of her magic to that same soil so it could support the next generation with crops; she was, therefore, both a grave and a womb at once.

Coatlique is often depicted with a child in her arms, and the first man was thought to have sprung from her as a result of divine conception. The story goes that, one day, the goddess was dusting and picked up a ball of lint dropped by a blue humming-bird, placing it inside her apron. As a result, she gave birth to the first mortal man 'without sin'.

Coblynau Also known as Koblernigh, these Welsh mining fairies are cousins of the Cornish KNOCKERS. Ugly but friendly, they are about eighteen inches high, always dirty and wear red handkerchiefs with yellow spots round about their heads. They are blessed with good humour and bring luck to mortal miners by knocking at spots behind the seam faces where rich ore lodes may be found. Although they carry mining tools and appear to be working industriously, they never actually do any digging themselves, preferring instead to dance a wild version of a Morris dance. Never neglect to thank a coblynau for indicating the whereabouts of ore deposits, else the next time you visit that tunnel it will be barred with mounds of stones.

Cockatrice Very like the BASILISK in appearance, the cockatrice is a monster with the wings of a fowl, tail of a DRAGON with a deadly sting at its tip, and the head of a cock. This chimerical creature was hatched by a serpent, or toad, from a cock's egg. With its livid, dangling wattles and its ability to kill with a glance, the cockatrice was referred to in the Bible as typifying evil. Witness *Jeremiah* viii.17:

> For behold, I will send serpents, cockatrices among you which will not be charmed and they shall bite you, saith the Lord.

According to legend, England was once infested with cockatrices, until a knight dressed himself with mirrors and walked the countryside thus attired. The cockatrices were destroyed by the reflections from their own eyes. The word is still used to describe a treacherous person with evil intent, as instanced by Shakespeare in *Twelfth Night*:

> They will kill each other by the look,
> Like cockatrices.

Colt Pixy A fairy, guardian of orchards and vegetable gardens throughout England. Most often, it takes the form of a white colt who will nip the heels of would-be thieves, and chase them from the trees.

Corpse Bird Many birds are regarded as being evil omens and portents of death, notably the magpie and the raven who are both thought of as the Devil's own pets. In Wales, the 'derwyn corp' is the name given to a large, ghostly bird which flies around a house where there is sickness, stopping only to tap loudly at a window if the patient is to die.

Crodh Mara Fairy cattle, or sea-cattle, which frequent the

Scottish waterways. They are usually hornless and have round ears. Fairies often bestow them as gifts upon favoured mortals for, when they mate with mortal stock, the offspring will enjoy superior stamina and strength. However, Crodh Mara cattle need to be closely penned in at night, else they will head for the nearest loch and dive in, followed by the rest of the herd. These cattle are much less domesticated than their mortal counterparts although, unlike the malignant fairy water-horse EACH-UISGE, they will remain loyal to humans if treated well. A story is told of a water bull who valiantly fought an Each-Uisge to the death in order to save the life of a servant girl who tended the needs of fairy cattle.

Cronus A Titan and the son of Uranus and GAEA, Cronus castrated his father and assumed domination of Olympus and the world. He was frightened by a prophecy that his downfall would be similarly brought about by one of his own children, so he ate them all at birth — HERA, POSEIDON, Hestia, DEMETER and HADES. His youngest son ZEUS was saved this fate, being raised in a secret cave and suckled by a she-goat. Ultimately, Zeus overcame his father and chained him to a rock midway between the earth and sea. There he ordered Cronus to vomit up the other children, who then became the gods of Olympus. According to myth, Cronus was placed in the heavens, where he may be seen as the planet SATURN.

Cughtagh A rather disagreeable type of GHOST found in the Highlands of Scotland. The cughtagh was once admired as a handsome and benevolent giant who distributed gifts to the needy folk in hill villages. However, he became embittered with age, losing his fine looks and noble habits, and becoming a surly, cob-webbed ghost who lived in dark caves. The cughtagh's presence is marked by a far-off tumble of pebbles and gravel as you stand at the opening to his cave. If you venture inside, be aware that the cold puff of air which comes to greet you is actually his sigh of exasperation, as he moves further inside the cave.

Cu Sith Scottish fairies may claim an enormous shaggy dark-green dog for their own. Thus was Cu Sith, and he differed from other dogs in having paws that left prints the size of a man's, and a long tail plaited in a flat braid which lay coiled upon his back. Cu Sith usually moved in complete silence, though would bark loudly three times when hunting his prey. His special task was to kidnap mortal women and take them back to the fairy mound where they would be employed as wet-nurses for fairy children.

Cybele Originally designated as a Phrygian nature-goddess of caves and waterways, Cybele was later thought to be RHEA, the wife of CRONUS and therefore the mother of the Olympian gods. Many fertility rituals were held in her name, and oak and pine trees were planted near her forest sanctuaries. Cybele was usually depicted in a chariot drawn by lions, with a crown on her head and a drum or set of cymbals in her hand.

Cyclops The name comes from the Greek for 'eye as big as the full moon'. Cyclops were giants with only one eye, like a lantern, in the centre of their forehead. Addison in *Milton Imitated* wrote:

> of the mighty family
> Of one-eyed brothers hasten to the shore
> And gather round the bellowing Polypheme . . .

Polypheme was their king, later slain by Odysseus. The cyclops were charged with the business of forging iron for Vulcan and working the underground quarries, where their singular eye cast light. Although dull-witted, they were fierce and cannibalistic warriors, their preferred weapon being the thunderbolt. Cyclops may have originated with the Arimaspians, a one-eyed race from Scythia who coveted gold and were constantly fighting gryphons for access to their caches of treasure. Milton in *Paradise Lost* wrote:

> when a gryphon through the wilderness . . .
> Pursues the Arimaspian, who by stealth
> Had from his wakeful custody purloined the guarded gold.

Cyclops were not unique to Greek mythology; appearing to Sinbad in *The Arabian Nights* was a huge monster:

> as tall as a palm tree and perfectly black [with] one eye which flamed like a burning coal in the middle of his forehead.

Cyoeraeth Also known as Cyhyraeth, the Welsh version of the BANSHEE. A horrible weeping woman with an emaciated face and black teeth, the cyoeraeth's wail announces the approach of death. This dreadful cry was described by Coslet as:

> a doleful . . . sound heard before the deaths of many and most likely to be heard before foul weather. The voice resembles the groaning of sick persons who are to die . . . It begins strong, and louder than a sick person could make; the second cry is lower, but not less doleful but rather more so; the third yet lower, and soft, like the groan of a sick man almost spent and dying.

The Welsh also believed the cyoeraeth was wont to amble along beaches on lonely , stormy nights, carrying a small inextinguishable candle and crying into the wind. Her appearance here would presage a shipwreck, the candle lighting the way for pall bearers who would follow. Strangely, she was also thought to appear by streams and lakes at night, and to splash loudly, thus warning any passers-by of the danger, with no thought to trap them.

D

Dagan The chief god of the Philistines, Dagan (or Dagon) is represented with the face and hands of a man or woman and the tail of a fish. Being a sea-faring folk, it was natural that the Philistines should idolise such a form, as Milton commented in *Paradise Lost*:

> Dagon his name; sea-monster, upward man
> And downward fish; yet had his temple high
> Rear'd in Azotus, dreaded through the coast
> Of Palestine, in Gath and Ascalon,
> And Accaron and Gaza's frontier hounds.

According to the Bible, *Samuel* 1:5, the Ark was desecrated by being placed in the Temple of Dagan, and Samson destroyed both the temple and the statue of the god in retribution before dying there himself.

Dagda An ancient Irish deity, Dagda literally translates as 'the good god'. He was the chief deity of the mighty fairy race, the TUATHA DE DANAAN, and therefore the father of both mortal and immortal folk, hence his epithet All Father. Among his sacred possessions were an enormous club which could raise the slain to life again; a magic harp whose music made its listeners forget sorrow; an inexhaustible cauldron from which no-one is turned away hungry; and two marvellous sheep — one eternally roasting, the other forever feeding in readiness for slaughter.

Dagda's generous nature was inherited by his daughter, Brigid, who was made a saint for her many good works. For instance, on St Brigid's Day in Ireland, she once filled a great lake with ale for the poor to enjoy.

Dando Dogs These ferocious beasts figure in a famous Cornish legend of an evil priest, named Dando. He enjoyed nothing so much as sensual pleasures, and drank and womanised to excess. One Sunday, he went hunting with his fierce black mastiffs, stopping only to swig at a flask of strong drink. As he finished, he smacked his lips and swore to spend Eternity in Hell, if only there was a ready supply of the drink. The Devil promptly granted his wish, and encouraged Dando and his dogs to terrorise the countryside in an attempt to snare other foolhardy souls.

Demeter The Greek goddess of vegetation and fruitfulness, Demeter gave the first seeds of wheat to mankind and taught him how to cultivate the soil and make bread from the grain. She had various consorts and was noteworthy for attempting to refuse the mighty ZEUS when she was engaged in seeking her abducted daughter, PERSEPHONE. While she wandered the earth all the crops withered, and Zeus, so that men would not starve, arranged for Persephone to return to her. However, since the girl had eaten six pomegranate seeds during her stay in the Underworld, she had to return there for six months every year. During this time, Demeter mourns her absence and the earth grows cold and barren.

Demeter's symbol is the ear of corn and she is also linked to the bee in Classical literature, due to her industrious nature and nourishing function. Fertility rites were held for her, from which men were excluded, and phallic symbols such as piglets, snakes and pine cones were used to decorate her shrine and thus encourage the generation of seed in the earth.

Demogorgon Also known as The Most High One; a terrible deity of ancient Greece, mentioning his very name was thought to result in abject disaster, as referred to by Nicholas Rowe (Poet Laureate, 1715) in *Lucan's Pharsalia VI*:

> Must I call your master to my aid
> At whose dread name the trembling furies quake
> Hell stands abashed and earth's foundations shake?

The Roman epic poet Statius, in the first century AD, claimed it was unlawful to know this god even existed. The Demogorgon's powers of wizardry were unequalled:

> When the moon arises [then]
> Cruel Demogorgon walks his round
> And if he finds a fairy lag in light
> He drives the wretch before and lashes into night.
>
> Dryden *The Flower and The Leaf*

He was believed to live atop the Himalayan mountains, attended by elves and evil fays. Every five years he called all souls to judgement to determine whether they were worthy to continue their lives on earth. Given that the Greek root of the word is *gorgo* (devil), the Demogorgon was probably a manifestation of Satan.

Demon Drummer The GHOST of a musician, hanged in 1660 in England for a misdemeanour. After his death, his family were plagued by POLTERGEIST-like pranks — hair and clothing were tugged at, doors slammed and china smashed. Far more wearing for the community at large was the incessant drumming which emanated from the jail-house. It is said that this ghost still beats his eerie tattoo during times of war.

Devi The great goddess of the Hindus, Devi is the consort of VISHNU and a two-fold personality, as demonstrated by her prime manifestations. In one, she is a proud and noble warrior maiden, astride a lion. She uses her twelve (or eighteen) arms and all available weapons to dispense and destroy evil, although she did not relish inflicting pain or death. Devi was thought very beautiful and to 'hold the universe in her womb'. More shocking is the goddess's manifestation as the horrific KALI, who wears a girdle of severed human heads and arms. Describing the fierce power of Devi in this form, Sarkara wrote:

> Your hands hold both delight and pain. The shadow of death and the elixir of immortal life are [both] . . . yours!

Devourer An awesome beast who figured in Egyptian legend, the Devourer sported the mane of a lion, the body of a hippopotamus and the jaws of a golden crocodile. Rather like the three-headed CERBERUS who guarded HADES, the Devourer attended MAAT, the Egyptian goddess of Truth, who assessed the dead before they were admitted to the afterlife. If the person's heart was heavy with misdeeds, the Devourer would consume the victim and they would never find peace.

Diana The Roman counterpart of ARTEMIS, a goddess of the moon, a virgin and a huntress, Diana was also the patroness of women and assisted mothers in childbirth. Her name was derived from 'diviana' (the shining one), and glittering shrines of gold and silver were made for her temple at Ephesus.

Dierach *see* FACHAN

Dionysius The god of fertility, wine and drunkenness in Greek mythology, Dionysius was known as Bacchus to the Romans. Thomas Parnell described the latter thus:

> . . . jolly Bacchus, god of pleasure
> [who] charmed the world with drink and dances
> and all his thousand airy fancies . . .

Dionysius means 'son of Zeus', a reference to the tale surrounding his birth. ZEUS was the lover of a mortal maid, Semele, who foolishly asked the god to appear before her so she might identify him. Being the god of lightning his appearance resulted in Semele being charred to ashes, so Zeus plucked the infant from her remains and sewed it up in his own thigh. HERA, Zeus' wife, was jealous of the child and cursed him to travel the earth, bestowing the gift of wine-making on those who were kind to him and sending insane those who treated him badly.

The rollicking god made more friends than foes, and his cult was very popular indeed, characterised by devotees being freed of their inhibitions and enjoying wild, frenzied orgies. His female attendants were known as Maenads, and they danced riotously through the woods. Such was their passion that they tore the hapless Pentheus to shreds in an orgiastic fury. Dionysius' male followers were the SATYRS and, in procession to honour their god, they carried phallic staffs twined with ivy and grape vines and tipped with green pine cones. Dionysius was usually depicted with the flanks of a goat or bull to symbolise his fertility aspect.

Djinn A type of spirit in Arabian folklore. They are most often described as the offspring of fire, though some sources claim they first arose from man's shadow. Djinn are governed by a race of kings named Suleyman, one of whom is believed to have erected the pyramids. They live on Kaf Mountain, in the desert wastelands. A good djinn often takes the form of a lovely woman, while a bad one appears as a monster with the head of a hyena and hind-quarters of a wolf. Quite often, the djinn are simply invisible, and may only be identified by a whiff of cinnamon in the air. They are much prized as servants, for their ability to turn onion skins into gold leaf and many other magical spells, and were imprisoned in brass bottles or finger-ring compartments from whence they were summoned to do the bidding of their captor.

Dobies Rather silly and stupid BROWNIES, found in England and Scotland. Very sincere and always willing to help a human, dobies are nonetheless inept at most tasks. Asked to stand guard over good or treasure, they would good-naturedly hand everything over to a perfect stranger. Similarly, they would clown their way through even simple household chores leaving chaos behind with spilled milk, broken eggs and unfed chickens. Country folklore has it that dobies were actually the sad little GHOSTS of unwanted or plain women, who would fumble around the house trying to be useful until their spirits had been exorcised.

Dog Men Dog-headed tribes of India were first mentioned in the Italian romance *Guerino Meschino*, as a result of Marco Polo's tales of his travels. Polo maintained that these people enjoyed a peaceful existence on the Isle of Andaman, engaging in the trade of nuts, apples and rice with India. Somewhat more sophisticated was the dog-headed tribe of the Isle of Macumeran described by fourteenth-century English traveller and writer Sir John Mandeville. Their king sported an enormous ruby pendant, carved in the shape of the tribe's deity — the ox — and his subjects wore head-dresses shaped like oxen.

Domovoi The popular Russian word for GHOST. Slavonic legend has it that at the time of the Creation of the World a group of malignant spirits staged a revolt against Svarog, the sky god. As punishment they were turned into leaves and blown hither and thither — some down chimneys, some into stables, others into newly turned earth. In time, these became domestic spirits and usually appeared as a rather homely married couple. The male domovoi traditionally lived by the front step and the female in the cellar, where she could best supervise the family's food supply. They were quite approachable and appreciated hearing their names mentioned or receiving gifts of wine and rice on festival days. Domovoi would cheerfully undertake household chores while the family slept, if they were treated with respect and gratitude. However, they would become noisy if ignored or neglected and downright troublesome if the family itself became lazy or rude.

Doppelganger The German term for a GHOST which is actually the 'double' or identical likeness of someone who is about to die. Sometimes, the doppelganger appears to friends or relatives of the dying, and their mimicry is so convincing that they are usually taken for the person involved. More often, however, they haunt that person alone and by so doing indicate some terrible tragedy is imminent. A doppelganger is invisible except to its owner and is not reflected in a mirror. Robert Kirk described one in *Secret Commonwealth of Elves, Fauns and Fairies* (1691) as follows:

> . . . in every way like the man, as a twin brother and companion, haunting him as his shadow, both before and after the original is dead; and was also often seen of old to enter a Hous, by which the People knew that the Person of that Liknes wes to Visite them within a few days. This Copy, Echo or living picture, goes att laste to his own Herd.

The doppelganger stands right behind its owner and always moves swiftly to dodge out of sight. Cats and dogs can see doppelgangers, and if one looks wide-eyed over your shoulder this is the likely cause.

Dragon Huge, scaly monsters of the reptile kingdom, variously described as being red, green or black, with flaming eyes, clawed feet and a snake's tail. Generally savage in nature, they were believed to have bred underground in the beginning of the world, their twisting movements resulting in a network of caverns and catacombs which led to the sea. Dragons are thought to have appeared above ground in China and Japan before moving to Europe. Some say that when dragons moved above ground, fairies assumed ownership of many of the caves and mounds and the treasure therein. The Greek *draca* (sharp vision) is a characteristic referred to by the Greek epic poet Hesiod (eighth century BC) in *The Shield of Hercules*:

> The scaly monster of a dragon, coil'd full in the central field — unspeakable, with eyes oblique retorted that aslant shot gleaming fire . . .

In Ireland the word 'drag' meant 'fire', and the Welsh 'dreigiaw' referred to 'silent meteors'. Hence Shakespeare says in *Cymbeline*:

> Swift, swift ye dragons of the night!
> That dawning may bare the raven's eye.

To the ancients, dragons represented malignant and destructive power. In Africa they were the hybrid offspring of an eagle and a wolf, and were usually the guardians of a fortune in gems, hidden in mountain caves or underground tunnels. Similarly, in Greek legend, dragons stood watch over the Golden Fleece and the Golden Apples of the HESPERIDES.

Other cultures claimed that planting dragon's teeth would cause a fierce army to burst forth from the soil, or that dragons were the form assumed by the cursed dead. To early Christians dragons symbolised paganism and sin, witness *Psalms* xci:13, where saints are said to 'trample the dragon under their feet'. The many allegorical stories about saints vanquishing dragons and freeing captive virgins, such as St George, arose at this time, and dragons were hunted mercilessly. In particular, the English dragons, known as Worms, were a menace to the countryside for they attacked stock and laid waste to villages by poisoning the water supply. They could only be killed with a spear through one small spot on their back, or in their mouth, that was not protected by scales. The huntsman could then claim the dragon's treasure hoard, and it is said that many of the noble houses of England were thus financed.

In China, however, dragons were perceived as benevolent. Their appearance in the sky was an omen of good fortune. These dragons were usually bright red, with golden-tipped scales and sheer, membranous wings. They were intimately connected with the elements and could be petitioned to control rain and wind on mortals' behalf. Oriental dragons were not bloodthirsty like the Worms in England, and a pretty story tells us that the beautiful colours of autumn leaves are a result of a nearby dragon yawning and tinging them with his warm breath, before settling down to his winter hibernation.

Duergar Scandinavian folklore describes the 'dwergar' as a demi-god who controlled echoes and shadows, thus creating a world of trickery and illusion. Similarly, the duergar is a malicious type of GOBLIN who dwells in the hills and rocks of Northumberland in northern England. They are noted for their strength, tenacity, magical powers and skills in metallurgy. According to ancient Gothic legend, duergars sprang from the maggots eating the flesh of the giant YMIR, and fled into the ground when the first light broke. Since then, they have represented the darker, subterranean forces of nature. Their evil habits are illustrated in the following tale: a traveller, lost and alone at night on a craggy moor, was invited by a duergar to sit by his fire and warm himself. As the fire burnt down, the duergar got up and took a log lying to the right of the fire and placed it amongst the embers. As this burnt down, the DWARF asked his guest to fetch another log, this time lying to the left of where they sat. Sensing a trick, the traveller refused and instantly the duergar and his fire vanished. The traveller then saw that he was sitting right on the edge of a cliff, and if he had leaned over to get the log he would have fallen to his death.

Dumuzi Sumerian monarchs received their authority from Dumuzi, the god of male fertility and strength. His mother was a dragon-headed cloud and his wife was INANNA. Their happy union ensured prosperity for the city and its people. Dumuzi was principally responsible for the country's agriculture, and he controlled the natural forces on earth, rather than the celestial powers of moon and stars. His periodic descent to the Underworld — as a result of quarrels with Inanna — and his return from there, symbolise the constant cycle of death and rebirth in nature.

Dunnie A mischievous fairy-beast who, like the COLT PIXY, most usually takes the form of a horse, although also as an old man or woman. The dunnie, or doonie, most especially delights in taking an unsuspecting victim for a wild ride and then tossing him into a pile of mud or manure. It does have a benevolent side to its nature, though, and will guide lost children home and rescue sick or trapped forest animals.

Dunter A rather vicious English GHOST which haunts ancient sites of keeps and castles along the Scottish border. In days of yore, such places were spattered with the blood of sacrificial victims to ensure good fortune in battle, and dunters are thought to be the spirits of these unhappy people. They make a constant rhythmic noise, described as the grinding of seed in a hollow stone mill, to warn away intruders. Should this noise become louder suddenly and be heard in the nearby town, it was an evil omen.

Duppy A type of voodoo GHOST found in the West Indies who is usually summonsed by villagers to undertake some act of revenge. This is done by pouring a glass of rum on the grave of a person newly dead, then calling their name until they appear. The duppy is the personification of evil and only capable of malicious acts; at the very least its fetid breath will cause a victim to vomit violently, though it is more often asked to kill via its pernicious touch. The duppy can only operate at night and will expect a reward on returning to its grave. Those who feared attack from a duppy would sprinkle tobacco seed in its path as a sure method of repulsion.

Dwarf Dwarves are powerfully built little people who live underground or in mountain caves throughout Europe, particularly Scandinavia. The menfolk have an aged, craggy appearance, being hunch-backed from their hard labour, and wear a long grey beard. Standing no more than a foot high, they seldom leave their subterranean homes, for exposure to sunlight will turn them to stone. They are usually dressed in long grey tunics and scarlet aprons that touch the ground, being extremely sensitive about showing their feet to anyone. This is because they are often deformed, either pointing backwards or shaped like those of a goat, or goose. Those looking for dwarves may sprinkle soft flour near a likely place at twilight, so as to study the footprints found there in the morning. According to some accounts, dwarves appear as toads during the day.

Dwarves mine for precious metals and work them into beautiful ornaments and jewellery. Among their many magical artefacts are Miolnir (the Hammer of THOR), Gram (Siegfried's sword), Brisingamen (FREYA's necklace) and the ship Skidbladnir, large enough to ferry all the Norse gods across the skies, yet small enough to be kept in ODIN's pocket. Dwarves were well-versed in all magical matters — witness RUMPELSTILTSKIN, who could spin gold from straw, and King Albrich, who could restrain an angry giant with an enchanted coat-thread.

The keepers of all precious stones and gems, dwarves are chary of speaking to humans for fear their treasures will be stolen. However, those wishing to learn the dwarves' skill in metallurgy or wood-carving should offer gifts of money or gold in exchange. When leaving the dwarves' lair, be quite sure to take nothing away, not even a pebble, for the dwarves will sense the theft and bring misfortune upon the offender.

Dybbuk The name given to a demonic or maniacal GHOST of someone who had been evil during his lifetime. Typically a dybbuk was not satisfied with life beyond the grave and would return to take possession of another person, changing their character and using them to wreak havoc. An old story of an exorcism of a dybbuk seems closely associated with Christian legend. It was said that a talented and gentle boy, named Israel, led his classmates into the forest to admire the birds and flowers, talking all the while of the holy scriptures. Suddenly, they were attacked by a dybbuk in the form of a hitherto placid woodsman who now wanted to eat the band of travellers. Israel proceeded to walk directly into the dybbuk's slavering jaws, down to where its horrible heart was. Unafraid, he plucked the heart and made his exit. Then, with a clap of thunder, the dybuk crumpled and resumed the form of the placid woodsman, the evil black heart having disappeared.

E

Each-Uisge A fierce and dangerous fairy water-horse found in Scotland. Very similar to the AUGHISKY of Ireland, it is treacherous to its rider, carrying a victim into the water to be devoured. Its skin is sticky and the rider cannot jump off. It preys on children in particular, one gruesome tale relating that an Each-Uisge made off with seven children, the only remains being their discarded livers when they washed ashore.

As with all fairy animals, the Each-Uisge has the ability to change its shape at will. A well-known story tells of a handsome young man who made love to a village girl on a river bank before they dozed together in the sun; as she combed his hair she found weeds and shells, thus identifying the dreaded creature. Stealthily, she drew away and began to run. As she neared her home, she heard the thunder of hooves behind her and turning saw the water-horse coming for her. She was saved by her aunt, who released the tame water-bull, the latter being a loyal servant, which chased the Each-Uisge towards the loch and battled with it (*see also* CRODH MARA).

Eale Also known as yale, an odd-looking creature found in the south of India. It had an elephant's tail and a boar's head which was bearded, goat-fashion. It also had two spiralling horns which could be pointed independently in any direction — a tremendous advantage in a battle. For this reason, eales were used as temple guardians to ward off evil spirits and looters.

Echidna In Greek mythology, Echidna was the wife of TYPHON, the hurricane deity. She was a horrific type of MERMAID, with the tail of a serpent and the torso of a beautiful woman. Her nature was most malevolent and her cursed offspring brought chaos and hardship to the world; they included the CHIMERA, the SPHINX, the GORGONS, the hell-hound CERBERUS and the hundred-headed dragon of the HESPERIDES. Living in damp caves beneath the earth, Echidna shunned the light of day; her presence could be tracked by rank, marshy patches, or cracks in the soil's surface.

El Also known as The First One and The Master of Time, El was the father of gods and men amongst ancient Syrians and Canaanites. He was omnipotent and instrumental in the fertilisation of the earth, having divinely bestowed the first rain. As a result, one of his sacred titles was 'He who causes the springs to flow'. El was usually depicted as a seated figure wearing bull's horns, the symbol of strength and fertility.

Elemental A supernatural spirit which haunts places or people without being the GHOST of a person himself. Elementals often appear as a moving light or a change in temperature, or they may take the form of an animal or bird and make it behave oddly for a period of time. They are drawn to places of power, often appearing at the site of some great battle or murder, or frequenting ancient shrines to nature spirits.

Elf Among the most ancient of fairy people. In *The Faerie Queene*, Spenser wrote of the first man and woman as 'Elfe . . . and Fay . . . [of] whom all Fayres spring':

> Of these a mighty people shortly grew
> And puissant kings which all the world warray'd
> And to themselves all nations did subdue.

Originating in Scandinavian mythology, elves are capricious sprites that dance on the grass, or sit in the leaves of trees and bask in the light of the full moon. They may be divided into two classes: the good Light Elves and the more powerful Dark Elves. Light Elves have fair, golden hair, sweet musical voices and magic harps. Unlike many fairy folk elves move about at will during the day, the young females taking particular delight in riding sunbeams through keyholes. They are invisible to humans, although a child born on a Sunday may glimpse them if he puts one foot inside a fairy ring. Dark Elves, however, are slightly more sinister. Short, ugly, long-nosed with dirty brown clothes, they also love to dance, but their feet poison and blacken the grass, making it unfit for animals to graze there. A single whiff of their breath will cause sickness or death, and the music from their demented fiddling will drive a man mad. Sick cattle or children are thought to have been harmed by a Dark Elf's arrow, as Collins wrote:

> There every herd by sad experience knows
> How, winged with fate, their elf-shot arrows fly
> When the sick ewe her summer food forgoes
> Or Stretched on earth the heart-smit heifers lie.
>
> *Popular Superstitions*

Birthmarks, or other natural defects, were thought to be marks or bruises left by elves, and Queen Margaret insulted Shakespeare's *Richard III* accordingly:

> . . . thou elvish-marked, abortive, rooting hog!

The word 'elf' was later applied only to small fairy boys; witness Titania's decision 'to make my small elves . . . coats'. The elves themselves disliked the name as a result, seeing it as patronising, and preferred to be called 'good neighbour' instead.

Elle Folk Usually considered to be a type of Danish ELF, although the story of their origin sets them apart, for they are believed to be the descendants of Adam and his first wife, Lilith. Elle Folk are great thieves of dough and other food, and are strange-looking indeed. Elle-women are beautiful and alluring from the front, though from behind they sport hollow backs and cows' tails. The Elle-men are stooped and old, and are happiest when lying in a pool of sunlight to warm their withered limbs. Also known as Huldre Folk, these elves are sensitive about their defects and should be treated with tact by mortals, else their cattle will die.

Ellyon A Welsh ELF. Dear little folk, tiny, with thin high-pitched voices, they sup on toadstools and 'fairy butter', the latter being a yellow fungus found in the roots of old trees. Ellyon are well-intentioned towards mortals and will sweep and clean the kitchen and tidy the shelves cheerfully each evening, dancing and talking the while. Their only condition is that their privacy be respected; if the householder spies on them as they work, they will vanish and never return.

Emma-Hoo Also known as Emm-O, he is the chief of Jigoku, the Underground Hell of Japanese myth. Emma-Hoo is depicted as riding on a water-buffalo and parading past lines of men to pass judgement upon them, reflecting their sentence back to them by means of a giant bronze mirror on his breast. A harsh judgement would occasionally be reprieved by intervention from his sister, who sat by his side where she judged the women. On the strength of a prayer from a loving soul, she would suggest an unfortunate soul be reborn and given a chance to reform, rather than be doomed to purgatory.

Empusae Menacing creatures of Greek mythology who took the form of beautiful maidens, the better to seduce and murder lone male travellers. In their natural state, empusae had the head and breasts of a lovely girl and the body and legs of a donkey. They would wait silently by the roadside for a victim and could only be identified if forced to speak, for then they would emit a loud bray.

Endymion Once a beautiful mortal youth, a shepherd who tended his flock on Mount Latmos, Endymion was beloved by the moon, Silene. Legend has it that ZEUS granted the boy immortality on condition that he remain forever slumbering. Thus each evening Silene bathes her white body in the ocean, then sets off across the skies to caress her sleeping lover. In *The Merchant of Venice* Shakespeare writes:

> . . . the moon sleeps with Endymion,
> And would fain be disturbed.

Enlil The Sumerian god of wind and air. Strongly associated with industry and growth, his gift to the people was said to have been the pick-axe, and his likeness was often placed by a new roadway or building. Enlil had an ambivalent attitude to mankind. On the one hand he smiled upon human endeavours; however, if irritated he enlisted the aid of the monster Labbu and wrought tempests, specifically floods or hail. In a particularly devastating tantrum, it was Enlil who was responsible for engendering the Great Flood, having first saved the moon and set her adrift in a boat. He held the 'tupismati' (tablets of destiny) and could be petitioned to determine the course of the world.

Eos In Greek mythology, the goddess of the dawn, also called the Dawn Maiden; to the Romans, she was Aurora. Sister to HELIOS the sun, and Silene the moon, Eos is described as ever-youthful and lovely. Homer called her 'rosy-fingered'. She sets out before the sun, driving a team of horses which pull her soft blue chariot up from the depths of the ocean, and shows her brother the way to rise. James Thomson, in his poem *Castle of Indolence*, wrote:

> You cannot shut the windows of the sky
> Through which Eos shows her brightening eye.

Eos abducted ORION to be her lover, and later wed Astareus the Titan and bore the Four Winds, Boreas, Eurus, Notus and Zephyrus. Both gods and mortal men found her captivating, and by her first husband Tithonius she became the mother of Memnon, King of Ethiopia and one of the Egyptian gods. Memnon was slain by ACHILLES at Troy and Eos has mourned her son ever since, her daily tears forming the morning dew.

Another well-known story about Eos concerns her mortal husband Tithonius. For him she begged the gift of immortality from her fellow gods, but neglected to specify eternal youth as well. As a result her handsome husband shrank into a shrivelled old man until he was so deformed the gods took pity on him and turned him into a cicada — one of the first creatures to excitedly greet the dawn on a warm summer's day.

Epona Originally a Celtic nature-goddess, depicted as a woman astride a mare, or a woman's torso with a horse's head. Epona was adopted by the Romans as a goddess of horses and mules. In Roman art she was shown with a cornucopia of grain, while in Eastern Europe and England huge horses were carved into chalky hillsides by devotees of her cult.

Erinnyes Also known as the Furies, Daughters of the Night, or the Angry Ones, these were avenging goddesses of the Underworld in Greek mythology. They sprang from blood spilled by the mutilated Uranus and were horrible indeed to behold, with snakes in their hair and bat-like wings. Their names bore apt testimony to their fearful nature — Allekto (she who is unremitting), Teisiphone (she who avenges murder), and Megaira (she who is envious). Each carried a whip and flaming torch with which to chivy both mortal offenders and recalcitrant gods. They were charged with dispensing justice and avenging violations of the natural order. For instance, they prohibited HERA from endowing her horse with speech, for they considered this unnatural; they would also return the sun to its true course, whenever it deviated for any reason.

Eros The Greek god of love who inspired physical attraction between the sexes and thus ensured the continuity of life. Eros was known as Cupid to the Romans. The son of APHRODITE and ARES, this mischievous god was married to the beautiful mortal maid Psyche, and liked nothing better than to meddle in human affairs. He carried a bow and a quiver full of arrows — golden ones which caused their victims to fall in love, and leaden ones which resulted in disinterest. Hesiod, the eighth-century Greek poet, in his *Theogony*, described him as 'the most beautiful and wanton of gods' bearing a quiver 'full of arous'd desires'. Eros was usually depicted in conjunction with Hymen, the god of marriage.

The ancient Spartan cult paid Eros great homage, regarding him as a great creative force in men's lives, the builder of dynasties and the establisher of friendships, as well as the creator of sexual desire. At one time, the Orphic cult of extremists regarded him as the Creator of the world.

Erymanthian Boar The capture of this hideous wild animal was one of the labours of HERCULES. Black as night, with flaming red eyes and tusks as long as a man's arm, the Erymanthian Boar had killed many people. However, its brain was minuscule and Hercules managed to trap it by pretending to be an army and getting the animal confused and tangled in foliage. Once trapped, the boar was delivered to the city of Mycenae, which it had long terrorised, and there it was ceremonially disposed of.

Estrie The medieval Hebrew version of a VAMPIRE. Travelling by night she took the form of a mortal nurse, the better to prey on children and suck their blood. In her normal state she had the head and teeth of a savage wolf and the wings of a bat, although she would endeavour not to allow any mortal to see her thus. To avoid being seen or attacked, she would clutch at bread or salt belonging to her victim's family and attempt to eat it quickly. If the mortal was able to stop her doing this, the estrie would die. To ensure she remained this way, her mouth would be packed with earth, thus assuaging her hunger in the Afterworld.

Etain The most romantic legend in the realm of fairies is the Irish tale of Midhir, King of the Fairy Hill, and Etain (or Edain) of the TUATHA DE DANAAN. A jealous rival turned the lovely Etain into a fly and she was carried away by the winds. After seven years the insect was blown into the Great Hall of Inver Cechmaine and was accidentally swallowed by the wife of that nobleman; she was reborn nine months later, again given the name Etain and growing to be an exquisitely beautiful woman. All the while, Midhir knew where she was and eventually came to reclaim his lost bride with the aid of fairy magic and wisdom.

F

Fachan Also known as Fachen, Fachin, or the Diereach, this evil monster from Scotland is so ugly that simply looking upon one could result in death from heart failure. J.F. Campbell, in *Popular Tales of the West Highlands*, described one thus:

> . . . one hand out of its chest, one leg out of its haunch and one eye out of the front of its face.

Other reports claim the fachan sported a tuft of dark blue feathers from its head, like a cock's comb, which it ruffled before attacking. Its sole gnarled arm was exceptionally strong and, wielding a flail of iron chain or leather thonging, he could destroy an orchard overnight.

Fafnir According to Wagner's opera *The Ring of the Nibelung*, Fafnir was an evil and ruthless giant who killed both his brother and father to obtain their gold. He then turned himself into an enormous DRAGON and settled down on top of the cache. The only mortal who was able to slay Fafnir was the hero Siegfried, who, by eating another dragon's heart and bathing in blood Fafnir spilled from his wounds, was endowed with supernatural strength.

Fairy Godmother A generic term for any good-natured fairy who performs kind acts for mortals, particularly babies and women, so they are always made very welcome at christenings. In classical literature, certain fairies acted as guardians for different gods. For instance, Tasso (1544-95) tells of Lucina, who was the protectress of Alidoro and his lady-love, the maiden warrior Mirinda, and of Urganda, the guardian fairy of Amadigi. Various other tales account for the origin of the fairy godmother — one has it that, like the Italian witch Befana, a fairy godmother was actually looking endlessly for the Christ Child. The Bulgarians sombrely suggest that she is a dead mother looking for her own baby, while the Spanish say she is the GHOST of an aunt or grandmother, looking to make a gift to her descendants. With the arrival of Christianity, the Virgin Mary was combined with most versions of the story and popularised as a spiritual benefactor, and guardian or 'godmother' to everyone.

Fairy Rade Since the days of the legendary TUATHA DE DANAAN, Irish fairies have enjoyed aristocratic entertainments — music, feasting, tournaments of skill, and literature. Another time-honoured pursuit is embarking upon a stately procession or 'rade'. This magnificent sight was described by Lady Wilde in her *Ancient Legends, Mystic Charms and Superstitions of Ireland*:

> Seven score steeds, each with a jewel in his forehead like a star, and seven-score horsemen all the sons of kings, in their green mantles fringed with gold, and golden helmets on their heads and golden greaves on their limbs and each knight having in his hand a golden spear.

No servant was allowed to ride a fairy steed; indeed, so proud were these beasts that 'a base-born churl [would be] thrown violently to the ground and killed on the spot.' These processions or rades are common to many aristocratic fairy families throughout the world.

Fates Also known as the Moirae, three goddesses whom the Greeks and Romans believed to arbitrarily control the birth, life events and death of every man. The daughters of the night, they were Clotho, who spun the thread of life; Lachesis, who would often add that little touch of luck to change a person's destiny; and Atropos, The Unchangeable, who used her 'abhorred shears' to cut the thread of life at death. The Fates were thought cruel, for they paid no heed to human suffering and were usually depicted as old and ugly women attended by the shadowy Nemesis, goddess of the inevitable. The Albanians tended to a more charitable view, describing the Three Fates as fairy-like creatures with butterflies' wings.

Faunus The grandson of SATURN, Faunus was worshipped by the Romans as a fertility god. He was also adopted by shepherds and herdsmen as a protector of forests and animals. He came to be identified with the Greek PAN and was depicted with horns and the legs of a goat or wolf. His attendants, the mythological fauns, were the patrons of wild animals and gave their name to the animal kingdoms in different countries — the fauna.

Fee A passionate and mysterious ELF, native to France. Few men have been able to resist their strength and beauty, and at one time would congregate at the base of the zigzag path which led to the French village of Faye, hoping for a glimpse. Francois Rabelais (*c.*1494-*c.*1553) accordingly wrote that 'they go to Paradise as the way is to Faye'(from *Gargantua and Pantagruel*). Also known as WHITE LADIES they dress in pure white and live by streams, so they may meticulously rinse their gowns clean every evening. To dry them, they don the clothes and embark on a wild, abandoned dance by the river-shore. Should any fellow be passing by, he must refuse their invitation or else they will dance him to a watery grave. Fees have beautiful faces with hypnotic eyes, though they may be identified by a physical flaw, such as a snake's tail or bird's feet. Originally nature spirits, fees would metamorphose into fog or cloud, mountain stones or moss at will. They would also mingle with unwary humans for spite, selling jewellery and magic cloth at the village fete — when the purchaser leant to pick up the item, the fee would twist his arm and fling him to the ground.

Feng-Huang A marvellous bird, sometimes called the Chinese Phoenix, which dwelt in ancient China. It was the sun's messenger and therefore acted as a herald of peace and prosperity, always to be seen flying overhead when a new Emperor ascended the throne. Its feathers were long, silken and of every imaginable colour, and were said to be infused with the glow of Paradise. The feng-huang's voice was also beautiful, and its song consisted of five perfect notes which echoed in the mountains as the bird soared the skies before returning to its home in the clouds with the gods.

Fenoderee Variously spelled Fenodyree or Phynoderee, the fenoderee is a hairy BROWNIE found on the Isle of Man. He is tall, with twisted, ugly features and a body covered in black hair. Tradition has it that the first fenoderee was actually a handsome prince from the proud fairy tribe of the Ferrishyn. His ill-looks are a punishment received when he failed to appear at a fairy festival, preferring to spend his time with a mortal maiden.

The fenoderee possess phenomenal strength and are favoured by farmers for helping with heavy agricultural tasks, in particular they are famous for their skill and thoroughness in harvesting crops, and have been known to thresh a barnful of corn in one night. When seeking mischief, the fenoderee will offer to shake hands, for easily crushing the bones of his victim's hand amuses him greatly. His strength is not matched by his intelligence, however, and humans wishing to avenge their broken or bruised fingers will instruct the fenoderee to fetch water with a sieve, or to round up a hare, using a flock of sheep.

Having helped the farmer with his labours, the fenoderee, like all brownies, should not be thanked or offered any gifts, for he will be greatly offended and leave at once. Nor will he tolerate criticism. John Rhys tells of a fenoderee who was given a suit of clothes; so disgusted was he with this 'bribe' that he placed a curse on the family for each item.

Fenrir A giant demon wolf, Fenrir was the brother of HEL, the Scandinavian god of the dead. He was exceedingly malicious and the gods had to restrain him with a magic chain, named Gleipnir, forged from:

> . . . the sound of a cat's footsteps, the roots of a mountain, the breath of a fish, the beard of a woman and the spittle of a bird.

This chain successfully bound Fenrir until Ragnarok, the Day of Judgement, when he broke loose and ran amok in the heavens, swallowing ODIN whole. For this crime, Fenrir was sent into exile forever more, though his leering face and slavering jaws may still be seen in rosy cloud formations at sunset.

Fetch A WRAITH, the disembodied GHOST of a living person, fetch is the common name used in England to describe a double (*see* DOPPELGANGER), and is inevitably a portent of death. It is similar to the Norse 'fylgia', the spirit follower who accompanied every man and woman through life and died with them. Queen Elizabeth I is said to have died after seeing her fetch 'pallid, shrivelled and wan'. John Aubrey, in his *Miscellanies* (1696) vividly describes a fetch's appearance:

> The beautiful Lady Diana Rich, daughter of the Earl of Holland, as she was walking in her father's garden at Kensington, to take the fresh air before dinner, about eleven o'clock, being then very well, met with her own apparition, habit and everything, as in a looking-glass. About a month after, she died of the smallpox. And it is said that her sister, the Lady Isabella Thynne, saw the like of herself also, before she died. This account I had from a person of honour.

While the English waited patiently for a fetch to appear, as a summons for mortals to proceed to the grave, it is interesting to note that the word was adapted by the Portuguese as *fetisso* (magician or oracle), and involved a concentrated worship of idols to determine the future, including the time of death.

Finn Originally known as Fionn MacCumal, this Irish mortal achieved divine status. As a child he touched the god's magic salmon and, upon sucking his thumb, became possessor of all knowledge. Finn and his son Oisin were heroes of the cycle of epic tales, *The Fianna*, which celebrated all the gods and kings of Ireland. Together they founded a band of tried warriors, known as Fenians or Finn's People. Few soldiers passed the entrance test: the candidate stood in a hole in the ground up to his waist, wearing no armour. Then, said *The Fianna*:

> . . . must nine warriors, having nine spears, with a ten furrows' width between them and him, assail him and at the same time let fly at him.

If the would-be Finian was wounded he was not accepted.

Finn married a witch called Saar, who usually manifested herself as a deer. Finn, in turn, often appeared in the guise of a hind or a hunting dog, and his children took the form of fauns (*see* FAUNUS) when wishing to escape danger.

Finvarra The High King of the Irish fairies. He headed the tribe of the Daoine Sidhe, originally the TUATHA DE DANAAN, who lived in the Hollow Hills. The palace court, called Finvarra's Rath, existed beneath the Hill of Knochma. Originally gigantic in stature, Finvarra and his court became, with the coming of Christianity, far smaller, and they regarded their ancient armaments and helmets with awe at their size. However, Finvarra's looks and virility were not impaired. Although he was married to OONAGH, the most beautiful woman to have ever lived, he frequently gave chase to pretty mortal maids and carried them off to his royal chambers. Only rarely, as in the case of Ethna the Bride, did these women ever wish to return home to their mere mortal husbands after a night with the Fairy King.

Finvarra possessed great intelligence and was a famed chess-player. Many mortals lost all they owned — including their own lives — in a game with him. This resulted in Finvarra often being regarded as the King of the Underworld and his court as the Company of the Dead. In Lady Wilde's tale *November Eve* (from *Ancient Legends, Mystic Charms and Superstitioins of Ireland*), she tells of a lad who was lured to a fairy revel where he met Finvarra and Oonagh. On sitting at the table to enjoy marvellous victuals and music, he saw that a servant was actually the GHOST of his recently dead neighbour. Resisting the blandishments of his host, he fell senseless to the ground, and:

> when he awoke, he was lying in a stone circle and his arms were black and blue with the marks of fairy fingers.

Fir Darrig Also known as Fear Dearg, this odd little fairy with the blue nose and red coat is a native to Ireland. For a fee of whisky he will help mortals caught in Fairyland to escape, or show them antidotes to spells and curses. He is, however, not a trustworthy sprite, and delights in practical jokes of a bizarre and sometimes gruesome nature. He is the unchallenged master of 'pishogue', the art of bemusing a man's sense, and can cast spells turning day into night, men into women, food into dust — in fact, everything to its opposite.

Firebird A gentle and benevolent bird fabled in Russia for its habit of appearing when mortals need its help. Storytellers described its eyes as flashing crystal, and its glistening feathers to be made of pure gold — a single one could light up a darkened room. The firebird dined exclusively upon golden apples and its powerful wings created strong winds when the bird took to the air; as he flew, all the other birds would fall silent in awe at his grace. Stravinsky's ballet *The Firebird* re-tells the most famous tale of this creature, who carried a prince to a land that had long lain asleep, there to rescue a princess and help her dispose of the witch who had enchanted her countrymen.

Flying Dutchman Immortalised in Richard Wagner's opera *Der Fliegende Hollander* (1843) and Captain Marryat's stirring *The Phantom Ship* (1839), this is probably the most famous GHOST ship of all. It is frequently seen in stormy weather off the Cape of Good Hope and considered an omen of ill fortune. King George V witnessed the spectral ship in 1881, making the following entry in his journal:

> July 11 1881: During the middle watch, the so-called 'Flying Dutchman' crossed our bows. She first appeared as a strange red light, as of a ship all a-glow, in the midst of which light her masts, spars and sails, seemingly those of a normal brig., some 200 yards distant from us, stood out in strong relief as she came up. Our lookout man on the forecastle reported her as close to our port bow, where also the officer of the watch from the bridge clearly saw her as did our quarter-deck midshipman, who was sent forward at once to the forecastle to report back. But, on

> reaching there, no vestige nor any sign of any material ship was to be seen either near or away to the horizon.

True to tradition, this sighting was followed swiftly by one of the crew suffering a fatal accident. There are several versions of the tale explaining why *The Flying Dutchman* is accursed. One is that the captain of the original vessel, caught in a shocking storm, cursed God and endangered his men. For his blasphemy and irresponsible behaviour, he was doomed to wander about like a sea-tossed ghost, never to rest again. Another story, from Sir Walter Scott, says the vessel was originally laden with precious jewels, then violent murder took place, followed by plague. As a result, no port would offer the boat shelter, and it ceaselessly traverses the Cape, seeking safe harbour.

Formorians Also known as Fomorians, hideous demons in Ireland made up of a motley of twisted beast and human flesh, who pre-existed the Great Flood. A quarrelsome tribe, they were led by King Conan and his malignant deputy, BALOR, into battle armed with clubs and stones. Balor had two eyes, one being invested with so much evil power that it took four men to lift the eye-lid.

In Scotland the Fomors were a race of giants, also skilled in enchantment and cruel rulers. In both countries the Fomors were defeated by warriors of a brave new race armed with golden spears and helmets, who were variously referred to as the Partholan or the TUATHA DE DANAAN. Symbolically, the Fomorians were thought to represent the old pagan beliefs that entailed human and animal sacrifices being submerged by a new age of enlightenment.

Fossegrim The name given to a plaintive GHOST of a young man who haunts European rivers, playing his flute and desultorily throwing pebbles into still water. He likes to admire pretty girls and will seldom harm them, sitting on a rock in the centre of the river to see them as they punt past. However, if one maiden is foolish or churlish enough to become upset by the sight of Fossegrim, he could well overturn the boat from spite. An old

French tradition, that each boat should carry an unsheathed knife in its prow to combat the Fossegrim, is still adhered to.

Freya An extremely lovely VALKYRIE, Freya became one of the wives of ODIN. She was the German goddess of love, fertility and childbirth, the Norse equivalent of APHRODITE. Freya is usually depicted wearing a magic necklace forged in the sun called Brisingamen, and a cloak made of falcon's wings. She travelled in a chariot drawn by cats, the latter being her sacred animal symbol and familiars. Despite her many affairs — one of her immortal duties being to entertain heroes slain on the battlefield — she loved Odin dearly and wept tears of gold when she lost him.

Fridean A form of Scottish ELF who lived by roadways. Travellers would offer them bread and milk to be sure of a safe journey.

Fuath A Scottish term referring to a group of fairies and fairy beasts which can be dangerous, or at least mischievous. They include the SHELLYCOAT and the URISK. Often male, fuath may assume the shape of a stallion; they always live near the water.

Fudu-myoo The guardian of wisdom, according to Japanese lore. He is usually portrayed with an exaggeratedly high forehead and awarded the title The Unshakeable Spirit. Fudu-myoo is single-minded in his pursuit of the truth, and his wrathful wielding of the Sword of Knowledge in his battle with human greed and ignorance is a fearsome sight to behold.

Furies *see* ERINNYES

G

Gabriel Hounds Also known as Gabriel Ratchet's Hounds, or Sky Yelpers, these were ghostly wolves with human heads who roamed the skies during storms. Sometimes thought to be the souls of unbaptised children and unrepentant sinners, their bloodcurdling howls were an omen of death to all who heard them. English country folk once believed these beasts would hover over a house as a warning to the inmates to mend their ways. It is now more widely accepted that the hounds are, in fact, night-flying geese. The flapping of their wings and the strange cries they make would indeed have been eerie for those who knew nothing of bird migration.

Gaea Also known as Gaeia, the Great Earth Mother and fertility goddess of Greek mythology. The most popular story concerning her conception was that a golden egg tumbled out of Chaos in the beginning of the world. When this split open, one half revealed Gaea, the other Uranus. From her union with Uranus were born Pontus the sea god, and the mountains. She also gave birth to CRONUS, the first ruler of Olympus, the Titans and the Cyclops. More unfortunate offspring included the monster TYPHON, as a result of her mating with the king of the Underworld, Tartarus.

Gaea was, ultimately, the source of all life; hence the ancient custom of placing a newborn child on the ground, that it might draw from her strength. In early religion she was worshipped as the patroness of marriage, her fecundity being petitioned with gifts of fruit and seeds.

Galleybeggar A headless GHOST which frequents Somerset in south-western England. The old word 'galley', from whence the ghost's name derived, means to scare or frighten. This would appear well-chosen, for the galleybeggar's main purpose seems to be to terrify anyone who sees it. Witness Ruth Tongue's story of the galleybeggar who would tuck his head firmly under his arm and then slide on a toboggan through the main street of a village, shrieking with laughter the while (from *Forgotten Tales of English Counties*). The galleybeggar appears to have no malice as motive, just mischief.

Galleytrot A GHOST which appears in the north of England. It usually takes the form of a huge, shaggy white dog, about the size of a bull-calf, which will pursue anyone it sees. Alasdair A. MacGregor in *The Ghost Book* (1955) speculated that the name 'galleytrot' came from the French *gardez le tresor* (to look after treasure). This could well be true, for most sightings of a 'galley' have been near the sites of ancient monasteries or graveyards, where coins or gold plate could be buried.

Ganconer Also known as the Irish Cancanagh, or Love Talker, an extremely handsome and dashing — though rather unprincipled — fairy. He wanders lonely valleys and isolated copses, where he plays enticing music on his flute. The Love Talker preys upon unaccompanied young women, such as shepherdesses or milkmaids, seduces them and then disappears. The girl having once experienced a fairy lovemaking is no longer contented in this world, and will pine and die for her fairy lover. Girls wishing to avoid such a fate should shun wearing or passing near fairy flowers, such as clumps of harebells or love-in-idleness. Most dangerous of all is the May bush — witness the old song:

> O my love wore a garland of May
> O my love wore a garland of May
> And she looked so nice and neat
> To her pretty little feet
> When she met her false lover in the dew.

Ganesa Also addressed as the Lord of the Host, Ganesa was the god of wisdom and success in Hindu mythology. He was the elephant-headed son of SHIVA, and usually portrayed as plump and amiable, no doubt resulting from his fondness for fruit and sweet rice cakes offered by his followers. He rides a rat, and is of a yellow colour, with four hands which hold a shell, a discus, a waterlily and a club. A legend explains his elephant's head as follows: when his mother, Parvati, was bathing, Ganesa was assigned as guardian for her privacy. Unfortunately he even refused entry to his father, Shiva, who sliced off his son's head in a fit of anger. So remorseful was Shiva that he took the head of the first creature he encountered and placed it on the boy's shoulders. By acquiring an elephant's head, Ganesa also assumed the elephant's sagacity and became the patron of literature. Even today, Indian students invoke a prayer to Ganesa when they start a new term at school.

Gans Spirits invoked by the American Apache Indian tribe. The SHAMAN who is offering prayers to the gans wears a black mask and a high head-dress made of wooden slats. The dancing takes place in ceremonial houses known as 'kivas'. Although early white settlers thought these were evil dances and that the gans were devils, in fact the purpose of the ceremonies was to drive evil spirits away from the tribe's vicinity. If the gans were sufficiently propitiated, they would use their considerable powers to attract good fortune.

Ganymede The extremely beautiful son of the King of Troy. Lustful travellers came from all over the world to watch him dance, naked except for a silk cap atop his curls. Ganymede was beloved by ZEUS, who assumed the guise of an eagle so as to spirit him up to Olympus; there he was given immortality and became the gods' cup-bearer, responsible for giving them their daily draught of the Elixir of Life. Holle wrote in his *Ariosto* of:

> . . . when Ganymede above
> His service ministers to mighty Jove.

Eventually he was rewarded for his long and faithful service by being placed in the heavens as the constellation of Aquarius.

Gargoyle We know this to refer to a decorated water-spout, usually found in church architecture. Early gargoyles were in the form of iron heads shaped like demons, and were found on temples in both Eastern and Western cultures. The Chinese specifically placed gargoyles over doors and windows to bar evil spirits from entering. These grotesque figures are usually half-human and half-bird or animal. A popular style is a fantastic dragon's head, with water flowing out of its mouth. This is a reference to Gargouille, the great French DRAGON who ransacked Rouen in the seventh century.

Garkain According to Aboriginal mythology in Australia, Garkain was an horrific spirit who haunted the thick northern rainforests. Most commonly, he assumed the form of a giant fruit-bat, with enormous wings and long, pointed teeth and a harsh cry. His horrible wont was to envelop his victim with his wings and suffocate him to death. VAMPIRE-like, the Garkain would then suck the victim's blood. In turn, the victim's GHOST would haunt the Garkain's jungle, attending the needs of its master and unable to warn away other folk who ventured too near.

Garuda The sacred god-prince of birds in Sanskrit mythology, Garuda is the enemy of snakes and loyal servant of VISHNU and LAKSHMI, his wife, who both ride upon his back. Its head, talons, beak and wings were all those of an eagle, or vulture; its limbs and torso were human. Garuda was believed to be enormous in size and, as it flew, the beating of its wings caused the earth to topple and monsoons to follow in its wake. Garuda was not only a devotee of Vishnu, but a divinity in its own right. Its mission was to skim low over the earth's surface and search out sinners, devouring them with a snap of its mighty beak. Garuda's golden colour meant it was also regarded as a sun-symbol.

Ghede In Haiti, the voodoo island of the West Indies, this god of death appears as a lean figure in black top hat, long black tail-coat and dark glasses. Ghede will live by the village crossroads, where the souls of the dead or enchanted pass by. Along with his female counterpart, Mamn Brigitte, Ghede will guard the local cemetery. He most often appears as a ghostly mosquito who will suck the blood of any white child living nearby and use this life-force to resurrect the dead.

Along with Erzulie, the goddess of erotic love, Ghede is noted for his unpredictable obscenity, behaviour which his acolytes imitate at secret rites where they raise the dead, fly through the air and supply love potions and death spells to those who desire them. Ghede has an enormous propensity for rum, and his whereabouts are usually marked by a number of bottles, along with phalluses carved on nearby trees or fences.

Ghillie Dhu A sweet-natured and docile wood-sprite from Scotland, the ghillie dhu is extremely shy. He lives alone in birch trees, clad in moss and leaves. The ghillie dhu is kind to children and will help those who are lost or frightened to find their way home, and show the hungry which berries and nuts are safe to eat. The Scots word 'gillie', referring to a stable-boy whose job it is to settle a pony and hold it for a child to ride, is derived from the fey and solitary ghillie dhu. Sir Walter Scott called barefoot and ragged wild mountain Scots lads 'gillie wet-foots', saying he could not tell them apart from the fairies who 'beat the bushes'.

Ghost The spirit of the deceased, appearing in a variety of different forms. The traditional ghost appears in a hazy white form, popularly believed to be ectoplasm. Others have taken the form of warriors, children, headless women, PHANTOM coaches, monks and many more. Usually, what all the ghosts have in common is a tragedy suffered during their life on earth, and they will reappear to a family descendant in the attempt to resolve what could not be resolved in life. For instance, those who experience a violent death (self-inflicted or otherwise) or are denied proper burial must remain earth-bound until they are exorcised. Similarly, desecrated shrines or graves are doomed to suffer from continued hauntings, and the ghosts of murdered lovers or deserted children assail the living in their quest for post-mortem justice.

Even people who have lived a normal and contented life are likely to see ghosts, sometimes called 'crisis ghosts', which appear to the living to warn of some imminent danger. Most unlucky are those ghosts of people who were violent or cruel during their lifetime. Their sins deny them rest and they will continue their nefarious behaviour beyond the grave unless formally exorcised.

Ghost Owl An eerie nocturnal predator who flew on silent wings, feared throughout the world as a supernatural bird of ill-omen. In Scotland the owl was called 'cailleach oidhche' (night hag), and in Wales 'aderyn y corff' (corpse bird). Its hooting was thought to presage death, for owls were the personification of restless spirits returning to earth to seek revenge. Anyone who kept a pet owl was suspected of being a magician, and farmers would nail an owl's body to a front door, with its wings outstretched, to avert thunder and hail. American Indians had more respect for the owl. They believed that, if beheaded or shot, poison-tipped gems and beads pour from the bird's body, killing the greedy hunter; they leave owls well alone.

Ghoul An evil GHOST who originated in Arabia. Ghouls have horrific faces and, despite being composed of vague grey matter, possess enormous strength which they use to disinter corpses and plunder grave-sites. Ghouls feed on the flesh of the dead and the living, usually frequenting churchyards and other deserted places. They are attracted to funerals where a great deal of wealth is displayed, and will stand by the graveside, invisible, biding their time until the mourners have departed. Then the ghoul will rob the corpse of the interred jewellery and devour the newly dead flesh with its sharp fangs. For this reason it is best to carry out funerals with a minimum of pomp and fuss.

Gilgamesh Once the King of Sumer in ancient Babylonia, Gilgamesh's many exploits were lauded in the important *Epic of Gilgamesh* written *c.*2000BC. Described as 'two-thirds a god and one-third a mortal', Gilgamesh attempted to achieve immortality by seeking and harvesting a briar plant which grew beneath the ocean. On returning to the surface, he carelessly looked away from where he had placed the briar and a snake ate it, whole. This is why snakes can shed their skins and pursue a new start in life, while men are condemned to the one covering which must eventually wither and die. Although Gilgamesh failed in his attempt to be a true god, the other gods took pity on his situation and appeared to comfort him with the news that he would live honoured forever as a shadow in the Underworld.

Glaistig A female water-sprite, with the face and torso of a most beautiful and seductive woman. Wearing a long, green, embroidered gown and cloak she is, however, hostile and dangerous and will lure men to dance with her by highland lochs before feeding, VAMPIRE-like, on their blood. The glaistig will occasionally assume the appearance of a kind BROWNIE, showing benign tenderness to children or old women and helping farmers to tend their cattle. She may be identified by the fact she has hairy haunches and cloven hooves, like a goat, concealed under her gown. Like the pipe-playing, nymph-ravaging PAN whom she resembles, the glaistig loves music and travels on the wind as well as by water.

Glam The name given to an Icelandic shepherd who worked for a farmer named Thorwall. A lonely and gruff soul, Glam was exceedingly ugly with rough hair and skin, though very loyal to his employer. One night, in the depths of winter, Thorwall demanded Glam go outside to settle the livestock who had been frightened by a WRAITH, or 'walker after death'. Unfortunately Glam was himself bested by the GHOST and he, too, became a surly and violent 'walker after death'. Glam returned to torment his employer whom he blamed for his death; Thorwall, however, was determined to exorcise Glam and attacked the wraith most savagely, stabbing it with daggers and throwing flaming torches through it. Although Glam was finally banished it was not before he had cursed his employer, saying he would 'see with a ghost's sight'. Thorwall died soon after, tormented by visions of GHOULS and PHANTOMS.

Glamis Castle A vision of stony dignity, with its mist-shrouded battlements, Glamis Castle in Tayside is probably the most haunted spot in Scotland. Secret chambers abound within, one of which is said to contain the skeleton of the Monster of Glamis. This is variously thought to have been a half-man, a half-beast, or a deformed child of one of the Earls of Strathmore. Many other GHOST sightings have been reported at Glamis Castle, including a Grey Lady who haunts the chapel, thought to be the sixth Lady Glamis who was wrongly burned alive as a witch; a tongueless woman wandering the grounds frantically trying to speak; a tiny page hovering by the gate; and the wicked first Lord Glamis, a rake who continues to raise merry hell with his drinking and gambling. Glamis Castle is most famous for its association with *Macbeth*, and Shakespeare's hero is said to still bemoan the murder of King Duncan, appearing to walk on the roof, taking a route known as The Mad Earl's Walk.

Glashans ELEMENTAL spirits found on the Isle of Man, they have a malicious habit of magnetising stones which mark the road's edges; these then exert a strong pull on passing motor cars, causing them to swerve off the road despite the driver's efforts.

Glastyn Also known as Glashtyn, a field sprite who frequents farmhouses on the Isle of Man. A glastyn is rather like a BROWNIE, helping the farmer with chores and asking only for a bowl of cream and some bread at day's end. He may also appear in the guise of a small grey water-horse or a lamb, always with an unusually long tail. As with all denizens of Fairyland, the glastyn may be perverse as well as benign by turn, and reports have been noted of those who have run amok, raping women and destroying crops if they have been slighted in any way. Such a reaction is most likely if the glastyn or his family has been hurt or injured when the farmer was clearing land. As a result, Manx farmers always walk around such areas and describe their intentions out loud, giving the glastyn ample time to relocate.

Gnome The word 'gnome' comes from the Greek *gnoma* (knowledge); thus the Knowing Ones or the Wise Ones. According to the medieval Rosicrucian system, and to Paracelsus' work before that, gnomes are one of the four ELEMENTAL spirits of earth; namely the SYLPHS of the air, the SALAMANDERS of the fire, the NYMPHS or NEREIDS of the water, and the pygmies or gnomes of the earth. These gnomes would move freely through the earth and were guardians of mines and quarries. Alexander Pope wrote, in his preface to *The Rape of the Lock* (1712):

> The four elements are inhabited by spirits called sylphs, nymphs, gnomes and salamanders. The gnomes or demons of the earth delight in mischief; but the sylphs, whose habitation is in the air, are the best conditioned creatures imaginable.

These small, wrinkled, bearded beings may be confused with TROLLS or DWARVES, due to their appearance. They revel in annoying mortals and playing practical jokes, particularly by using their magical picks and shovels to relocate planted seeds or undermine a house's foundations.

Goblin A general name for the familiar demon or mischievous spirit who dwells in private houses or in the chinks of trees. Goblins are generally small and quite odd-looking, being swarthy and bowed, with caps pulled way over their eyes and extremely large, gnarled hands. In Germany, goblins were often called Hodeken ('little hat') due to their habit of pulling on their felt hats so snugly. Goblins may adopt the shape of an ugly animal to torment humans, especially on Hallowe'en. They are thought to be the Devil's companions and to tempt men to death or illness by offering them bewitched foods. In *The Goblin Market* (1862) Christina Rossetti wrote:

We must not look at goblin men
We must not buy their fruits
Who knows upon what soil they feed
Their hungry, thirsty roots?

They are not always malicious towards mankind, being known as 'kobold' or 'demons of the mines' in Germany, and 'coblyns' or KNOCKERS in Wales and south-western England, because of their habit of tapping on the shaft wall to identify the whereabouts of a rich lode of ore.

Golden Fish An enormous fish who lived in the Black Sea. As big as two cathedrals it was covered with scales of pure gold. One day it became stranded in shallow water and was rescued by a humble fisherman. When the Golden Fish offered this man a reward he asked only for bread, which the creature promptly provided. The fisherman's wife, however, chastised him for this simple request and returned to the shore, there to harangue the Golden Fish with her demands for jewels, wealth and status. The Fish patiently granted her requests until she greedily asked to be created as God. Suddenly all the gifts disappeared, and the pair were left only with the humble fisherman's hut they owned to start with.

Goosey A whimsical story is told by Whitby farmers from Yorkshire in northern England of the GHOST of a young man who wanders the town at Christmas time. This foolish lad was said to have gorged himself on an entire goose one Christmas Eve and, upon staggering home, was robbed and murdered. Ever since, he has been unable to rest and bemoans his gluttony and foolhardiness.

Gorgon In Greek mythology there were three unusually hideous gorgons who lived beneath the sea. They had bronze scales, lolling tongues and yellow tusks, and serpents on their heads instead of hair. Medusa was the Queen and so hideous was her face that anyone who looked upon it was turned to stone. She was killed by PERSEUS when he held up his shield to her and she gazed at her own reflection. As she died, the winged horse PEGASUS sprang from her blood and the hero was able to escape on the steed. Homer in *The Odyssey* refers to the horrid creature:

> Lest Gorgon rising from the infernal lakes
> With horrors armed, and curls of hissing snakes
> Should fix me stiffened at the monstrous sight
> A stony image in eternal night.

The word 'gorgon' has more recently come to mean anything that is exceptionally abhorrent. Shakespeare used it in *Macbeth* to describe the murdered body of Duncan:

> Approach the chamber and destroy your sight
> With a new gorgon . . .

Graces, The Three The Romans believed there were three sister Graces, befriended by the MUSES. They were named Euphrosyne, Aglaia and Thalia, and were usually shown embracing each other, demonstrating that where one is, all are welcome. They preside over the affairs of men, taking special interest in decorum, purity, happiness, goodwill, kindness and gratitude.

Graiae Daughters of the sea-god Phorcys, the Graiae were sisters of the GORGONS. They were named Pephredo, Deivio and Enyo, and were depicted as three grim-looking old women; they had only one eye and one tooth between them, which they constantly passed around. They alone knew where the evil gorgons were to be found and jealously protected their whereabouts until PERSEUS forced them to reveal their secret when he stole their eye.

Grampus An aquatic monster, the grampus frequented English lakes and could be seen spouting huge columns of water as it wallowed in warm, muddy water. It had a head rather like a dolphin, with a blunt-ended nose.

Green Children Discovered near the mouth of a pit in

Coggleshall, eastern England, during the sixteenth century, according to Thomas Keightley in *Fairy Mythology*:

> . . . they differed in the colour of their skin from all the people of our habitable world, for the whole surface of their skin was tinged with a green colour.

Brought to the home of a knight, this girl and boy wept a great deal, spoke in strange syllables and would only eat green beans which, according to Celtic superstition, are the food of the dead. They eventually learned to speak English and explained they had come from St Martin's Land, a twilit, subterranean place. One day they had wandered to the cavern's mouth and there they were struck unconscious by the bright sunlight. The girl eventually was baptised and, significantly, lost her green colouring though she remained 'rather loose and wanton in her conduct'. The boy, however, pined and died.

Green Lady A tree ELF, most often to be found in elm, oak, willow and yew, but also in pine, holly, ash and apple. The old English folksong demonstrates that they could often be sinister in their intent, waylaying passers-by and snatching at the wind with skinny, white hands:

> Ellum do grieve, oak he do hate
> Willow do walk, if yew travels late.

All such plants must be treated with respect, so as not to offend the Green Ladies. For instance, permission should be sought before lopping a branch from a tree which is known to be frequented by a Green Lady; superstitious Derbyshire farmers plant primroses at the foot of such trees each Midsummer's Eve, so as to be rewarded with wealth and longevity.

Green Lady is also used to describe a greyish-green GHOST or PHANTOM often found in Scotland. These were said to haunt families when a death in the family was imminent, such as the Green Lady of Caerphilly who would assume the shape of a bunch of trailing ivy, and wander thus through ruined castles and graveyards.

Gremlin Probably the species most recently to enter the catalogue of supernatural beings, for it was only during the Second World War that these misty GNOME-like creatures were blamed by British and American pilots and navigators for any trouble which assailed their aircraft. The pilots nicknamed them 'gremlins' and felt, generally, that they were friendly pranksters rather than dangerous antagonists. Witnesses describe gremlins as looking like rabbits or bulldogs, sometimes wearing spats, top hat and breeches, and with long, webbed feet that enable them to move quietly. More recently, stories have circulated that mechanical or electrical faults in factories are due to gremlins taking over the working of machines.

Griffin The griffin, also spelled gryfin or gryphon, originated in Indian and Arabian lore. It is the offspring of a lion and an eagle, with the hindparts of the former and the head, neck, wings and claws of the latter. Eight times larger than a lion, the griffin has an acute sense of hearing, and its talons are highly prized for their ability to change colour when they come into contact with poison. Sir John Mandeville, fourteenth-century English traveller and writer, described it in detail:

> . . . they have the body upwards of an egle and benethe as a lyonn . . . but one griffoun hath the body more grete and stronger than one hundred egles such as we have amonges us. For one griffoun there will be flynge to his nest a great hors, or two oxen yoked togidre . . . he hath talouns so grete upon his feet . . . so that men maken cuppes of hem to drynke of . . .

The creature was sacred to the sun and drew the chariot of the Sun god across the sky each day. The griffin also had a lust for treasure and hoarded caches in lofty mountain caves. This, and the fact that the females laid eggs of agate in nests of pure gold, meant the griffin was hostile to aggressive treasure-seekers and swift in its attack. It was also the mortal enemy of horses and would rip them apart in seconds with its mighty talons.

Griffins were recently adopted by the Christian church as a symbol of Christ, the leonine part signifying his mortality and the eagle's head and wings representing his divinity soaring skywards.

Gruagach There are two distinct species of this Highland Scots fairy. The first is a female spirit with long fair hair who travels from village to village by water, visiting farms and helping to tend cattle. Her mode of transport means she will arrive drenched at the door of a farmhouse to beg shelter and ask leave to dry herself by the fire. Should she be allowed in she will be lucky around the house, and serve the family well. The second type of gruagach is male, and he will also help with farm work, wearing a jerkin of bright red and green leather. As with the BROWNIES, gruagachs will happily serve their masters for nothing more than a cup of milk.

Gulon A ferocious beast living deep within the Scandinavian forests. Resembling a feral cat, it could be identified by its fox's tail and shining, mirror-like eyes. Unlike most other fabled beasts it preferred to scavenge carrion from the forest floor rather than kill for fresh meat. Hunters would pursue it relentlessly during the snow season, for its winter pelt was especially prized in coat and hat making.

Gwraggedd Annwn Also known as Gwrageth Anoon, these beautiful blonde water-maidens live in rich palaces beneath the many lakes of Wales. Stories tell of certain flowers or stones by a lake which can be touched in a special way to reveal a secret passage to the middle of the lake. There the Gwraggedd Annwn hold court, surrounded by beautiful gardens, and a visitor will be entertained with music and offered fine victuals. However, if he takes as souvenir so much as a blade of grass the entrance to this charming kingdom will close forever more. They are not as dangerous as MERMAIDS or NIXIES, and on nights of the full moon will dance in the meadow flats, wafting scarves of silver mist above their heads.

A predominantly female race, they have been known to take mortals to be their husbands. Children born of these unions were often gifted in the art of healing and became famed physicians. A lovely story is told of a young herdsman who saw one of the Gwraggedd Annwn rowing on a lake in a golden boat. They fell much in love, and her father gave her a fine dowry of fat lake-cattle and his blessing for a happy marriage, with the proviso that the groom never raise his hand to the water-fairy. Many happy years passed, but eventually the Gwraggedd Annwn's curious fairy ways were her undoing. For laughing and singing at a funeral her husband gave her a reproving tap, and she had to return to her home in the lake.

Gwyllion Forbidding and evil-intentioned Welsh mountain fairies. Quite hideous to behold, the female gwyllion is closely allied with the goat and can assume this animal's shape. They only come out when the sun sets, and their favourite past-time is to lurk amongst the rocks on either side of a mountain path at twilight. From this vantage point they will silently spy on travellers, offering wrong directions if asked and placing obstacles such as stones and logs on the path. They are afraid of storms and will ask for shelter when it rains — invariably they are received hospitably, for folk are afraid of retribution from a gwyllion. As with any other evil-intentioned fairy, they may be repelled with cold iron or an opened Bible.

H

Hades The Greek god of the Underworld, or Unseen World, whose name has become synonymous with the infernal regions themselves. Hades was later known as Pluto or Orcus to the Romans. Son of CRONUS and husband of PERSEPHONE, Hades was charged by his father with ruling The House of Shades, or the dead. He was gloomy, stern and deaf to all appeals. Worshippers used to avert their eyes from his statue when making a sacrifice to him, so deep was their respect for his fierce nature. His kingdom was a treasure trove of jewels and gold, and ancient folk revered it as a source of other wealth, such as crops, minerals and fresh water. However, those who passed through the entrance gates where Hades stood might never return to the mortal world.

This god's symbol was a two-pronged fork, which popular folklore adapted as the Devil's pitchfork. Hades also possessed a magical helmet which rendered him invisible during his travels on earth.

Hag So-called from 'hak', a species of snake, developing into the term 'hagge' during the sixteenth century to describe 'a succubus who sits on a man's chest and gives him nightmares'. Any horrible old woman dabbling in the supernatural during Shakespeare's day would have been derided with Macbeth's greeting:

> How now, you secret, black and midnight hags?

This is the most popular view of the hag — an ugly old crone who is allied with the devil and practises her occult spells to the detriment of mankind. However, hags could assume many appearances; often they were thought to be of enormous proportions, such as the giantess Grendel of Scandinavian legend, or the Blue Hag of the Highlands in Scotland, whose grey-blue cape was the swirling mist of the glens. Such hags were ugly, with massive twisted features and great strength. Like the nature goddesses of old, they were responsible for storms and rock-falls. Paralleling the seasons, such hags can metamorphose into beautiful — though treacherous — young maidens in the spring time. Some appear as GHOSTS, while others turn into cannibalistic monsters like the witch BLACK ANNIS who was said to be a descendant of the Celtic winter goddess, Anu or Danu.

Hag of the Dribble Also known as the 'gwrach-y-rhibyn', this sorrowful spirit is the Welsh version of a BANSHEE. A hideous old woman with wild hair, long skinny arms and a ghastly, toothless grin, she haunted the banks of the River Dribble. Some sources claim she was derived from one of the old Welsh water-goddesses, others that she only haunts descendants of the more noble families. Her piercing cry is a death omen and she will hover near the person she is attempting to warn, crying 'My husband! My husband!' if a man is to die, or 'My child! O, my little child!' if a baby is endangered.

Hahgwehdiyu The Iroquois Indians believed Hahgwehdiyu to be the Most Divine One, responsible for creating the world. Along with his evil twin brother he was born of Ataensic, the earth goddess. He shaped the horizon using the curve of his hand, and took sand from his mother's face and breasts to create the moon and stars, respectively. Hahgwehdiyu was constantly trying to control his wicked brother who would use forces of darkness, thunder, wind and rain to destroy all the good work achieved. They fought a duel using huge thorns of the sacred crab-apple tree, and Hahgwehdiyu emerged victorious. He banished his brother to the west, along with his servants of darkness, although the spirits of thunder and lightning gave their allegiance to Hahgwehdiyu instead; henceforth this god was depicted with a drum and a forked head-dress, representing these forces of nature.

Hairy Hands A very peculiar monster which haunts Devon in south-western England. In pre-automobile days, a disembodied pair of hairy hands would tear at horses' manes, frightening them and causing them to rear. More recently Hairy Hands has been reported as wresting steering wheels from drivers' hands and forcing them off the road, often causing appalling accidents. Local lore has it that the hands belong to a convicted highwayman who would hold up carriage-travellers in the early nineteenth century. For his felony, his hands were cruelly lopped and thrown away. As they were denied Christian burial the hands proceeded to assume a life of their own.

Hameh In Arabian mythology, a bird formed from the blood and brains of a murdered prince. It has beautiful purple and green plumage, but its voice is strident and it threshes its wings frantically overhead when in the presence of any other murder victim, crying 'Ishkoonee!' ('Give me a drink!' — of the murderer's blood). It will not rest until the death has been avenged and the murderer punished, when it will fly to the Afterworld and inform the victim of his murderer's fate.

Hanuman Formed like a monkey and with the heart and soul of a god, Hanuman was the son of the Indian god Vayu. He led an army of men and monkeys against the many-headed evil Ravana, who was Lord of the Underworld and commanded a tribe of malformed spirits, to rescue the goddess Sita. His first move was to build a causeway to the enchanted isle (Sri Lanka), and then place Ravana's citadel under siege, ripping up trees and toppling walls in mischievous monkey-fashion. Ravana captured Hanuman and set fire to his tail, but the monkey avenged himself by growing to the size of a giant and setting fire to the city. He then flew to a nearby magic mountain to gather healing herbs for his troops, which ensured their success in battle. Henceforth, men and monkeys remain staunch companions.

Hap, Hapi *see* APIS

Harpy Monstrous storm goddess of Classical origin, a black-winged creature with the head and breasts of a woman and the body and limbs of a vulture. Harpies were fierce and loathsome, living in stinking filth and contaminating anything they neared. Virgil described them thus:

> Of monsters all, most monstrous this; no greater wrath
> God sends 'mongst men; it comes from depth of pitchy hell:
> And virgin's face, but womb like gulf insatiate hath,
> Her hands are griping claws, her colour pale and fell.

The daughters of Electra and the sea-god Thaumas, the harpies personified whirlwinds and storms. Their names were Ocypeta (Rapid), Celeno (Blackness) and Aello (Storm). They were infamous for tormenting and starving the blind king Phineus, until the warrior hero defied them and let the king rest at last.

Latterly the word 'harpy' has come to mean any person who is cruel or merciless, or who hungrily tries to appropriate the food or belongings of a weaker person. In *Pericles, Prince of Tyre* Shakespeare wrote:

> Thou art like the harpy
> Which do betray, doth wear an angel's face,
> Seize with an eagle's talons.

He used the motif again in *Much Ado About Nothing*:

> I will do you . . . any embassage . . . rather than hold three words' conference with this harpy.

Hathor The Egyptian sky-goddess, represented as a woman with cow's horns, between which was suspended a solar disc. She sometimes appeared on earth as a hippopotamus, too, and her epithet was The Golden. The mother and wife of RA, the sun god, Hathor presided over matters of beauty, love and marriage, and attended childbirth. She was also the tutelary deity of music and love, usually depicted with a drum or rattle.

The legend has it that, in the guise of a cow, she gave birth to the entire world and all its inhabitants. Another extraordinary tale says that Ra, convinced mankind was plotting to overthrow him, sent Hathor to kill them all. However, Ra squeamishly refused to witness the slaughter, so he flooded the fields where his subjects were with beer which had been dyed red with pomegranate juice to resemble blood. Both Hathor and her potential victims became exceedingly drunk and merry, so she failed at her task.

Hathor was also thought to dispense food and drink to the dead as they passed into the Afterworld, and some papyri show her either licking a newly dead soul or offering comforting suck from her udder, whilst in her guise as a cow.

Headless Horseman The tradition of ghostly horsemen minus their heads, or carrying their heads under their arms, is a very ancient one. Early Norse folklore describes such GHOSTS, swathed in black cloaks, thundering across the skies. Woden, the Scandinavian war god, was thought to lead this band of spirits, all of whom were once kings ruling different fiefdoms and all of whom were killed in battle. More recently, the American writer Washington Irving (1783-1859) described the ghost of a cavalryman 'whose head had been carried away by a cannonball in some nameless battle' during the American War of Independence. This ghost, in the absence of a head, carries a huge flaming pumpkin to light his way as he tears after late-night travellers at break-neck speed to see whether they have his head secreted in their luggage. As with many ghosts this headless horseman is only permitted to travel between midnight and dawn. For the rest of the time, he and his steed must return to the churchyard where his mortal remains lie.

Hecate One of the Titans, and strongly associated with the moon and witchcraft, Hecate had three bodies and three heads (those of a lion, dog and mare). She was also a triple deity, being goddess of the occult, the Underworld and of crossroads. She was sometimes referred to as Trivia and offerings of black lambs, honey and new-born puppies were left for her at crossroads. Shakespeare referred to her three-fold nature in *A Midsummer Night's Dream*:

> And we fairies that do run
> By the triple Hecate's team.

Originally thought to have a beneficial effect on flocks, Hecate was once the patroness of herdsmen. Latterly, however, she became a powerful spirit and practitioner of witchcraft, witness Shakespeare's Macbeth's reference to her as a 'secret, black and midnight hag'. She is thought to travel across the night sky bearing torches, and the mythological dragons who pull the dark clouds of night across the sun are called Hecate's Team.

Hel Also known as Hela, the goddess of the Ninth Earth and guardian of the Underworld in Norse mythology. The daughter of the evil LOKI and sister to the terrible wolf-demon FENRIR, Hel dwelt beneath the roots of the sacred ash, Yggdrasil. She had a demonic nature, cursing all her subjects to dreadful sickness and painful deaths. The only souls who escaped her torments were those who were pure in thought or who had died for a noble cause. Her face and body were the livid blue of a cadaver, and her ghastly attendants were aptly named Gangla (Decay) and Ti (Slowness). Hel lived in the land of Elvidnir (Den of Sleet and Black Clouds), eating the brains and bones of mortals with a bewitched knife, Sult (Starvation), and sleeping in a vile bed named Kor (Sickness). Thomas Gray, in *The Descent of Odin* (1768), wrote:

> . . . down the yawning steep he rode
> that led to Hela's drear abode.

Gray noted, also, that Hel's kingdom was banished so far from Asgard, the home of the gods, that it took ODIN nine days and nights to reach it.

Helios The Greek sun god, known to the Romans as Sol. Son of the sea god Hyperion, Helios' sisters are Silene the moon goddess, and EOS the goddess of the dawn. He drove through the heavens, from east to west each day to his palace in Colchis, in a golden boat drawn by four winged white horses. Helios was such a dazzling sight that few mortals ever glimpsed him in detail, and he was known to have struck sinners blind with the rays from his golden helmet and breast-plate.

Helios was thought to see and know everything, and he was often invoked in blessings; his fault was that he could not keep a secret. He was not as promiscuous as the other classical gods, and actually rejected the lovely NYMPH Clytie who pined for him until her body became a beautiful flower — the heliotrope — which turns to watch the sun's progress across the sky each day.

Hephaestus The son of ZEUS and HERA, Hephaestus was the Greek god of fire and the protector of blacksmiths and craftsmen. He was to become Vulcan to the Romans. Hephaestus was crippled and ugly, having had the temerity to interfere in a quarrel between his tempestuous parents, and been flung from Olympus to the Island of Lemnos below for his pains. Milton described the god's mishap as follows:

> . . . from morn to noon
> He fell, from noon to dewy eve,
> A summer's day, and with the setting sun
> Drop't from the zenith, like a falling star,
> On Lemnos, the Aegean isle.

Hephaestus was a talented artisan. Among his many fine artefacts were the armour of ACHILLES, a golden throne for his mother, the necklace of Harmonia and the axe which split Zeus' skull, facilitating the birth of ATHENE. He also forged the Fire-Breathing Bulls for King Aetes, and moulded the clay which formed Pandora, the first woman. His workshops may be found wherever molten lava or metal spills onto the ground, and smoke occasionally belches forth from his underground chimneys, known as volcanoes.

A bitter and sad god, he was repeatedly cuckolded by his wife APHRODITE, whom he had blackmailed into marrying him. In his humiliation he forged a magical net which caught her *in flagrante delicto* with her lover, ARES, and exposed them to the derision of the other gods.

Hera Daughter of CRONUS and wife to ZEUS. Through her status as Queen of Mount Olympus she was the patron of all womanly activities, including childbirth, and the guardian of wedlock. She was jealous of her husband's many romantic liaisons and was a formidable opponent, with many stories being told of her harrying Zeus' mistresses and persecuting his illegitimate children. For instance, she sent two serpents to kill the baby HERCULES, who was Zeus' son by the mortal Alcmene, but he succeeded in strangling them.

Hera was also the protectress of the home and domestic industry. Devotees of her cult represented her as a cow crowned with a diadem, a literal earth-mother. Her personal attendants are the graceful Hons, who ensure that the seasons and events follow their allotted schedule. Hera was vain and vindictive, if incited. For instance, when Paris designated the wanton APHRODITE as the most beautiful of the goddesses, Hera's morals were affronted and she arranged for the Trojan Wars to occur as just recrimination for the slight.

Hercules A demi-god, Hercules was the greatest of the Greek heroes. He was the son of ZEUS and the mortal princess Alcmene, and possessed many fine qualities, including extraordinary wit and great strength. However, he was the butt of HERA's wrath and she drove him to madness. The Delphic Oracle advised Hercules that the only way to rid himself of her curse was to undertake twelve gruelling tasks. These 'Labours' were sung of by bards as follows:

> The Nemean lion first he killed
> Then Lerne's Hydra slew;
> Th'Arcadian stag and monster boar
> Before Eurystheus drew:

Cleansed Augea's stalls,
And made the birds from Lake Stymphalis flee;
The Cretan Bull, and Thracian mares,
First seized and then set free;
Took prize the Amazonian belt,
Brought Geryon's kine from Gades;
Fetched apples from the Hesperides
And Cerberus from Hades.

BREWER *Dictionary of Phrase and Fable*

When Hercules completed his tasks he was welcomed to Olympus and granted the gift of immortality. As was fitting for one so widely travelled, he became the patron of trade and voyages.

See AMAZONS; CERBERUS; ERYMANTHIAN BOAR; HADES; HESPERIDES; HYDRA; NEMEAN LION; STYMPHALIAN BIRDS. *See also* ANTAEUS; ATLAS.

Herla The King of England in ancient times, he figures in fairy legends as follows: a mysterious creature covered in hair and cloven-hoofed, paid a visit to King Herla on the occasion of his marriage and showered him with many marvellous gifts. As he left the court, he asked the King to visit him when he, too, wed in a year's time. This King Herla and his retinue duly did, bearing many gifts and well-wishes. So greatly did they enjoy the celebrations that they stayed for three days. The pygmy king gave Herla a small dog to set on his saddle as a parting gift, and told him not to get off his horse until the dog did. On returning, Herla found all had changed, for in truth three-hundred years had passed and not three days. When two members of his party jumped to the ground they crumbled to dust. As a result, King Herla rides the countryside with his ghostly retinue still, hoping the dog will indicate where it is safe for him to stop.

Hermaphroditus The son of HERMES and APHRODITE, Hermaphroditus was an extremely beautiful boy. The NYMPH Salmacis was especially besotted by him, and Ovid (43BC-AD18) wrote that she 'prayed that the twain might become one flesh' (from *Metamorphoses*). This did indeed occur, for when she went to embrace him the bodies of the lover and the beloved merged forever, becoming a double-sexed being — a youth with the breasts of a woman. The cult of this twin deity reached its height during Roman times, when the god symbolised the joint sacred rule of emperor and consort.

Hermes The son of ZEUS and the nymph MAIA, Hermes was the messenger of the gods, as well as being the god of good luck and wealth, and therefore the patron of both merchants and thieves. He was precocious and enjoyed mischievous pursuits. For instance, his winged sandals helped him to steal cows belonging to APOLLO, and his wit ensured the stock walked backwards so that no trace of their movements could be found.

Hermes' musical talent ensured he remained a favourite with the gods, and he was credited with inventing the lyre from a tortoise shell. His mercurial personality was likened to quicksilver, to which was lent his name, according to Hoole's *Ariosto*:

> So, when we see the liquid metal fall
> Which chemists by the name of Hermes call.

An ingenious inventor in his own right, Hermes was an alchemist by trade. We still refer to certain compounds as being 'hermetically sealed', in reference to the touch of his magic caduceus which he latterly bestowed upon AESCULAPIUS, the god of healing. Hermes also watched over travellers, and roads often sported wayside shrines or *hermaeia* which featured a bust of the god, or the herald's staff which was his emblem. The Greek philosopher Theophrastus (*c.*372-287BC) wrote of a travelling friend's respect for Hermes:

> . . . he goes by the carved shafts at cross-roads, pours oil on them from his flask, falls on his knees, makes an obeisance, and only then moves on.

An extrapolation of this responsibility saw Hermes designated as the conductor of the souls of the dead to HADES, as well as being a god of sleep and dreams.

Herne the Hunter A famous PHANTOM said to gallop on horseback through Windsor Park, near London. Tradition has it that he was one of King Henry VIII's forest wardens. He offended the king in some way and was summarily hanged, appearing since as a shaggy man, wearing a great set of stag's horns and blowing a trumpet. Shakespeare describes his appearance in *The Merry Wives of Windsor*:

> There is an old tale goes that Herne the Hunter . . .
> Doth all the winter-time at still midnight
> Walk round about an oak with great raged horns
> And there he blasts the tree, and takes the cattle
> And makes milk yield blood and shakes a chain
> In a most hideous and dreadful manner.

Other sources claim Herne was more likely a woodland spirit, whose home was a particular oak tree now long gone. Still others claim he was adapted from tales of the Norse god ODIN, and his fleet-footed mount Sleipnir. It remains a surety that sightings of this spectral figure — the most recent by a London youth in 1964 — portend ill.

Hesperides Charmingly known as Children of the Evening Star, these three lovely Greek goddesses guarded the golden apples which HERA received as a marriage gift. Milton wrote of:

> Hesperus and his daughters three
> That sing about the golden tree.

Along with the hundred-headed DRAGON Ladon, the Hesperides lived in a beautiful orchard, referred to by Robert Greene in *Friar Bacon and Friar Bungay* (1598):

> Shew thee the tree, leafed with refin'd gold
> Whereon the fearful dragon held his sete,
> That watched the garden of the Hesperides.

HERCULES, as one of his Twelve Labours, was charged with slaying the dragon and, outwitting the three sisters with the help of ATLAS, procuring the apples for Eurystheus.

Hillmen Also known as Mound-folk, the Hillmen are Scandinavian in origin and refer to a class of beings between ELF and human. Most live in caves or under hills and mounds in a typically village environment, farming blue-skinned cattle. They are master smiths and have superior mystic ability in interpreting runic knowledge. Like GNOMES, hillmen avoid the sunlight, for it can strike them blind. On the Isle of Man they were known as Hogmen and tended to be far more aggressive, kidnapping women and children and setting fire to barns. However, if well treated, they made generous neighbours and always marked the birth of a neighbourhood child with a pouchful of gold sovereigns.

Hippogryph Also known as the 'hippogriff', these were winged creatures born of the union of a male GRIFFIN and a filly. The name comes from the Greek *hippos* (horse). Poets referred to the hippogryph as a symbol of love, presumably because of its soaring habit and fantastic, gleaming appearance. Milton wrote in *Paradise Regained*:

> So saying he caught him up and without wing
> Of hippogrif, bore through the aire sublime
> O'er the wilderness and o'er the plaine.

Hob Though most usually the name given to kindly domestic spirits, there are a few exceptions. Most notable is the GHOST named Hob who haunted several of the rivers in Yorkshire. Thought to be the spectre of a horseman who once drowned nearby, Hob is condemned to plague other travellers by re-directing signposts, extinguishing lights and placing boulders in their path.

Hobgoblin Also known as hobmen, the name hobgoblin is thought to be a corruption of 'Rob-goblin', i.e. Robin Goodfellow, or PUCK. Shakespeare wrote in *A Midsummer Night's Dream* of:

> Those that hobgoblin call you, and sweet Puck
> You do their work, and they shall have good luck.

Generally, hobgoblins are a more friendly species of the oft-malevolent GOBLIN. Domestically inclined spirits, they are happiest when warmly ensconced by the grate or hob over a kitchen fire, and are more at home in the country than in a city or town. If treated well, they will protect the household from evil spirits and undertake chores in the kitchen, though they do not like to go outdoors. Like BROWNIES they are happy with an offering of bread and milk at the end of the day. Ill-treated hobgoblins can cause strife and discord, though, souring milk, tangling clothes and muddying floors for spite. A Herefordshire hobgoblin would avenge himself for any insult by stealing all the family's keys and refusing to return them until his favourite cake had been baked and left on the hob for him to eat.

Hobyah Amongst the most evil and dangerous of fairy spirits. Very similar to BOGIES used to chastise children, hobyahs kidnapped people and imprisoned them in caves, where they had to mine for fairy gold before they were eaten for their pains. According to K.M. Briggs, hobyahs were 'terrified of dogs, and with good reason, for they were finally all eaten up by a large black dog' (from *The Fairies in Tradition and Literature*).

Hooper An eerie spirit who frequented a certain beach cave in Cornwall, south-western England. Thought to be the GHOST of a local fisherman named Hooper, the spirit appeared as a soft, grey cloud and emitted strange cries to warn of coming storms. Should any other fishermen ignore the warning of Hooper and sail out into the weather, they could find themselves drawn inexorably back to shore, even against the tide. The spell was broken one day by a particularly stubborn fisherman who used clubs to beat his way through the grey mist. His boat never returned from its trip, nor was the Hooper ever seen again.

Hop O'My Thumb The name given by Kane O'Hara in his poem *Midas*, to a tiny little boy thought to have pixy blood:

> You stump o'the gutter, you Hop O'My Thumb
> Your husband must from Lilliput come.

Horla The protagonist of Guy de Maupassant's definitive story of a POLTERGEIST-like haunting, *Le Horla* (1887). The horla became increasingly malevolent towards inhabitants of the house, moving furniture and breaking crockery, and filling the house with a sense of dread. Described as having no 'clearly defined outlines', but rather 'a sort of opaque transparency', it was VAMPIRE-like and sapped energy from the household inhabitants. The horla became stronger than they, and eventually the family left the house to the devices of this 'malevolent force from an unknown dimension'.

Horses of Power A very old Russian folk tale claims that once a year the night sky is filled with the thunderous sound of hooves, as magnificent horses, once ridden by famed heroes, ride again. It is also said that in times when Russia has need of strength in battle, these horses will awake their masters and carry them to where they are needed.

Horus The Egyptian god of sunlight and daybreak, Horus was usually depicted in hieroglyphics by a sparrow-hawk, a bird which was sacred to him. Other epithets name him He Who Is Above or He Who Is After. One of his eyes was the sun and the other the moon. Horus continually waged war with Seth, the god of darkness and evil, and eventually won the privilege of assisting his father OSIRIS in the Judgement Hall, where he was responsible for weighing the hearts of all arrivals on the Scales of Truth.

Host The Host of the Unforgiven Dead, also known as the Sluagh, is the term used by people from the Scottish Highlands to describe the spirit world. Evans Wentz in *Fairy Faith in Celtic Countries* described the Host as:

> . . . travelling in the air above places inhabited by people. The host used to go after the fall of night, and move particularly after midnight . . .

The Host are forbidden to enter the Kingdom of Heaven until

they have repented of their early sins. Particularly recalcitrant spirits may refuse to do so, returning to earth each night in the form of black clouds which block out the light of the moon. They become bitter and evil, fighting each other and poisoning animals and humans with venomous darts. Evidence of the Host's appearance is said to be the red crotal (lichen) stain found on rocks the morning after a heavy frost, which is blood they have spilled during their aerial spats.

Huitzilopochtli The mighty Aztec god of war. He was depicted as the sun, a young warrior who was born each day, defeated the stars of the night and was resurrected again and again by the souls of warriors in his care. Huitzilopochtli was born of the goddess COATLIQUE, and she was made aware of his conception when a wreath of blue humming-bird feathers fell from the sky. His acolytes wore head-dresses of these feathers and carried gold staves and shields in temple processions. The sixteenth-century Franciscan historian, Bernadino de Sahagun, wrote:

> The priests offered [this] idol flowers, incense and food and adorned it with wreaths of flowers and garlands of feathers
> *History of Things of New Spain*

Such libations were probably not the norm, however; other records speak of ceremonial statues made of flour mixed with sacrificial blood, and battle prisoners were disemboweled on Huitzilopochtli's temple steps to appease the god, when he was angered.

Hydra The offspring of TYPHON and ECHIDNA, Hydra was a nine-headed serpent who lived in the marshes of Lerna. It ventured forth only to kill cattle or flatten crops, poisoning the air with its fetid breath. HERCULES' second task was to kill this monster. However, as soon as he struck off one of its heads another two shot up in its place. Finally he managed to overcome the Hydra by cauterising the necks after each decapitation, and burying the heads beneath a rock. By dipping his arrowheads in the monster's blood, he ensured they would become poisonous.

Hyter Sprites These fairies from East Anglia in eastern England are very well intentioned. Sand-coloured with green eyes, they can readily assume the form of sand-martins and, thus disguised, will rescue lost children and return them to their homes. If the child has become lost or frightened as a result of parental neglect, then the adult in question may expect to be admonished by the fairy, who dislikes irresponsibility and carelessness.

I

Idun In Scandinavian mythology, Idun was the goddess who held the magical Apples of Youth. These she kept in an ivory box, and the gods ate from them as often as they wished to renew their youth. She was kidnapped by the storm god but the other gods commanded LOKI to retrieve her, for they all began to age rapidly without her supervision.

Imp Also known as impet, a little demon, devil or evil spirit. The word 'imp' means a graft or shoot, hence is sometimes used to describe a child, as in Cromwell's comment about Prince Edward when writing to Henry VIII:

> Let us pray for . . . our King's most excellent majesty and for . . . our Prince, that most angelic imp.
>
> *Pathway to Prayer*

More common is Milton's use of the word, describing the serpent in *Paradise Lost* as 'the fittest imp of fraud', for imps are thought to sprout from Satan and to frequently adopt various animal forms in order to serve their evil master. Theirs are the more menial chores in Hell — the fetching and carrying of water, for instance — and their reward is to suckle at a witch's nipples.

Inanna The Sumerian goddess of love and war. She was identified with the planet Venus and thought to be the daughter of the sky god, for another of her epithets is Mistress of the Sky. Inanna made a pilgrimage to The Land Without Return, a hell below the earth's surface presided over by her sister, the mistress of death. Inanna's request for water was denied and her sister, inflamed with jealousy, had her turned into a corpse and hung on a stake. Inanna was restored by her loyal subjects, but was forever accompanied by a ghastly demon-servant and had to periodically go into hiding so her evil sister could hold sway and unleash her temper — thus explaining the continuing paradoxes of life and death, illness and health, harvest and famine.

Incubus A ghostly spirit, or demon, who assumed a man's form in order to have sexual intercourse with mortal women. The word comes from the Latin *in cubo* (to lie heavily upon), which probably referred to the powerful nightmare which would assault the victims after seduction. The incubus appeared either as a handsome young stranger, or in the guise of a trusted family friend — even a member of the clergy — to best gain the woman's confidence. Their task was to impregnate the woman so she would eventually produce children who could serve Satan. The great magician Merlin was said to have been born of a union between an incubus and a nun; happily Merlin used his other-worldly powers of wizardry for good, rather than evil.

Iris The Greek goddess of the rainbow, or the rainbow itself. Iris was most often depicted as a NYMPH with golden, winged sandals and a herald's staff, for she was employed as a messenger for the gods. When she had a missive for delivery the rainbow was a bridge let down from heaven for her to travel upon. Sometimes it plunged into the depths of the sea, indicating she was taking a command to the sea-gods from ZEUS; at other times a blessing from HERA would take the multi-hued arch directly to the door of a worthy mortal family.

Ishtar A wanton Babylonian goddess whose cult was marked by lascivious excesses. The Classical historian and traveller Herodotus (*c.*480-425BC) wrote:

> The foulest Babylonian custom is that which compels every woman of the land once in her life to sit in the temple of Ishtar and lay with some stranger . . . after sexual union has made the woman holy in the goddess' sight, she returns home . . . Hand-

> some women are, of course, soon free to depart, but it happens that the uncomely sometimes have to wait several years . . .

The wife of Tammuz, Ishtar was a powerful goddess whose annual death, resurrection and marriage dates paralleled the agricultural calendar. Her bad temper was notorious, and she was often depicted with a beard and a bow and arrow, testifying to her warlike character.

Isis The Egyptian goddess of the earth and moon. Wife of OSIRIS and mother of HORUS, she possessed great magical powers and her epithet was She Who Is Rich In Spells. Isis was usually depicted as wearing a large pair of cow's horns — an animal which was sacred to her — between which a disc representing the moon was suspended. Isis is thought to have invented spinning and weaving and was the tutelary patron of childbirth, meting out the fate of mortals as they entered the world. Erasmus Darwin referred to her domestic powers in his *Loves of the Plants* (1789):

> Inventress of the woof, fair flax flings
> The flying shuttle through the dancing strings . . .
> Taught by her labours, from the fertile soil
> Immortal Isis clothed the banks of the Nile.

The Romans tell that Isis appropriated a portion of the sun god's power when she grew weary of worldly affairs and thereafter adorned the heavens as the constellation of Sirius. Apuleius believed she was mother to the gods of the Roman Empire — DIANA, MINERVA, Venus, HECATE, etc. — and awarded her the additional responsibility of ensuring the welfare of sailors through the use of a celestial wooden rudder which controlled the wind and waves.

Izanagi and **Izanami** Two supreme deities who were the brother and sister Creators of the World, according to Japanese mythology. Out of the original ocean of Chaos they were born, symbolising the interactive forces of Yin and Yang. Izanagi possessed a magical jewelled spear and this he flung into the endless water, creating the first land-mass from its point. Here the couple built a magnificent palace and begat many other Japanese gods. Izanami died when giving birth to the fire god, and the distraught Izanagi followed her to the Land of Gloom, where he was appalled by the sight of her body infested with maggots.

Izanami henceforth became the Earth Mother, the prime goddess of Shinto, and presided over the Underworld. Izanagi fled back to the earth's surface, pursued by an army of thunder gods and headless warriors. He managed to rout them by tearing his clothes off and setting them to sail down a river, then blocking the river with a mighty boulder. By his actions he ensured temporary respite for mortals from evil forces, though they periodically seep past the stone to plague the world, at Izanami's behest.

J

Jack In Irons A giant Yorkshire PHANTOM who haunts lonely roads. He is swathed in chains, from which hang trophies — namely the heads of his victims, hanging by their hair. Jack is thought to be the GHOST of some poor manacled prisoner who died in a dungeon and has henceforth sought to torment other humans. His favourite custom is to loom out from the wayside and startle travellers. With his cumbersome chains he does not move very quickly, though, so a quick sprint will save a potential victim from Jack's clutches.

Jack O'Lantern Also known as Jacky Lanter, this is an English term used variously to describe WILL O'THE WISP or PUCK. In some parts of the West Country Jack's magical lantern, glimmering in the marshes, is regarded as a lucky charm. An old saying runs:

> Jack O'Lantern, Joan the Wad
> Who tickled the maid and made her mad
> Light me home, the weather's bad.

Elsewhere the GOBLIN lights are regarded as dangerous, leading travellers into trackless wastelands and to their deaths.

Jaguar A beast worshipped as a powerful god in pre-Columbian South America. Its staring eyes and double row of fangs feature in many religious icons, and its skin has magical healing properties. Warriors still hunt the jaguar in ritualised fashion; they must stalk it for three days and it may only be killed with a wooden spear. The jaguar represents the ancient power of the jungle, and must be treated with absolute respect. Its power is formidable and it has a direct effect on the fertility of crops and mankind — witness statues of jaguars coupling with women as a means of ensuring the tribe's continuity.

Janus A Roman god, Janus guarded doorways and was therefore the god of auspicious beginnings. He had two faces, each looking in opposite directions. This had symbolic significance on the double-gated temple in the Roman Forum, which was open in times of war and closed when peace prevailed. This simile continued in use even in recent times, with *The Times* newspaper commenting on the American Civil War as follows:

> Slavery was the hinge on which the gates of the temple of Janus turned.

Janus developed into a god of all beginnings, and accordingly the month of January was named in his honour. He is usually depicted with a bunch of keys — hence our word 'janitor' — and extremists of his cult called him Janus Quadrifrons (Four Heads) believing he also controlled the four seasons.

Jenny Greenteeth A malignant water-sprite, native to the north of England. As with many BOGIES her presence is used to discourage children from misbehaving. In this instance, Jenny Greenteeth is a HAG with long green fangs and sharp claws who drags children who stand too close to the river's edge to a watery grave. Her presence is signalled by the green scum found on the top of stagnant pools, and apparently her favourite delicacy is bare feet — a thinly veiled admonition to keep those shoes and socks on, no matter how hot the day.

Jersey Devils These monsters are found only in New Jersey, USA, and are said to be the descendants of the illegitimate offspring of a woman named Mother Leeds. With twelve children to her credit, she became pregnant for the thirteenth time by a British soldier. As a result of her infidelity and disloyalty to her country, the child was cursed from birth, rapidly growing to be over six-foot long with a snake's tail and bat wings, and the head and mane of a black stallion. A snorting and savage beast, it promptly ate all Mother Leeds' other children and plunged into the New Jersey forest, from whence it emerged regularly to tear clothes hanging out to dry, and trample vegetable gardens.

Jimmy Squarefoot A creature only ever seen on the magical Isle of Man, Jimmy Squarefoot has a formidable appearance, with the head and tusks of a large boar, the body of a man, and large square feet swathed in calico bands. In days of old, he was thought to have been ridden by one of the Foawr, fabled giants who threw stones at the earth as they passed overhead. More recently he appears to prefer amiably wandering the countryside and doing no harm.

Julunggul The god of Creation in Aboriginal legend; known as Yulunggu, he appears as a rainbow snake who arches himself across the sky early in the rainy season. His appearance is essential to the tribes' fertility, and he is petitioned in initiation rites for young boys at puberty. Dreamtime legends tell that the Julunggul, in his guise as a gigantic serpent, dug out many rivers and waterholes as he writhed through the desert sand. This is why the rivers have many curves, because they follow the wriggling tracks of the serpent; similarly, waterholes are round because they are in the shape of a snake coiled up to rest.

Julunggul has a violent temper if his rest below the earth is disturbed. Once, he chased a young girl up into the Milky Way. So angry was he with her that he flung a handful of the stars after her, and they fell to earth with such force that they formed a row of waterholes across the country.

Juno In Roman mythology, the venerable Queen of Heaven and wife of JUPITER. Originally a moon goddess, Juno presided over matters of fecundity, childbirth and marriage. She was venerated by women in a feast named Matronalia, and the month of June — once called Junonius — was considered most auspicious for weddings. Juno was the guardian of the home and with the title 'Regina' was once lauded as the Queen and Mother of all Rome.

Jupiter The god of sun and sky, Jupiter also controlled rain, thunder and lightning. Any place struck by a bolt of lightning was considered sacred to him. He was the guardian of property and guarantor of oaths taken in his name, and became the patron of the Roman empire, taking a special interest in games and sports. The Ides, or days when there was a full moon, were sacred to him and his shrines were placed high on mountain tops.

In the latter days of the Roman Empire his powers were assumed by the Emperor, or Divine Guide of the World. Cicero, who had his head and hands cut off for recommending a return to republican principles, ruefully referred to Jupiter as 'the awful presence of the supreme mind', perhaps foreshadowing Christian beliefs.

K

Kai-n-tiku-aba The Samoan people explain the mythos of Creation as follows: as Na Atibu, the father of the gods, lay dying, he decided the world was ready for mankind and that it was time for mortals to settle the earth. His spine then became a great tree with many branches, known as Kai-n-tiku-aba, and the first people sprouted as so many blossoms and fruit. At first, all was well. Then a surly man named Kourabi shook the tree from spite and broke the main branches which were heavy with another generation of 'fruit'. Thus the people were scattered far away from their original home, and bitterness and a capacity for battle entered their souls.

Kali A Hindu goddess named after her home Calcutta (Kali-kutta, or Kali's village). She was the wife of SHIVA in Hindu mythology; the Queen of Death and Terror, she is usually represented as drinking the blood of a victim and dancing on his corpse. Kali wears a girdle of severed human heads. Her skin is blue-black, she has a long red tongue, and snakes twine about her body. She has four arms, making her an inescapable foe — one hand holds a sword, one a human head, one is raised in a gesture of peace to trick the unwary, and the other forms a claw, ready to pinion its next victim.

Kali was worshipped by the fearful Thuggee cult, religious extremists who killed in her name, believing that only through destruction as personified by Kali could the creative life-force be revealed.

Kama The Hindu god of love, Kama is the husband of Rati, the goddess of sensual desire. He is represented as a plump youth riding on a sparrow or a parrot, and he carries a bow of bee-encrusted sugar cane and five arrows, which represent the Five Senses. Festivals in his honour are marked by a plethora of flowers, and the lusciously scented frangipani is held sacred to him. Kama also bears the epithet The Bodyless, a reference to his run-in with the god SHIVA, who reduced him to ashes for an act of impertinence.

Karkadann A ferocious beast which padded the plains of Persia and India in search of prey. A solitary predator it resembled the grey wolf, except that it had two horns — one long ivory one in the centre of its forehead, and the other a squat and curved tusk at the tip of its nose. The karkadann was strong and vicious, and could slay even elephants. A prized trophy was its horn for, like the UNICORN's, this would sweat in the presence of poison. The karkadann, despite the violence of its temper, could be seduced by the gentle song of a ringdove, and it would lie perfectly still when this music was heard. Huntsmen rapidly learned this trick and would carry a pair of ringdoves with them to render the karkadann helpless before their attack.

Kelpie (or Kelpy) A Scottish water spirit. Although sometimes appearing as a short man covered in hair, it is most often identified as a wild young bogey-horse, or a cross between a horse and a bull displaying two long, sharp horns. Kelpies may be readily identified by their hoof-marks, for their strange inverted pad leaves the reverse of those of normal horses. A magical beast by any account, J.F. Campbell in his *Popular Tales of the Western Highlands* (1890) writes:

> . . . his back lengthens to fit any number; men's hands stick to his skin and [when] he is killed nothing remains but a pool of water.

A magic bridle may be used to tame a kelpie temporarily, though this will engender great rage in the creature. The kelpie grazes beside rivers and streams, luring unsuspecting humans to ride him. As soon as they mount, he dashes into the water — at best he will give them a ducking, at worst he will drown and then eat them. Graham in his *Sketches of Perthshire* wrote:

> Every lake has its kelpie or water-horse, often seen by the shepherd sitting upon the brow of a rock, dashing along the surface of the deep or browsing upon the pasture or its verge.

In several fables the kelpie appears as a handsome young prince, who lures maidens to a watery fate worse than death. A sure indication of such a disguise, though, is that the seducer's hair will be wet and full of weeds or shells.

Keres According to Greek mythology keres were VAMPIRE-like spirits who attacked the body when it was time to die. These spirits were begotten of Nyx, the goddess of night, and they wore robes stained scarlet from the blood of their victims. Keres were often described as hovering, on outstretched wings, above a battlefield, for their favourite pastime was to swoop upon a warrior at the point of his death and suck the blood from his mortal wounds.

Khu The ancient Egyptian name for a GHOST. They believed that as soon as a person died their spirit attached itself to the family left behind. The god of the dead spirits, Chontamenti (He Who Is In The Utmost West), is often depicted with the head of a dog or jackal and newly dead spirits sometimes assume this form also, howling as the cortege passes. If the person had lived and died peacefully, then his khu would likely be benevolent, although an unpleasant death might result in a violent khu. Ritual offerings of meat, spices and wines were made by the mortal family to propitiate the restless spirit.

Killmoulis A particularly ugly BROWNIE or sprite from Scotland who acts as a guardian for a mill. Every mill has a killmoulis or mill-servant, who is devoted to the welfare of the family it serves. They are characterised by having no mouth and an enormous nose — to eat, they presumably snort up their food. Dwelling in a favourite cosy spot by hearth or oven, the killmoulis would wail if sickness or misfortune threatened the family. However, he could also be a tiresome prankster and thus often more of a hindrance than a help about the house — Briggs tells of practical jokes such as 'blowing ashes over shelled oats spread out to dry' (from *The Fairies in Tradition and Literature*). In Amsterdam and Copenhagen these brownies are known as Kabouters or Kaboutermannikins. Although somewhat dim-witted they are marvellous workers and willingly light fires, cook and clean. They are also talented wood-smiths, carving toys for children and ornate pipes and spoons for adults.

Kirkgrim A GHOST thought to haunt churches, where its appearance was an ill omen. Sometimes described as a pig or a horse, it was doubtless derived from the ancient custom of sacrificing an animal when a church was being built and burying the carcass in the foundations, in turn being a memory of pagan rituals. T. Thistleton Dyer comments that it was once customary to inter a lamb beneath the church's altar; the kirkgrim or churchgrim, in the form of this lamb, would latterly appear in the pews to indicate a coming funeral.

Knockers Cornish GOBLINS who dwell in mines of south-western England and point out rich veins of lead, silver and tin. Miners say that they indicate the whereabouts of the ore by tapping on the shaft walls with their antler-picks, hence the name. Also known as 'coblyns' or 'coblynau', Cornishmen have long left pieces of traditional miners' fare — the Cornish pastie — for the knockers to eat. However, whistling and swearing offends them and they will shower the guilty person with pebbles and gravel until he stops. Another tradition has it that the knockers are afraid of the sign of the cross, an idea which probably stems from the legend which says that knockers are the GHOSTS of the Jews who took part in the crucifixion of Jesus and were punished by being sent to work in the mines.

Kobolds A German species of KNOCKERS who also live in mines. They are, however, far more malicious in their intentions, and wilfully frustrate miners by causing rockfalls and accidents, cutting ropes or extinguishing lamps and thus stymieing their labours. Interestingly the blue metal deposit, cobalt, was so named by miners because it was useless and troublesome, reminding them of harassment suffered at the hands of these GOBLINS.

Koki-teno The legendary fox spirits of Japanese superstition, they can either assume human form or enter the living body of a man or woman, most often appearing as beautiful women in long white gowns. To accomplish this, the spirit has to wander old cemeteries until it finds a human skull, put it on its head and then turn to the North Star. Legends tell that the Koki-teno can seduce any mortal man and that their victims will eventually become subject to 'fox possession', running about growling and easily frightened by dogs.

Kraken A huge sea-monster, variously described as a serpent or squid, said to have been seen off the coast of Norway and on the North American coast. It was described by Bishop Pontoppidan in the eighteenth century as being over a mile and a half in circumference; he also said the sea all around it was darkened by the jets of ink it spat out. Pliny spoke of the kraken in the Straits of Gibraltar, where it basked on the warm surface of the water and was mistaken for a series of small islands. The animal was thought to have many tentacles and to spend most of its time sleeping. Tennyson, in his poem *The Kraken* (1830), speaks of:

> Below the thunders of the upper deep
> Far, far beneath in the abysmal sea
> His ancient, dreamless, uninvaded sleep
> The Kraken sleepeth [until]
> Once by man and angels to be seen
> In roaring he shall rise and on the surface die.

The most recent sighting was in 1977 by Indonesian fishermen.

The kraken is generally believed to be a type of giant cephalopod which normally lives and feeds at the bottom of the ocean. If, however, their food sources are jeopardised, they will rise to the surface preceded by a boiling mass of water, there to menace ships and grasp and eat sailors. One of the theories about the abandoned ship *Marie Celeste* is that the crew were plucked off by a hungry kraken.

Kuei Evil Chinese GHOSTS, spirits which draw their form and power from the forces of darkness, misfortune and death. They are usually the ghosts of people who lived evil lives during their time on earth, and are undeserving of entry to Heaven. Thus they become malicious and bitter. At best a displeased kuei will overturn furniture or pinch children's faces; at worst it will bring sickness or death to the home. Rather like English fairies, kuei will shy away from weapons made of iron or steel, and will not trouble a house where these are placed in the doorway. Nor are they especially intelligent. Although it was once thought only Confucian scholars could outwit a kuei, a deterrent popular amongst all Chinese is to set it to solving a riddle. The kuei will usually give up and leave a house in high dudgeon.

The most efficient means of diverting a kuei is to sculpt upward-turning eaves on a roof. This spirit can only travel in a straight line, so when it slides down the roof in the hope of gaining entry to a house, it will be swept up in the air again by the curving gable. Similarly, a screen placed across the inside of a doorway will hinder their progress, for they cannot move sideways.

Kukulkan According to Mayan tradition, one of the most important gods. Depicted as a feathered serpent, he was the chief god of life, as well as controller of the winds. Kukulkan was attended by spirits of earth, water and fire, and was responsible for the sprouting of maize crops and the mating of fish — in short, in his hands he held the key to the tribe's survival.

A beneficent deity, Kukulkan was once held to have been a king from another land, who arrived in Yucatan by sea and elected to stay rather than risk the return voyage. In this guise he was more of a cultural hero, and reportedly taught the people how to compile a calendar of the seasons and to consult the heavens for weather information.

L

Lakshmi (or Laksmi) One of VISHNU's many consorts, she was the goddess of good fortune, wealth and beauty, usually depicted as a full-breasted maiden sitting upon a lotus flower, or carrying one in her left hand as a symbol of her involvement in agriculture and harvest. A gentle, flower-garlanded goddess, Lakshmi spent a great deal of her time in contemplating the universe and bestowed gifts of calm and wisdom upon those mortals who sought to emulate her through transcendental meditation. A myth of creation states that Buddha was born of a thousand-petalled gold lotus, which hereafter became Lakshmi's womb, and a source of both mental and physical succour for pilgrims seeking solace.

Lamas A type of benevolent and protective DJINN, or spirit, who supervised the welfare of mortals. The lama was found in ancient Chaldea and was usually depicted as a female, her likeness being carved beside portals to sacred chambers to repel evil. In later myths the lamas assumed different shapes and names, such as Nigal who had a lion's head, and Kirub who had a bull's torso. Most often, though, lamas were stylistically portrayed as winged hybrid creatures and may have been linked to the later goddess-spirit who presided over the home and heart, Lamaria.

Lambton Worm The Saxon word for DRAGON was 'worm', and one of the best known tales of the creature is sourced from fourteenth-century Lambton, a village in England's north country. There the heir of Lambton, a devil-may-care lad who delighted in offending people, sat down to fish one Sunday morning in full view of all the local folk who were dutifully attending church. Cursing his ill-luck in not having caught a fish, the heir suddenly felt a tug on his line and struggled to land a horrid creature, described by a passer-by as being:

> Like a great eft [newt] . . . except that it's got nine holes around its mouth . . . and bodes no good . . .
>
> TRADITIONAL

The heir tossed the creature in a well and went away to fight in the Holy Land. During his absence the worm grew to massive proportions, coiling itself around the hills and terrorising the countryside. It was said to drink the milk of at least nine cows daily. On his return, the heir of Lambton asked a neighbouring witch how to destroy the monster. She told him he had to cut the worm to pieces and fling them into a swiftly flowing river, ensuring they could not join together again, a method consistently used from then on by knights in their pursuit of dragons.

Lamia A female monster of Greco-Roman mythology, not unlike the GORGON or the Scottish GLAISTIG fairy in her gruesome habits. Originally the Queen of Libya, she was seduced by JUPITER; jealous JUNO murdered her children and cast a spell which turned her into a beast with the head of a woman, the body of a snake, strange cloven hooves and a flowing lion's tail. The Lamia also had a peculiar ability to take out her eyes and hold them in her hand. As a result of this curse, she set about devouring any children she came across, in perverse vengeance for having lost her own. Thus the Lamia was long used as a BOGIE to frighten naughty children.

Other of Lamia's offspring have become known as Lamiae. These lovely girls with long fair hair were actually blood-sucking VAMPIRES who preyed exclusively upon young men as they lay sleeping. Some accounts claim that the Lamia was actually Lilith, Adam's first wife, who refused to bear his children and was cursed for deserting him.

La Milloraine The country name given to a large, sad-faced GHOST who haunts the Touraine area in France. No-one is quite sure of the origin of the PHANTOM, who is female and thought to be quite overweight with flabby arms and many double-chins. However, she is quite dolorous, and sighting her, or hearing her crying as she slowly shuffles by, are both very bad omens. The sight of this ghost usually indicates an outbreak of fever or disease close by.

Lazy Lawrence A GHOST who is said to be the guardian spirit of Somerset orchards, in south-western England. He can change his shape at will, sometimes assuming the form of a spirited colt who will chase children or other thieves away from the crop. Lazy Lawrence is a powerful spirit and widely thought to inflict 'crampe and crookeing and fault in their footing' upon wrong-doers, as this local saying testifies:

> Lazy Lawrence, let me goo
> Don't hold me summer and winter, too.

His presence is also still felt in the phrase 'Lazy Lawrence's Load', which is how a farmer would describe a worker who struggled under a too-heavy load of fruit. Apparently this was the wont of the original Lazy Lawrence, a lackadaisical labourer who would avoid making an extra trip if he could. His ghost, therefore, is always described as being hunch-backed.

Leanan-Sidhe A shadowy and seductive fairy, the Leanan-Sidhe may be ruthless and dangerous to those who fall under her spell. She is capricious, elusive and quite irresistible. In Ireland her behaviour is as a benign MUSE, her beautiful voice and exquisite music inspiring poets and singers to brilliant, albeit short, lives. On the Isle of Man, she is known as Lhiannon-Shee and appears as a blood-sucking VAMPIRE.

Le-eyo The great god-ancestor of the Masai tribe in Africa. Le-eyo was distinguished by an error which mankind has been trying to right ever since. Charged with meting out rights and privileges for all beings and entities at the time of Creation, he carried a small leather pouch on one hip containing the charms for immortality and reincarnation, while a large stone bucket to his other side contained materials for instigating death and decay. The moon and man stepped up to Le-eyo together, and the god became confused, saying 'Man, die and remain away; moon, die and return' as he sprinkled them with the reversed charms. The moon has henceforth had the ability to return to earth, while man's right to do so was forfeited.

Lemures Also known as 'larvae' these were the evil spirits of the dead during Roman times, as opposed to the good natured 'lares'. Milton, in his *Ode On The Nativity*, wrote of:

> The lars and lemures [who] moan with midnight plaint . . .

They were most active during the month of May, when they would return to torment the living. During this time, many offerings were made to MAIA, the goddess of the dead, to assuage her, and a constant din of drumming was to be heard which frightened off her attendant GHOSTS. Black beans would be burnt on the graves of those recently deceased to stop them from becoming lemures, for they were known to detest this smell.

Leprechaun The best known of Irish fairies, shoemakers by trade, the word 'leprechaun' coming from *leith bhrogan* (the one-shoe maker). These solitary cobblers are often found under a dock-leaf working merrily on a shoe, although, like their cousins the CLURICAUNS, they can frequent wine cellars and have been known to over-indulge in heather-ale. Leprechauns usually wear a cocked hat, breeches, and shoes with large buckles. William Allingham described one thus:

> I caught him at work one day, myself
> In the castle-ditch, where the foxglove grows —
> A wrinkled, wizen'd and bearded elf
> Spectacles stuck on his pointed nose
> Silver buckles to his hose
> Leather apron — sole in his lap —
> 'Rip-rap, tip-tap,
> Tack-tack-too!'

Leprechauns are extremely wealthy and hide crocks of gold and jewels about the countryside. They can be persuaded to reveal the whereabouts of this treasure by holding their eyes in a fixed stare, though they will disappear the instant the mortal blinks. Rarely, however, has anyone been able to outwit a leprechaun, for they are characteristically sly and tricky and enjoy playing practical jokes on mortals. One story is told of a man who saw a leprechaun bury a purse of gold in a field of ragwort. Excitedly he tied his red neckerchief to the plant's stem and ran home to fetch a shovel. When he returned, every ragwort plant in the field sported a red banner.

Leviathan The great sea-monster of Biblical legend. In the *Book of Job* 41:19, we learn that:

> His breath kindleth coals and a flame goeth out of his mouth [and] he maketh the deep to boil like a pot.

The Leviathan's skin was made of chain-mail and repelled any arrows or spears. His eyes were so bright they glowed beneath the sea, and when he moved he was preceded by an evil-smelling fog on the surface of the waves. The Leviathan was a ruthless and cruel creature, with 'a heart as hard as a millstone', and it destroyed anything which came in its path. Some accounts have it that the Leviathan was actually the mate of the land beast BEHEMOTH. God separated the pair for fear they would reproduce, and eventually forced them to do battle with each other. Other records describe the Leviathan as an enormous salt-water crocodile; the word was used to describe DRAGONS also, and was used as a title for the later Kings of Egypt.

Liekkio A ghostly flame which hovers over bogs and meadows at dusk in rural Finland. Rather like the English WILL O'THE WISP, this light bobs at eye level and invariably presages death or mishap to any traveller who follows it, mistaking it for the lights of a welcoming farmhouse.

The Finns tell of a long-ago New Year festival where children would sing while marching through the village holding candles above their heads. This custom ended suddenly when a witch took the opportunity to kidnap several of the children, who were never seen again. The little flames of Liekkio are, therefore, thought to be the GHOSTS of those lost children, still carrying their candles. Since they may only return to earth by replacing one of their number with a living child, mothers warn their offspring never to follow the lights.

Limbo From the Latin *limbus* (the edge), it is the name given to the region inhabited by those spirits who can go neither to Heaven because they are not baptised, nor to Hell because they have committed no great sin. Unbaptised infants are thought to live in limbo, and their spirits may be summoned or used for either good or evil purposes.

Lobs Shakespeare called PUCK 'the lob of spirits', inferring he was a prankster who essentially meant little harm. Lobs are BROWNIE-like creatures with long tails. Large and amiable their strength makes them very useful for heavy farm work, such as threshing and mowing. The Lob-lie-by-the-fire of Scottish legend was a particularly large specimen, as was Milton's *Lubbard Fiend*:

> . . . then lies him down, the Lubbard Fiend
> And stretch'd out all the chimney's length
> Basks at the fire his hairy strength.

Like brownies, they prefer to work during daylight hours and snooze in a warm spot by the hearth during the day, only hoping for a bowl of milk as payment for their labours. Known as 'lubberkins' in Elizabethan times, the more doltish lobs were relegated to the simplest of tasks and took their refreshments outdoors, so clumsy and ill-mannered were they.

Loch Ness Monster Possibly the most famous 'fabulous beast' in our world today, the belief in the much-sighted 'Nessie' continues to linger. Expeditions to the bottom of the peat-filled loch in 1976 resulted in many photographs of what appeared to be a herd of giant sea-creatures with paddle-like fins, long necks and calf-like heads. The most likely explanation is that these creatures are a form of large sea-cow, though monster-watchers around the world still hold firmly to the view that the ancient loch is home to a family of plesiosaurs, a remnant of the Mesozoic era.

Loki A mischief-maker by nature, Loki was the Norse god of evil. The son of Farbauti, who ferried the dead to the Underworld, Loki was shunned by the other gods and roamed the world sowing disharmony in retribution. He was fickle and false, clever and cunning, and was usually symbolised by the tricksy flame of a forest fire, a classical emblem of wanton destruction.

Amongst his many escapades, Loki artfully contrived the death of BALDER the Beautiful through his cunning use of a mistletoe dart. He used his handsome appearance to seduce an ogress who bore him three dreadful children, FENRIR the Wolf, the Midgard Snake and HEL, all of whom caused travail to the other gods. Loki was caught and punished by ODIN several times, once being imprisoned beneath the earth's surface where he shook so violently that the world trembled. However, his incorrigible nature meant he was unrepentant, and Loki ultimately formed an army to fight THOR and Odin in the Ragnarok, the battle which destroyed the First World.

Looe In Cornwall, south-western England, it is said that a giant white hare named Looe gambols along the clifftops on evenings when there is a full moon. Some say it is the form assumed by the GHOST of a girl disappointed in love, who fruitlessly searches for her sweetheart, a fisherman who was drowned. This belief means it is quite common today for a newly wed bride to be terrified by the omen of a white hare appearing in her path, for this augers ill for her marriage. Looe could also be a variation on witch-lore, for witches were thought to use hares as familiars. However, the 'great white hare' is most likely a ruse invented by long-ago Cornish pirates and smugglers who wanted to deter people from walking along the shore on a brightly moonlit night.

Lorelei One of the most beautiful water-spirits known, Lorelei is said to have been a German girl who was unlucky in love and drowned herself as a result. She then assumed the form of a MERMAID, or SIREN, and was often seen sitting on the banks of the Rhine strumming a wistful song on her harp. Some tales say men who have seen the Lorelei lose their minds or their sight, or both. Others say she avenges herself of the insult offered by her erstwhile lover by luring fishermen and other sailors to their doom.

Lunantishee An Irish tribe of fairies that frequent blackthorn trees, guarding them from harm from careless passers-by. Woe betide anyone who breaks a branch without first asking permission of the lunantishee, for they will torment the offender, prodding him unmercifully with their bony white fingers. Taking a cutting from the tree on Hallowe'en or May Day when the fairies are about is also extremely foolhardy.

Lung The great, glittering DRAGON-god of China, present at the Creation of the World. The *Pan Ts'ao Kang Mu*, a sixteenth-century Chinese medical almanac, offers the following description:

> Its head is like a camel's, its horns like a deer's,
> its eyes like a hare's, its ears like a bull's,
> its neck like a snake's, its belly like a clam's,
> its scales like a carp's, its claws like an eagle's,
> and its paws like a tiger's . . .

The lung's emerald scales number eighty-one, a very potent lucky number. He flew the skies as master of the winds and rain, and served mankind well by controlling monsoons and hail. To propitiate him, the people offered Lung roasted swallows' hearts and red lotus blossoms.

Lutin A GOBLIN who figured prominently in French folklore, particularly around the Normandy region. Sometimes appearing as a beautiful horse, saddled ready to ride, Lutin was better known as a hearth sprite. 'To lutin' means to tie hair in ELF-locks; sometimes he would tangle a horse's mane so badly it had to be cut.

Lybardde *see* CAMEL-LEPARD

M

Maat The goddess of truth and justice in Egyptian mythology, Maat was the personification of world order and was determined to impose her own exemplary standards of legality upon wayward mortals. She was the daughter of RA, and honorary consort to the Pharaoh, who was charged with 'Honouring Maat, by living through her laws'. Maat wore a single ostrich feather in the centre of her forehead; one of her tasks was to weigh the souls of dead men for OSIRIS, and she would use this feather to test and redress any imbalance in the Scales of Truth.

Mab Mab is the Queen of the Fairies in England, having originated from the Irish warrior-queen, Maeve of the SIDHE. The latter was exquisitely beautiful, so much so that it is dangerous for any mortal to look upon her. Queen Mab, however, is more popularly featured as a mischievous sprite than a royal personage, for the word 'qu'en' in Saxon meant, simply, 'female'. Ben Jonson described her as follows:

> This is Mab, the mistris-Faerie
> That doth nightly rob the dayrie
> . . . this is shee that empties cradles
> Takes out children, put in ladles . . .

Shakespeare termed her 'the fairies' midwife', whose office was to deliver the brain of dreams or, simply, to send dreams — often erotic ones. Thus, when Romeo says 'I dreamed a dream tonight', Mercutio replies 'O, then, I see Queen Mab hath been with you'. Sir Walter Scott followed the same track, saying 'I have a friend who is extraordinarily favoured with the visits of Queen Mab'.

Macha According to Irish religion, Macha (or Machas) referred to a compound trinity of goddesses who concerned themselves with childbirth, agriculture and war. Following Macha's own death when giving birth to twins, she grew to prefer the fields of war and death and would be heard celebrating her morbid surroundings in a howling ecstasy of grief. Early warriors would petition Macha's aid before a battle by impaling skulls of prisoners on staves carved in her honour, in the hope she would be well pleased by the sight and not claim their lives. It was Macha who taught Irish women how to keen over their dead, taking the notes of her own awful cry from the shrieks of widows and groans of women in childbirth.

Mafulke The Polynesian natives explain the origin of fire as follows. The Great Earth Mother Mafulke lived in the Underworld and tended the enormous fires which blazed there. She alone was able to start fires, bearing sparks in all her fingers and toes. There was no light or warmth on the surface of the earth, for she selfishly kept it all to herself. The first man, Maui, begged Mafulke for a little fire and she reluctantly gave him one of her fingers. Maui claimed to lose it, so she offered him each of her fingers and toes, one by one, until she realised she had been tricked. In a thunderous rage, she sent rain to the earth to extinguish Maui's fires; however, the man managed to hide Mafulke's two thumbs from the deluge, and ever since, man has been able to make fire by rubbing two squat sticks together.

Maia The daughter of ATLAS the Titan, Maia was one of the beautiful Pleiades who appear now as stars in the northern hemisphere. She was deified by the early Romans as a fertility goddess and was combined with the Phrygian goddess CYBELE in a cult which also worshipped Vulcan. Usually represented by a mound of earth or a mountain, Maia wed ZEUS and their offspring included HERMES. Some sources claim the fifth month, May, was named for her, and that she latterly came to oversee the transit of the newly dead to the Afterlife.

Manabozho The principal god of the Algonquin Indians of North America; also known as Michabo, or the Great Hare. The grandson of Nokomis, the Earth Mother and the Creator of Fire, Manabozho was credited with many inventions; for instance, he taught braves how to read signs and omens in the forest, and he taught women the healing benefits of many herbs. Once, observing a spider spinning its web, the god devised the art of making mesh for fishing nets. Large and white, Manabozho was believed to live on an iceberg, the smoke from his pipe taking the form of mist on the surrounding water. He was also a brave warrior and killed the evil Great Fish that menaced his people by plunging a barb of ice down its throat and into its heart.

Manes The Romans called the spirit or GHOST of a dead person his *manes* or *mares*, and believed it was also interred deep in the earth in its master's grave. The manes rarely slept quietly, however, and would appear via a cave or chasm if its surviving relatives had left any of its wishes unfulfilled.

Manes were generally of a benevolent temperament. The Romans referred to them as 'the good people', and each household had its own retinue of such ancestral ghosts. However, the Romans took care to appease the manes wherever possible, making offerings to them known as 'religiousae' if they became troublesome, causing household disturbances or illness. From this custom came the saying 'to appease his manes'. An example saw the head of the household getting out of his bed at midnight on 13th May, filling his mouth with black beans and then spitting them to the floor, saying:

> With these beans, I ransom me and mine
> Ancestral ghosts, begone!
>
> TRADITIONAL

Thus the manes would be stopped from interfering in the family's affairs.

Mangar-Kunjer-Kunja The great Australian tribe of Aranda

Aborigines believed a complex tale of Creation. First, amidst the primeval chaos, there existed only two mute creatures, rolled together and ignorant of sight or sound. Like symbiotic grubs they lay twisted together in a ball, until Mangar-Kunjer-Kunja appeared in the guise of a lizard. With his sharp claws he separated the two beings and swiftly carved nostrils, eyes, ears and genitals, thus creating the first man and woman. He also taught them the arts of circumcision and sub-incision, used to produce the traditional tattoos sported by Aranda menfolk. Lizards remain sacred to these tribesmen, and death is said to result from accidentally killing one.

Manipogo The Canadian version of the LOCH NESS MONSTER. First sighted in 1909 in Lake Manitoba, it was described as a giant sea-serpent with a yellowish-brown hide and a caterpillar-like 'humping' action. Eye-witnesses believe it could come from the same family of beasts as Ogopogo, Tazama and Pohengamok, who all dwelt in lakes throughout British Columbia. Indians reported that, before taking a canoe on any of these lakes to fish, they would place a dog or a pig in the prow. Thus, if the lake monster surfaced, the animal could be quickly offered as a sacrifice, allowing the boat to make a quick return to shore.

Manitou A powerful guardian spirit of American Indian tribes. As distinct from a personal tutelary spirit, who watched over an individual brave, the manitou patronised the entire tribe and was thought to be the long-ago founder of that tribe. Most often, the manitou appeared as a nature-spirit and was depicted by its tribe with fetish-charms of certain animals, trees, stones, stars or water. Thus, in lay terms, the manitou was a mascot or luck-bringer, responsible for protecting the tribe's welfare. It was very important that its totem animal — often an eagle or a snake — not be harmed, for the manitou itself would be deeply angered by such an action. The tribal SHAMAN was responsible for calling upon the manitou at special ceremonies, offering such gifts as tobacco, usually accompanied by a ritual prayer:

> Thou are Manito. We give thee to smoke . . . We are often sick, our children die; we are hungry. Have mercy upon us. Hear me, O Manito, I give thee to smoke . . .
>
> SPENCE *Myths of the North American Indians*

Manitous were rarely evil, though they were known to delight in practical jokes. Usually a particular area was declared holy in the manitou's name, such as a group of rocks or a lake. Often the manitous could be heard in these places, and they would mimic passers-by rather like an echo.

Manticore Also known as a mantiger or montegre, this creature had the body of an heraldic tiger with a mane, and the head of an old man with either one or two spiralling horns. It was first described in Tylor's *Primitive Culture* as being:

> . . . bred amongst the Indians, having a triple row of teeth, in bigness and roughness like a lion's, face and ears like a man's, a tail like a scorpion's, with a sting and sharp-pointed quills . . .

Aristotle added that the manticore's voice was 'like a small trumpet' and that it was very wild, although if its tail was bruised it could be tamed without any trouble. Sometimes it is shown as having bat wings as well, and Indonesian records describe each quill in the beast's tail as being tipped in poisonous juices of the upas tree for added impetus. In India, it is still believed that certain people are able to assume the shape of a manticore, which then circles villages looking for human prey. When a manticore captures a victim the terrible rows of razor-sharp teeth make short work of bones, clothing or any other clues, thus explaining how occasionally individuals simply disappear without trace.

Maras Originally a Norse term for GOBLINS who attacked sleepers, robbing them of their faculties so when they finally awoke they were bereft of speech. It was similarly used in long-ago England to describe night-riding demons, usually female, who preyed upon men and gave them bad dreams. Our legacy today is the word 'nightmare'. These spirits were also known as 'mahrs', and could assume a more erotic personality. Most often, they were souls of jilted girls who visited their erstwhile lovers while they slept, stimulating them to nocturnal emissions and general restlessness. Fairyland was once called Mirryland or Marayland, and it was here witches claimed to ride at the time of their Sabbats.

Marduk A great hero of Babylonian legend, Marduk was the son of the water god Ea and the goddess of harvest Hinlil. He was half man and half fish; because he could live on both land and sea he was created Lord of the World and renamed Bel by the Sumerians. (As Bel, he was thought to have created the world as a result of his battle with the fearsome water monster TIAMAT, who had gripped the world in chaos. Bel went on to fix the planets' courses and rationalise the universe, alarming Tiamat's DRAGONS in heaven from whence their fiery breath became lightning.) Marduk was also a mortal king, whose children travelled the earth as ambassadors of their country. An important son was Nebo, who was later deified as the god of learning, for taking the gift of written language to other kingdoms.

Mares of Diomedes Horses belonging to the ruthless King of Aetolia in ancient Greece, named Dinos (Dreadful) and Lampon (Bright-Eyed). Diomedes' mares differed from mortal horses in that they would feed only on human flesh, a trait encouraged by their master who ordered them to eat any stranger who trespassed in his kingdom. It was HERCULES who broke the mares of their sordid habit, by killing the king and feeding his flesh to the horses. So bitter and rank was this meal that the mares lost their taste for eating humans.

Mars The Roman god of war. Unlike the popular Greek deity ARES, Mars was thought a noble god. He was regarded as the patron of herdsmen and their flocks, and, as the father of ROMULUS AND REMUS, was the honorary patron of Rome. At one time he was a sheep-farmer himself and, upon his deification, placed his flock in the heavens so as to keep a close eye on them. Hence the constellation of Aries is close to the planet Mars. Carrying a lance and attended by a wolf Mars did, however, have his bloodthirsty moments. Ptholomeus wrote of the Romans:

> . . . these men of Mars causeth warre and murther and battayle. . . .. He is red and angry . . . a maker of swordes and knyves and a sheder of man's blode.
>
> *Compost of Ptholomeus*

Mauthe Dhoog A very famous spectral hound which haunts the ancient castle of Peel on the Isle of Man. Soldiers present in the guard-room which it frequents describe it as a black spaniel who would enter the room when candles were lit and disappear at daybreak, trotting up the hallway. It is thought to have once belonged to a member of the castle's guard, and soldiers treat the little dog with much respect, refraining from swearing within its earshot. This superstition harks back to when a drunken trooper inadvertently cursed the Mauthe Dhoog, only to be struck dumb and die three days later, a fact referred to by Sir Walter Scott in his *Lay of the Last Minstrel*:

> For he was speechless, ghastly wan
> Like him of whom the story ran
> Who spoke the spectre-hound in Man.

Mermaid The best known of all the fairies who live in the water. Traditionally both the sexes have a human head and torso, and the tail of a fish. The maids are lovely to behold, combing their long tresses and gazing at themselves in hand-mirrors, while singing with exquisite sweetness on a rock near the water's edge. Browne wrote of:

> Ye mermaids fair
> That on the shores do plait
> Your sea green hair.

Mermaids are not unique to the ocean, however, being found also in lakes and freshwater streams. It is said that if you visit the

Mermaid Pool of Derbyshire just before dawn, you will see them swimming gracefully in the dark waters below.

Most commonly, tales are told of mermaids who fall in love with mortal men and painfully shed their tail in order to be able to live with them on land. Children of such a union are said to be born with webbed feet or scaly skin, although as with any fairy/mortal mating the child will be uncommonly gifted. Mermaids are also able to lure men to live with them beneath the sea, particularly if they are young and handsome, for mermen are often ugly and fierce. The story is told of Lutey, a Cornish fisherman, who rescued a mermaid stranded in a tidal pool and returned her to the ocean. As he approached the water she begged him to come with her and tried to drag him into the sea. He stopped her with the threat of his drawn knife and she sorrowfully sang:

> Farewell, farewell!
> For nine long years, I'll wait for thee
> And hold thee in my heart, my love
> And then I shall return!
>
> TRADITIONAL

The mermaid did indeed return to claim Lutey and it is said that every nine years hence, one of his descendants is lost at sea.

Mermaids were sometimes captured and kept for the knowledge they could bestow upon humans, particularly their understanding of herbal lore and their gifts of prophecy. Chambers wrote of a mermaid who gave a lad medical advice for his sweetheart's illness:

> Would ye let the bonnie May die in your hand
> And the mugwort flow'ring in the land?

Mermaids can, however, be destructive. Believed to be the GHOSTS of drowned men and women, the females frequently cause shipwrecks for love of a human sailor; a person soon to die by drowning is said to see a mermaid cutting a caper upon the water's surface, in anticipation of fresh company.

Mermecolion A rather tragic member of the leonine race,

found in Asia. It had the head of a lion and the body of a great bull ant. However, because the ant's stomach could not digest the meat that the beast caught and ate with its lion-mouth, the mermecolion would swiftly starve and die after birth.

Merrows Irish mer-people, also known as the Murdhuacha. The females are very beautiful, like MERMAIDS, with long flowing hair, sweet voices and jewelled webs between their fingers. They often appear as an omen before storms, though they are more gentle-natured than mermaids. The male merrows, though quite amiable, are extremely unattractive to behold. Croker wrote of them:

> They are nothing worth looking at, for they have green hair and green teeth and little pigs' eyes and long red noses and short arms more like a flipper than any respectable arm that could do a day's work.

Merrows differ from other sea-fairies in that they wear red feathered caps to swim underwater. If their cap is stolen, they cannot return to the sea and may wander the shores in the form of hornless cattle.

Mimicke Dog An endearing creature with curly ringlets instead of fur, the Mimicke Dog was featured in Edward Topsell's seventeenth-century *Historie of Foure-Footed Beasts*. An appealing and playful pet, it would imitate men's voices and their habits, creating confusion and mischief within a household. Often, one would be trained to carry out chores normally done by a kitchen maid. The Mimicke Dog was thought to be raised by apes in Africa, from whence it was imported to England as a treasure for Queen Elizabeth I.

Minch Men *see* BLUE MEN

Minerva The Roman goddess of education and business, Minerva was linked strongly with the Greek ATHENE. Her name was derived from the Latin root *mens* (thought). She had various responsibilities: as Minerva Medica, for instance, she was the patron of doctors and medicine, while her irascible temper meant that the spoils of war were also dedicated to her. Minerva, like Athene, was usually depicted wearing a helmet and armour and carrying a lance and shield.

Minotaur With the body of a man and the head of a huge bull, this creature was the result of a frenzied union between Pasiphae, Queen of Crete, and a white sea-bull. The Cretans named it Minotaur, meaning 'bull-son of the King Minos'. This Minotaur was imprisoned in a labyrinth beneath the Palace of Knossus and, as it would eat only human flesh, each year seven handsome youths and seven beautiful maidens were sent in to the monster's lair to meet their doom. The Minotaur was finally slain by Theseus, who found his way out of the labyrinth by trailing a skein of thread given him by the king's daughter, ARIADNE.

Miraj A strange and often savage creature from an island in the Indian Ocean, the miraj was a large hare with yellow fur, who sported a single spiralling black horn in the centre of its forehead. Unlike mortal hares, the miraj was both predatory and carnivorous, pursuing deer and antelope with great ferocity.

Mithra The Persian god of daybreak, also known as Mitra. His epithets include The One Who Dispels Darkness, a reference to his appearance as the light which preceded the sun as it rose. Contemporary sources described Mithra as having 10,000 ears and eyes, and as riding a gleaming white chariot above the clouds. During his travels, Mithra was thought to see all – nothing could be concealed from his gaze. The word 'mithra' was also used to describe a friend, and this god was thought to be a true friend of man, protecting and warming him in life and death.

Mithra was later adopted by the Romans, who designated him to oversee all legal affairs and transactions. He was usually depicted as a young man with a Phrygian cap and short tunic, thrusting a sword into the neck of a bull and thus demonstrating his triumph over the forces of evil. Mithra was merciless to his enemies, wielding a huge mace and firing poisonous darts as he rode into battle, attended by the virulent boar Verethraghna which was 'sharp in tusk, unapproachable, a raging beast'. An old prayer to Mithra sums up this duality in his nature:

> Mithra — evil you are, yet most good to the nations
> Mithra — evil you are, yet most good to man
> In the world, you have power over peace and war.

Moirae *see* FATES

Moloch The primitive Canaanites worshipped Moloch with rather gruesome rituals, including child sacrifice. The statue of Moloch in Carthage had large outstretched hands for children to be placed on before they tumbled to a blazing fire below, where they would be 'purified' and blessed by that god. Reference is made in the Bible, *Kings* 2, 23:10, to man making 'his son . . . or daughter to pass through the fire to Molech'. The word 'moloch' is still used to refer to any supreme sacrifice and was, in fact, used to describe the Crucifixion of Jesus, God's first-born son.

Monongahela Monster One of the best documented tales of the sighting of a sea monster occurred in 1852, when a whaling vessel, the *Monongahela*, netted and took aboard a creature which was rather like a cross between a snake and a crocodile. Over one-hundred feet long, with ninety-four teeth, it had a long tail and four webbed paws. The creature was sketched and the drawing witnessed by all the crew before it was decapitated. The head was then pickled in a ten-foot long tin box, and the rotting body returned to the ocean. Although the drawing made it back to civilisation the pickled head, along with the rest of the ship, was lost.

Morag A dun-grey monster, very similar in appearance to the fabled LOCH NESS MONSTER, believed to live at the bottom of the thousand-foot deep Loch Morar. According to a local song:

Morag, harbinger of death
Giant swimmer in deep green Morar
The loch that has no bottom
There it is that Morag lives.

Although this creature has not been reported as actually killing any people, its appearance is a frightening one with eye-witnesses testifying to its huge head and swelling shoulders, and the fearsome groans it emits.

Morgan le Fay A famed enchantress, known also as Morgaine le Fee, or Morgana the Fairy. Daughter of the Queen Igrayne and half-sister to King Arthur, she revealed to him the intrigue between Lancelot and Guinevere by giving him a magic draught which opened his eyes to the perfidy. She was ill-intentioned towards Arthur, constantly plotting his undoing and the destruction of Camelot.

Apart from the Arthurian legend, Morgan was the name of a Celtic sea-fairy; an echo of this belief is last seen when Morgan le Fay is one of the four fairy queens who spirit the body of King Arthur across the water to the Isle of Avalon.

Mumiai A type of POLTERGEIST. It is best known for persecuting Indian peasants, especially the lower castes or 'Untouchables', who may have stolen from a neighbour or have demonstrated dirty habits. These poor scapegoats are regularly beset by mumiai who toss their belongings in the air, break pottery and trample on gardens, so as to force the peasant to move out of the village.

Mura-Muras Ancestral spirits of Aboriginal tribes who accompany their descendants in their daily life. They may be petitioned by men to help with hunting animals, or by women seeking assistance with childbirth or illness. Most commonly, mura-muras are asked to send rain, for it is well known that if one is offended he will hold up a huge bark dish to the heavens and catch all the rain on its way to earth, out of spite. He may be placated, an acceptable tribute being pebbles doused in the blood of six young men, then placed high up in the branches of a tree so the mura-muras may reach them. The blood symbolises water, or life-blood of the tribe, and the spirit will respond with a like gift of his own 'blood', the rain.

Muryans A Cornish word for ants. Cornish people of south-western England believe souls progress through various stages, reducing in size each time until they reach the last stage of the cycle before passing to Heaven or Hell. During this final stage they appear as ants, which are really fairies in disguise. Therefore it is considered extremely unlucky to step on one.

Muses Nine young goddesses, daughters of ZEUS and Mnemosyne, the spirit of memory. They attended APOLLO. The Muses dwelt upon Mount Olympus and each was charged with supervising a particular artistic talent, fostering it wherever it was found amongst mortals. Their fields of expertise were: Calliope, epic poetry; Erato, erotic poetry; Euterpe, lyric poetry; Polyhymnia, religious poetry and hymns; Clio, history; Urania, astronomy; Terpsichore, dance; Melpomene, tragedy; Thalia, comedy.

Myndie Snake During the Dreamtime, Australian Aboriginals say, different creation ancestors gave the country its form. One of these was the dreadful Myndie Snake, the servant of Pundijl, who was the spirit ancestor of man, having created the first mortal from clay. The Myndie Snake was ten miles long and moved swiftly across the desert, often travelling just below the surface of the burning red sand. Aboriginals still point to various rocky outcrops or sandstone gullies which trace the Myndie Snake's progress through the outback. Its task was to destroy all those who broke Pundijl's laws, and its way was swift and terrifying. Transgressors would see the enormous snake bearing down on them, so they would break camp and attempt to hide in water holes or caverns. The Myndie Snake would find them and drip venom upon them, poisoning the water and burning them where they hid.

N

Naga A tribe of deities who are half-human, half-snake, they were found in India and on the Malay Peninsula, where they lived in a great underground city called Bhogavati. By travelling below ground and occasionally coming to the surface for air, they have created the great underground caverns and tunnels of South-East Asia. The Naga maidens have exceptionally lovely faces and are often successful in luring mortal men to their domain, though Naga men are less attractive with slate-coloured skin and cold, serpentine eyes. It is the latter who cause terrible nightmares about snakes. Naga are very covetous and will often steal jewellery and precious gems to adorn themselves and their buildings.

Narayana The seven-headed serpent believed to live in the legendary continent of Mu (thought by some scholars to be the lost city of Atlantis, and by others to be the Garden of Eden). Unlike its biblical counterpart, however, the snake Narayana was quite benevolent and generous to mankind, bestowing gifts of intelligence and memory. It was also known as Supreme Spirit and credited with creating coral and other gems.

Navky Known also as nakki, piteous sprites found by lakes in Finland and Yugoslavia. They were usually thought to be the GHOSTS of infants who had died unbaptised or, more tragically still, been murdered by parents unable to feed them. They appeared as young children or pale, pretty girls clinging to branches of riverside trees like willows, where they would cry and moan most unhappily. Sometimes they took the form of huge black ravens who cried out in human tones to passers-by, begging for baptism. More vengeful navky would attempt to entice a victim into the water, pretending itself to be drowning. In some parts of southern Russia, sacrifices were made regularly to a navky who thirsted for revenge against the living. Even today it is not uncommon for a tourist to be shown the respectful manner of asking the navky's leave before plunging into the lake or stream it has made its home.

Nemean Lion A fierce beast who terrorised the Greek countryside and kept the people in a state of constant alarm for twelve years. No-one was able to harm it because its hide was impregnable to spears or arrows. It was HERCULES who finally overcame this monster, first strangling it, then using one of its own claws to peel off the skin, which he wore as a lucky mantle from then on.

Neptune In Roman mythology, the god of flowing water. Although closely linked with the Greek POSEIDON, god of the salt sea, Neptune was worshipped as a fertility agent, for he was also thought to control rain and dew. Festivals were held in his honour during the northern summer to avoid drought.

Nereids Graceful sea-NYMPHS native to the Mediterranean, descendants of the fifty grand-daughters of Nereus the sea god, and Gaea the earth mother. They are extremely beautiful and usually very vain, spending their days riding tritons and dolphins through the waves, combing their rippling green hair and admiring their slender white arms. Unlike MERMAIDS they can be quite soft-hearted and virtuously save ships from being wrecked. Camoens wrote that when Vasco da Gama's ship was inadvertently steered towards a rock, the nereids lifted the prow from the water and turned it around. The most famous nereids are Amphitrite, who wed POSEIDON, and Thetis who became the Queen of Thessaly and mother to ACHILLES. Interestingly, nereids disdained marriage to mortals and would frantically assume different forms — a flame, a black hen, a fish, even a camel — to avoid capture. For this reason most have remained virgins, and women should protect their newborn babies against possible theft by a nereid who may spirit it away in the guise of a storm.

Nibelungen The 'children of mist or darkness', from the Norwegian *nebel* (darkness). They were subterranean dwarves of Norse folklore, descended from the dwarf Nibelung who was famous for having slain twelve giants. A jealous and selfish race, they hoarded a mass of treasure in their underground lair, a fact remarked upon in the thirteenth-century German epic poem *Nibelungen-lied:*

> 'Twas as much as twelve huge wagons
> In four whole days and nights
> Could carry from the mountain
> Down to the salt-sea bay . . .
> It was made up of nothing but
> Precious stones and gold . . .

Similarly, in the nineteenth century, they featured in Wagner's opera *Ring of the Nibelungs*, which referred to a much-prized ring bestowing fertility.

Nike The Greek goddess of victory. She was mostly depicted as a winged messenger of the gods, and carried a palm-leaf in one hand and a laurel garland in the other.

Nimue One of the names attributed to the mysterious Arthurian enchanter who lived in the midst of an imaginary lake surrounded by knights and damsels. The surface of the lake was a mere illusion, concealing her palace whereabouts from passers-by. She is believed to have brought up the young Lancelot du Lac, bestowing upon him the gifts of strength, valour and beauty. She is also believed to be the water fairy who presented Arthur with his sword Excalibur and to have reclaimed it from his knights at his death, when she was one of the four fairy queens who took him to Avalon.

Nixies German water sprites with fine gold hair and blue eyes the colour of the sky. They usually sit in the sun on river banks to play their harps and admire their reflections. In keeping with the ambivalent nature of women, which can be both beautiful and dangerous, nixies can be treacherous, and if a mortal man dares to spy on their frolicsome play he will be blinded. The tale is also told of a nixie who fell in love with a man and enticed him to follow her to the depths of the river, never to rise again. Male nixies, or nixen, are rarely seen, with only a ripple on the water's surface indicating their presence. They are often moody and will appear one day as a golden-haired youth, the next as a bad-tempered ELF who scatters debris in the water.

Noggle A mischievous beast, most common in Wales. They usually take the form of a dappled grey horse, differing from mortal horses in that they are barely three-foot high. They may also be identified by the sour smell which surrounds them and the fact that their tail curls up over their backs, rather than falling down between their legs. If a guile-less mortal ignores these warning signs and attempts to ride a noggle, he will find himself pitched unceremoniously into the nearest lake, while the beast disappears leaving only a sulphurous blue cloud behind. If a noggle is unable to find a human to torment, he will go to the local mill and stop it from running; the only deterrent is a steel knife in the millhouse door.

Norns In Scandinavian mythology, three sisters whose names were Fate, Being and Necessity. They are responsible for tending the Tree of Life, Yggdrasil, and also mete out man's destiny, representing respectively the past, present and future. The Norns attend the gods when they visit the well of Urda to sit in judgement of mortals; they also appear by a crib when a baby is born and play a game of dice to determine its future.

Nuckalavee Surely the most horrible of sea monsters. Found in Scotland it had the torso of a man and the legs of a horse, with an enormous lolling head. Long, powerful arms swung to the ground and there were flippers growing from its legs; it had fiery, staring eyes and a huge mouth exuding poisonous breath.

The worst aspect, however, was that it was skinless, so the creature's black blood could be seen coursing through its yellow veins, its powerful muscles and sinews were exposed and scraps of rotten flesh were dropped in its wake. The nuckalavee was completely malignant and thought to spread plague amongst livestock, poison crops and murder any straying humans. There was, however, an effective defence against this noxious beast — it could not bear fresh running water, so one could escape a nuckalavee by crossing a mountain stream.

Nun The Egyptian father of the gods, Nun personified the primeval waters of the ocean. In tomb illustrations he is portrayed as a man standing in water up to his waist, with his arms upstretched to support the sun. Because of Nun's ability to move over and under mud and earth he was sometimes depicted with a frog's head, and this animal was sacred to him.

Nut The Egyptian sky-goddess. She was usually depicted as a naked giantess who arched over Geb, the god of the earth, supporting the heavens upon her bent back. Her epithet was The Sow Who Eats All Her Piglets, a reference to her custom of 'eating' the sun every night, then giving birth to it from her womb again the following day. Nut was therefore strongly linked with the Egyptian cult of the dead, for she symbolised the continuum of resurrection.

Nymph A beautiful female nature-spirit who frequents the Greek countryside, usually serving a superior god or spirit. There are several different groups: the sea-nymphs are known as oceanids or nereids, the wood nymphs as dryads, mountain nymphs as oreads, and those which lived in rivers or springs were called naiades. A popular water nymph was Egeria, whose chuckling voice was heard when streams tumbled over stones. Pregnant women prayed to this nymph for an easy delivery, believing she would show them a way past every obstacle in their labour. A famous mountain nymph was Echo, whose voice may still be heard in valleys.

O

Oakmen A country rhyme runs as follows:

> Fairy folks
> Live in old oaks!

An oak coppice, where a felled oak sent up tightly packed shoots from a stump, is not considered a safe place to wander after dark, because they assume the shape of oakmen angry at the loss of their parent tree. Beatrix Potter, the authoress (1866-1943), described them as dwarves with red noses who wore red toadstools as caps. They are likely to offer delicious food to passing mortals, but this must be refused for when the fairy magic is reversed it will be seen to be poisonous fungi in reality. Oakmen are also believed to guard the wild animals of the forest and to dwell near clumps of bluebells.

Oannes Beings from another world, held by the ancient Chaldeans to be sea-gods. They had the head and body of a fish and the legs of a man. Oannes lived amongst men during the day and built the Sumerian civilisation, teaching art, science and engineering. At night they returned to the Persian Gulf to swim in the ocean.

Oberon High King of the Fairies, whose wife was TITANIA in Shakespeare's *A Midsummer Night's Dream*. His name may have been anciently derived from the German Alberich, King of the Elves, and Auberon or Oberycom were both names used to describe witches' familiars during the Renaissance. Oberon was a tiny DWARF, only three-foot high, with a humped back and a charming face. According to the fifteenth-century romance *Huon of Bordeaux*, Oberon's lineage was very impressive.

Cephalonia, mistress of the Hidden Isle, married Neptanebus the King of Egypt, and bore him a son who became Alexander the Great. Seven hundred years later Julius Caesar fell in love with the same lady and she bore him a son also — this was Oberon. At his christening, Cephalonia's ladies-in-waiting bestowed various fairy gifts on the babe. One was the ability to read men's thoughts, another to transport himself to any place on earth, instantly. However, a malicious fairy placed a curse upon him which resulted in his low stature. A lusty king, Oberon pursued amorous affairs with mortal and fairy maids, and when in the fullness of time he fell asleep in death, the angels carried his soul to Paradise.

Odin Also known as WOTAN or Woden, the chief god of the Scandinavians, called All Father. Handsome and eloquent he was also the god of war and patron of heroes, and credited with the invention of the magical runic tablets. He was always dressed in a shining breast-plate and helmet of gold, and was attended by the VALKYRIES and his twin oracular ravens, Hugin (Thought) and Munin (Memory), who whispered in his ear of all that they saw on their daily circuit of the world. Nor was Odin ever without his golden spear Gungnir, which never failed to hit its mark; his magic ring Draupner, which every ninth night dropped eight rings of equal value; or his eight-hooved horse Sleipnir, who was rarely far away.

Odin is believed to have sacrificed one of his eyes in order to gain wisdom, offering it to the evil Mimir who was the guardian of the cauldron of knowledge. His other eye became the sun. Many myths tell of Odin travelling in various worlds, most often disguised as an old man with one eye, a floppy hat and wooden staff. Odin was married to FREYA, goddess of love and the home. At Ragnarok, the Day of Judgement, Odin was swallowed by the demon-wolf FENRIR.

O'Iwa A famous and very old Japanese ballad tells the saga of a wicked nobleman, Iemon, and his tormented wife, O'Iwa. Iemon loved another and deserted his wife as she lay in child-bed, to be with his paramour. As he left he put a horrid curse upon her, causing her eyes to roll in her head and her hair to fall out in bloody clumps, before she died in agony. O'Iwa's tragic ghost could not rest until it had enjoyed revenge, and this came about when her erstwhile husband was about to marry his new love. As he pulled back the bridal veil he started in horror, as he beheld the livid face of O'Iwa. He drew his sword and attacked the spectre, only to realise O'Iwa had duped him for he had, in fact, decapitated his new bride.

Omniont To the American Indians this was a giant snake-god, one of the most powerful of all deities. Usually depicted with its tail in its mouth, forming the shape of the sun, Omniont had a strange curved horn growing from his forehead. Many SHAMANS claimed to possess a fragment of this horn — though it was more likely to have been a shard of buffalo horn — and used it in magic to bring sunshine and harvest. Omniont's name could never be spoken by mere tribesmen, and gifts and sacrifices were necessary to keep the great snake in good humour, for when angered Omniont would shake his rattle and leap across the sky to attack villagers in the form of thunder and lightning, vomiting rain and hail as he went.

Oni The demon spirits who lived in Jingoku, the underground hell of Japanese folklore. They were fierce and frightening to behold, being green or red with a horse's head on top of a skeletal human torso. Oni could change their shape or become invisible, at will. Their task was to travel the skies in chariots made of flames, to seek sinners. They also spread disease and stole from the bodies of the recently dead. Their recruits were judged by EMMA-HOO, King of the Jingoku, who arbitrarily meted out torture and punishment to be administered by the Oni. These demons eventually destroyed themselves with their evil ways — an old curse stated that they would never be able to eat or drink, nor rid their bodies of poisonous waste, so eventually, when they were bloated with their own toxins, the Oni dissipated as foul gas from the ground. These noxious fumes still arise from certain chasms and cracks in the earth in Japan, and these areas are studiously avoided by those who know what is good for them.

Oonagh The beautiful wife of FINVARRA, King of the Irish fairies. Lady Wilde, in her *Ancient Legends, Mystic Charms and Superstitions of Ireland*, describes Oonagh thus:

> Her golden hair sweeps the ground and she is robed in silver gossamer all glittering, as if with diamonds, but they are dewdrops that sparkle over it . . .

Despite her beauty Finvarra remains an incorrigible womaniser; not only does he have several other fairy wives and mistresses, but he enjoys seducing mortal women, first lulling them to slumber with gentle music and then spiriting them away to his underground rath, or castle.

Orfeo The mythological tale of Orpheus and Eurydice was re-worked in an English Gothic romance, whereby Orpheus became King Orfeo and his Queen, Dame Heroudis, was kidnapped by the fairies when she slept under 'an ymp tree'; that is, a magical grafted apple tree. King Orfeo embarked upon a search for Heroudis which lasted for ten years in the wilderness. Finally, he arrived at the underground palace of the Fairy King and played his harp most sweetly for the Court's pleasure. The Fairy King promised Orfeo any reward he desired, so he re-claimed Heroudis.

Orion A handsome giant of Greek mythology, the son of POSEIDON and known as a mighty hunter. Orion was also renowned for his beauty, and in *The Iliad* Homer described a handsome youth as being 'as fair as Orion'. Not always successful in matters of the heart, he was rejected by all the Pleiades and then blinded by a mortal father whose daughter he was wooing. He regained his sight by wading through the ocean to the eastern-most point and exposing his eyeballs to the sun. Thereafter he was beloved by EOS, goddess of the dawn, and she abducted him to be her lover. The gods elevated Orion and his trusty dog Sirius to the skies, where they appear as constellations.

Orthos The fierce two-headed dog of Greek mythology. Sired by TYPHON and ECHIDNA, he was brother to CERBERUS and like him was set to guard over the treasures of the Underworld. It was while Orthos was shepherding giant red cattle that he was captured and killed by HERCULES, who tricked the animal into attacking his own reflection, shown in Hercules' shield. Amongst Latin scholars Orthos' name became a synonym for the world after death.

Osiris In life, Osiris was the first ruler of Egypt. As brother and husband of ISIS he was worshipped in the form of an ox. He was responsible for establishing many of the social and agricultural rules of ancient Egypt, building towns and temples, teaching the people how to sow grain and make beer, and patronising the development of art, music and perfume-making. Then came the fall and apotheosis — he was killed by his brother Set, the god of evil, who cut his body into fourteen pieces and scattered them throughout the land. Isis invented the technique of embalming in order to restore all the pieces to life. The revived god became the Judge of the Dead and Ruler of the Underworld. He was usually depicted as a figure swathed in mummy's bindings, holding a scourge and a crooked staff. All souls came before Osiris and Isis for judgement, and he continued to cast a kindly eye over the living by monitoring the water levels of the Nile.

P

Pan The ancient Greeks worshipped this SATYR, the horned, goat-legged god of fields and wood. According to Phornutus, Pan's nether regions symbolised 'the spermatic principle of the world', his upper 'the hegemonic nature of the world'. The son of HERMES and a NYMPH, Pan was lusty, playful and energetic. Milton, in *Paradise Lost* described him thus:

> Universal Pan,
> Knit with the Graces and the Hours in dance
> Led on the eternal spring.

He claimed to have seduced each of the maenads and various other nymphs, including Echo. It was his pursuit of the unfortunate Syrinx that led to Pan's creation of his trademark, the Pan-pipes. The hapless nymph changed herself into a clump of reeds in order to avoid his advances, but Pan promptly cut the reeds and carried them close to his heart always afterwards.

If Pan was feeling amiable he would play a leisurely game of knucklebones with one or other of the goddesses; if irritable he would blow terrible notes on a conch shell to frighten men and their flocks.

Peg O'Nell An evil-intentioned GHOST who haunts the River Ribble in England. She is said to have been a maidservant at the nearby manor house. Argumentative by nature, she cursed her mistress when asked to fetch a bucket of water from the river one evening, grumbling that she would slip and break her neck. This she surely did, for the river bank was wet and icy, and her ghost returns every seven years to claim a victim in the Ribble — preferably a descendant of her erstwhile employer. Deaths of local children and livestock have long been blamed on Peg

O'Nell, though it is possible to avert such a tragedy by drowning a dog before Peg's anticipated appearance.

Peg Powler A horrific water-demon inhabiting the treacherous River Tees in England. An ugly, green-skinned HAG with long flowing hair and sharp teeth, she is insatiable for human life, dragging her victims to the bottom of the river where she devours them. Rather like JENNY GREENTEETH and other BOGIES, Peg Powler is said to especially favour children who were playing — despite their parents' instructions to the contrary — on the river's banks, particularly on a Sunday. The greenish foam or scum seen on top of the river is locally described as 'Peg Powler's suds', indicating the wicked sprite is below, laundering winding sheets for her victims.

Pegasus A poetic creation of the ancients, Pegasus (or Pegasos) was a magnificent white stallion with golden wings, a silky mane and warm breath that smelt of wild flowers. He sprang from the blood of the Medusa and was captured by BELLEROPHON with the aid of a magical golden bridle; together the pair slew the fire-breathing CHIMERA. However, when Bellerophon arrogantly attempted to ride Pegasus to heaven he plunged to his death, while the winged steed continued upwards, there to assume the responsibility of pulling ZEUS' thunder-cloud chariot across the sky.

Pegasus was also the horse ridden by the MUSES when they visited earth. As such, he symbolised poetry and literature and it was said that when he struck the side of Mount Olympus with his hoof, the waters of the Hippocrene sprang forth. This spring has long provided inspiration to anyone who drinks from it. Thus a poet will say 'I am on my Pegasus', meaning he is writing verse. This sacred fountain's modern name is Kyo Pegad (cool water), while its ancient name does indeed translate as 'sprung from the horse'.

Pegasus also came to represent swiftness and deftness. Shakespeare, in *Henry IV* referred to a rider being able to:

> Turn and wind a fiery Pegasus
> And witch the world with noble horsemanship.

Similarly the ease and strength of Pegasus' movement was referred to by Shakespeare in *Troilus and Cressida* thus:

> The strong-ribbed bark through liquid mountain cut
> Like Perseus' horse.

Peris Delicate, good, gentle DJINN, or spirits, of Eastern mythology. They were begotten by fallen angels and born in fire, and they lived on the scent of aromatic wood-smoke from religious sacrifices. They were lovely creatures, who would favour certain mortals with lucky charms or amulets, sending fabled beasts like the SIMURGH to assist their troubles. Using their wands, the peris pointed out a path amongst the stars by which the pure in mind could make their way to heaven. Thomas Moore in *Lalla Rookh* (1817) describes their habit thus:

> Like peris' wands, when pointing out the road
> For some pure spirit to the blest abode.

Peris opposed the wiles of evil djinn, or devas, and their battles could be witnessed overhead, as they would often fling stars and fireballs at each other across the night sky.

Persephone The daughter of ZEUS and DEMETER, Persephone (Proserpine) was abducted by HADES and became the unwilling Queen of the Underworld. The story goes that, as a small girl, Persephone bent to pick a lush flower, little realising that it was the hundred-blossomed narcissus offered by the earth to lease the god of death. She was seized by Hades and thereafter spent six months of every year below the ground. During this time plants and crops withered in mourning, only to burst forth joyously at her annual rebirth, a cycle continuing today. Milton describes this in *Paradise Lost*:

> . . . that fair field
> Of Enna, where Proserpin gathering flowers,

> Herself a fairer flower, by gloomy Dis
> Was gathered — which cost Ceres all that pain
> To seek her through the world.

Another story denotes her sweet nature: she is said to have taught the Underworld attendants to sing sweetly, in order to console humans on their way to stand before her husband's judgement.

Perseus The adventurous son of ZEUS, who coupled with his mortal mother Danae in the form of a shower of golden rain. Perseus' god-like strength and formidable wits meant he successfully undertook many adventures, including killing the horrific Medusa and rescuing the Princess Andromeda. ATHENE's nymphs bestowed upon him a sickle-shaped magic sword, winged sandals and a helmet of invisibility as tributes to his status as a warrior-god. Perseus was also famed for his navigational skills and his boat was thought the fastest in the world, being referred to by Shakespeare in *Troilus and Cressida* as follows:

> The strong-ribbed bark through liquid mountains
> cut . . . like Perseus' horse.

Peryton A large, deer-like beast with the wings of an eagle and antlers which would grow again immediately if lopped or damaged. Quite familiar to Classical scholars, the peryton was believed to be the spirit of a man recently dead, for the shadow it cast as it flew overhead was that of a man. Most often, this was taken to be the spirit of a fellow who had died whilst far from his home and family, so the wives of sailors or soldiers would view the appearance of a peryton askance. Nor would the travellers themselves welcome the beast's appearance, for perytons were known to swoop to earth and entangle a man in their antlers, carrying him far away before dropping him to his death.

Phantom A spectral apparition or ghostly figure which reappears at certain times due to pressure or circumstance.

Sometimes, when history threatens to repeat itself, a phantom of a long-ago parallel occurrence will materialise. These are usually intangible, transparent, cloudy figures. Phantom armies have appeared on battle grounds and fought side by side with mortal troops. Phantom bells from long-gone churches have been known to toll when warning of danger or invasion. Horse-drawn coaches, travelling at great speed and in complete silence, usually herald danger or death, having once been strongly associated with highway robbery and murder. Most famous of all are the phantom ships which haunt the world's oceans, appearing to doomed vessels. Sir Walter Scott epitomised the seaman's fear of these ghostly vessels in *Rokeby*:

> Or of that phantom ship, whose form
> Shoots like a meteor through the storm;
> When the dark scud comes driving hard,
> And lowered is every topsail yard . . .
> And well the doomed spectators know
> 'Tis t'harbinger of wreck and woe.

Phi According to Thai folklore, ancient nature spirits have survived since the time before Buddha. These fairy-like beings frequent trees and waterfalls, and will influence man's fortunes for both good and evil. Evans Wents in his *Fairy Faith in Celtic Countries*, points out that the Phi 'correspond pretty closely to the TUATHA DE DANAAN of Irish mythology'. For instance, the chao phum phi ('gods of the earth') are BROWNIE-like creatures who frequent houses and barns.

Phoenix A fabulous bird which dwelt in ancient Arabia and Egypt and symbolised all that was rare and marvellous. The size of an eagle, it had a golden head and iridescent feathers which reflected all the colours seen in fire — scarlet, gold, lavender and bright turquoise. Thought, variously, to live for between 300, 500 and 1000 years the phoenix would then build a pyre of fragrant spices such as frankincense, myrrh and cinnamon in a palm tree, also known as 'the phoenix tree'. Shakespeare refers to this tree in *The Tempest*:

And will I believe . . . that in Arabia
There is one tree, the phoenix throne — one phoenix
At this hour reigneth there.

The nest was then ignited by the sun and the bird self-immolated, singing gloriously as it died. Its sweet music was said to be due to its having many orifices in its slender beak, through which it played rather like organ pipes. Out of the ashes a worm would emerge, the embryo of the new phoenix, which would gather the ashes and take them towards the sun.

The appearance of the phoenix was said to be analogous with different stages of the world's progress, re-descending from Heaven at the beginning of each new era. It was last seen heralding the commencement of the reign of the Emperor Constantine in 334AD. Thomas Moore, in *Paradise and the Peri*, wrote:

The enchanted pyre of that lovely bird
Who sings at the last his own death-lay
And in music and perfume dies away.

The phoenix's behaviour meant the ancients believed it represented the powers of the universe, being able to command the heavens and ensure its own immortality. It was, therefore, a very popular motif in heraldry. Queen Elizabeth I adopted the *rara avis* in her medals and tokens, sometimes with the motto 'The Sole Phoenix Of The Whole World', and her portrait engraved on the reverse. Shakespeare wrote these words about the baptism of the Princess Elizabeth:

. . . as when the bird of wonder dies, the maiden phoenix
Her ashes new create another heir,
As great in admiration herself.

King Henry VIII

The word continues to be used to describe a fine woman or a paragon:

If she be furnished with a mind so rare
She is alone the Arabian bird.

Shakespeare: *Cymbeline*

The Christian church also adopted the phoenix as emblematic of Christ's death-to-life cycle, and magicians have long used it to symbolise their profession.

'Fun' or 'fung' were names given to the phoenix by the ancient Chinese. To them it was one of the four symbolical animals which presided over human destiny, and was sacred to the element of fire. It was often used as an embroidered or appliqued motif on cloaks for mandarins and emperors. The Chinese believed the phoenix's body was inscribed with the Five Virtues, and that it had:

> . . . the forepart of a goose, the hind-quarters of a stag, the neck of a snake, the tail of a fish, the forehead of a fowl, the down of a duck, the marks of a dragon, the back of a tortoise, the face of a swallow, the beak of a cock, is about six cubits high and perches only in the Woo Tung Tree.

Phooka The lore of Phooka or Pooka is clearly linked with the mischievous PUCK, who would assume the horns and hind-quarters of a goat when teasing mortals. However, this spirit has a more malignant disposition, and the Irish word 'phouka' was once used to describe the Devil. He takes various forms, sometimes appearing as an ass, a bull, a bat or a goat. He has also been known to take the form of an eagle, carrying men on his back and jettisoning them from high cliffs. Most often the phooka is a friendly pony who offers mortals a ride — to their detriment, for, with a wild chuckle, the horse takes a terrifying gallop across rough country and tosses the rider in a ditch or creek.

Piast Possibly the Irish version of the LOCH NESS MONSTER. A type of sea-serpent described as up to ten foot long, the piast has a large head, a humped back and a long neck adorned with a mane tangled with seaweed and kelp. It lived in the deep, dark Lough Ree, one of the three Lakes of Shannon. It was very shy, having only been seen ashore once. Piast was thought to propel itself through the water with large, paddle-like flippers, creating a strong wake. Time was, when fishermen would take a jug of whisky in their boats and pour a dollop in the piast's path, should its movements threaten to upset their craft . . . well, that was their story!

Pilosi A fairy found in ancient Gaul who was extremely hairy with the lower part of his body ending in goat's hooves. Stemming from the old pagan deities, pilosi brought good fortune to a home and were encouraged, like BROWNIES, to live by the fireside. So revered were they that the early Church was frightened of their popularity and tried to ban the heathen practice of nailing a horseshoe to the hearth, which signified the fairy was welcome, a practice still followed today to bring good luck.

Pixies The word 'pixy' is a diminutive of PUCK, or the Old English 'pouke'. Spenser, in *Epithalamion*, wrote:

> Ne let the pouke nor other evil sprites
> Fray us with things that be not.

Variously known as pigsies, puggies, piskies or pisgies, they are mainly found in Devonshire and Cornwall in south-western England. There they have given their names to many landmarks and their bells can be heard tolling beneath the moors.

Pixies are more homely in appearance than most fairies, and often the same size as humans. They usually have red hair and wear green coats and enormous pointed hats to shield their squinting, light-sensitive eyes and turned-up noses. Country lore has it that they may take the form of hedgehogs during the day. They revel in misleading travellers — in fact, in England and Ireland, to be misled or to become lost or confused is described as being 'pixy-led' or 'Puck-ledden'. Drayton wrote:

> This Puck seems but a dreaming dolt
> Still walking like a ragged colt
> And oft out of a Bush doth bolt
> Of purpose to deceive us
> And leading makes us to stray

Long winters' nights out of the way
And when we stick in mine and clay
He doth with laughter leave us.

A favourite prank played by pixies is to place a magical piece of turf in a mortal's way — as they step upon it even the most familiar surroundings become strange and confusing. Another mischievous game sees them standing in front of a fence-gate or stile, thus masking it from sight, while their puzzled victim circles the field fruitlessly looking for a way out.

The traditional method for countermanding pixy power is to turn your coat inside-out, or to hold up an iron cross (the latter referring to the belief that pixies are the souls of children who died before being baptised). In fact, some pixies have a greater sense of charity than do humans, and will leave posies of wildflowers on untended graves.

Mischievous pixies are known to steal horses at night and ride them in circles, or 'gallitraps', until exhausted. If a human steps into this gallitrap he will be imprisoned by the pixies forever. However, they can be industrious and emulate their friends, the BROWNIES, by threshing corn and the like, though they are likely to become bored quickly and stop work if given the opportunity. A pixy who was presented with a new set of clothes donned them gleefully, his work forgotten:

New coat, new waistcoat, new breeches!
You proud, I proud, I shan't work any more!

BRIGGS *The Fairies in Tradition and Literature*

Plague Maiden During the Middle Ages, bubonic plague ravaged the European countryside. Thousands of people died a miserable, lingering death and whole villages were exterminated overnight. In these credulous times, people looked for scapegoats and, in the village of Petherwin in Cornwall, one was found in the form of a local witch, Dorothy Dinglet. Witnesses testified that she had appeared as a flame, emerging from the mouths of the dead and flying from house to house, trailing a red scarf behind her. Hapless Dorothy was hanged by those who hoped this act would arrest the spread of the plague.

However, her GHOST did not rest easily, appearing to her accusers and crying:

> Before next Yuletide, a fearful pestilence will lay waste your land, and myriads of souls will be loosed from their flesh.
>
> BRIGGS *The Fairies in Tradition and Literature*

The Plague Maiden's prophecy came to pass, for the summer of 1665 was extraordinarily hot, exacerbating the spread of fever and plague as rats and fleas multiplied apace, and the village which persecuted her needlessly was, like hundreds of others, wiped out.

Poltergeist (from the German *polter*, meaning to knock noisily or tumble about). Poltergeists tend to disrupt households, throwing tantrums where crockery is tossed about kitchens, doors slammed, items stolen, window panes rattled, dust-balls blown around the ceiling — even shoes and clothes seeming to be worn and moved from room to room. A poltergeist is rarely malevolent, showing a predilection for mischief rather than revenge. It is not, therefore, believed to be a GHOST or spirit of a dead person as such; rather, a poltergeist will appear as a manifestation of some household tension, invariably in households where a child has reached puberty, and will make that girl or boy the focus of their activities. The German 'Quicksilver', for instance, pesters families with adolescent daughters. Her favourite game is heating pebbles and throwing them at people passing by the house. She has also been reported as sketching her initial 'Q' in lipstick or crayon on bathroom mirrors, leaving taps running and tearing clothing. Harry Price, in his *Poltergeists Over England* (1945), speculates that poltergeists are:

> able . . . to extract energy from living persons, usually from adolescents, especially if they suffer from some mental disorder . . . or by using these young people as a fulcrum, lever or support to increase and nourish this energy.

Portunes A happy little tribe of English fairies who were roughly half an inch tall, originally hailing from France. They looked like wizened old men, but they were invaluable on a farm, being quick and efficient workers. At night, great numbers of them would gather round the farmhouse fire and roast newly hatched frogs for supper. However arduous the labour set for them by the farmer, they would undertake it good-naturedly, although they did have one naughty habit. Like PIXIES, they delighted in leading travellers' horses astray, preferably into a muddy ditch or pond where the animals would become bogged. The portune would then be heard to giggle, before disappearing.

Poseidon Son of CRONUS, Poseidon was the Greek god of the sea, known to the Romans as NEPTUNE. Originally a god of earthquakes he mellowed to contentedly rule over the waves, usually favouring respectful travellers with a safe voyage. He rode the seas in a chariot pulled by splendid sea-horses, attended by beautiful MERMAIDS, mighty TRITONS and dolphins. Once armed with lightning flashes, Poseidon came to be more often depicted with a trident, the symbol of fishing, and he would blow a conch shell to call up the trade winds. Poseidon shared his coral palace beneath the sea with Amphitrite, and fathered many creatures. In particular he begat the winged horse PEGASUS and other part-equine beasts, a possible reference to the 'maned' waves which break on the shore like so many white horses.

Poseidon had a turbulent nature and used his trident to stir the waters, creating storms and whirlpools. So angry was he at the defeat of his subjects, the Atlanteans, by the Athenians that he is said to have buried that legendary city beneath the waves.

Prometheus Also known rather pragmatically as He Who Thinks Things Out In Advance, Prometheus was a Titan who stole fire from heaven in order to give it to men. For this crime ZEUS chained him to a rock in the Caucasus where a vulture tore at his liver, as described by Shakespeare in *Titus Andronicus*:

> Faster bound to Aaron's charming eyes
> Than is Prometheus tied to Caucasus.

In later literature this god's suffering in order to be a friend to mankind was alluded by poets, who used Prometheus as the personification of generosity which refused to be bowed by tyrrany.

Prometheus was thought to have created the first man from clay and to have warned mortals against accepting the gift of the woman, Pandora. For his talents he was made the tutelary patron of craftsmen and potters.

Ptath Also known as Ptah, the chief of the ancient Egyptian gods. With the epithet 'Lord of World Order', Ptath was thought to have created the earth by kneading mud made with the help of water from NUN. He was usually depicted as having a ram's head and holding an ankh, the symbol of life and generative forces in the universe.

Some sources claim Ptath was a craft-god, using his heart and tongue in conjunction with a smithy and potter's wheel; hence, he was sometimes called 'sculptor of the universe'. The Greeks identified him with HEPHAESTUS for this reason. Ptath was married to SEKHMET, the lion-goddess, and then to BAST, the cat-goddess, and was thought to have worked with OSIRIS in formalising the ritual procedures for mummification.

Puck In early times, the general term used to describe a devil. Later, thanks to Shakespeare, this HOBGOBLIN became a well known individual in his own right — a fairy and merry wanderer of the night, 'rough, knurly-limbed, faun-faced and shock-pated, a very Shetlander amongst the gossamer-winged fairies about him'. Also known as Robin Goodfellow, Puck is King Oberon's jester and spends much time playing pranks on mortals, though he does feel some compassion for lovers. Slightly larger than a human being, Puck is able to change into any person or animal he wishes. Closely related to the Welsh BWCA and the Irish PHOOKA, Puck usually appears naked, or sports a goat's haunches and horns. He may be glimpsed one moment, sitting on a tree stump and playing a haunting air on his pipe, only to embark upon mischief the next. Witness his self-description in Shakespeare's *A Midsummer Night's Dream*:

> . . . sometime I lurk in a gossip's bowl
> In very likeness of a roasted crab;
> And when she drinks, against her lips I bob,
> And on her withered dew-lap pour the ale.
> The wisest aunt, telling the saddest tale,
> Sometimes for three-foot stool mistaketh me;
> Then slip I from her bum, down topples she,
> And cries, and falls in to a cough;
> And then the whole quire hold their hips and loffe;
> And waxen in their mirth and neeze and sear,
> A merrier hour was never wasted there.

Python The name given to the monstrous serpent who was the pet of HERA, sent by her to frighten Leto, who had become pregnant with APOLLO and ARTEMIS by Hera's husband ZEUS. Both children survived, however, and Apollo later slew the snake in her cavern within Mount Parnassus, founding the Pythian games in honour of his victory.

Pythons, along with other serpents such as adders and vipers, recur in myth and allegory through time, largely as a symbol of evil or treachery to be overcome by man. This is particularly the case in Christianity, where snakes were emblematic of Satan and first appeared as the tempter of Eve. However, they were also believed to have great healing power, an age-old reference to Apollo's son AESCULAPIUS, god of medicine, being represented with a serpent twined around his staff.

Pythons were also believed to have oracular gifts. During Classical times, these snakes were worshipped by priestesses known as Pythonesses, in temples at Claros. During ceremonies of worship, the priestesses would wait until the spirit of the Python came upon them, then their moans, cries and babble would be interpreted and used to set out policies of war and government.

Q

Questing Beast An extraordinary amalgam of parts, this animal was prominent in the England of King Arthur (fifth/sixth century AD), being pursued by King Pellinore and Sir Palomides. It was described as having a snake's head, the body of a lybbarde (or leopard) and the hindquarters and tail of a lion. Fleet as a deer, it was said to 'roar as loudly as forty hounds'. It was a good omen to see one before a hunting expedition, as it would rapidly run the prey to ground. In fact, its name was a derivation of the Old English words for the 'hunt' and the sound of dogs' barking — 'the quest'.

Quetzlcoatl The plumed serpent god of Central America who presided over the sun, air and wind. He most frequently appeared arched in the sky, a marvellous sight with his multi-hued scales and bright feathers reaching from his head to his tail. Quetzlcoatl also occasionally appeared in the guise of an old man with a white beard and broken walking staff, or as a handsome young man richly arrayed in a cloak of feathers from the quetzl bird. He was thought to have once been a mortal king, reported Bernadino de Sahagun in his sixteenth-century *History of Things of New Spain*:

> In the city of Tollan reigned many years a king called Quetzlcoatl. . . . He was exceptional in moral virtues. . . . The Place of these kings amongst these natives is like King Arthur amongst the English.

This mighty ruler brought many gifts to his people, starting the cultivation of maize, teaching them how to make ceremonial feather mantles and how to study the stellar systems and the zodiac. He also revealed the great treasure troves of gold and precious stones which lay beneath the earth's surface, and taught craftsmen how to cut and polish the gems they found, and then to forge fine jewellery.

Quetzlcoatl was defeated by TEZCATLIPOCA and immolated himself upon a funeral pyre. Rare birds are said to have risen from his ashes and his heart is thought to still watch from the firmament, where it twinkles as the morning star.

R

Ra Variously known as Re or Ria, the great sun-god, one of the supreme Egyptian deities. He was the guardian of the god kings, who styled themselves as Sons of Ra. Ra was usually depicted as a bearded man crowned with a red disk to symbolise the sun. His emblems included the falcon and the scarab, or dung beetle, and he travelled the sky in a huge golden barge. The sun was thought to be the eye of Ra. The husband of Maut, Ra begat the sky and sunlight, along with Maat the goddess of truth. He lost some of this power to ISIS who poisoned him with a snake made of dust and his own saliva; she then demanded he bestow his gift of light upon her son, HORUS, in exchange for an antidote.

Rakim In the Micronesian Islands the first god was named Rakim. He was thought to have arrived upon a cloud and come to earth in the form of a flying snake. Through his aid, people learned the arts of carpentry and, particularly, how to carve fine canoes. The prow of each such canoe is still marked with a serpent's eyes, so it can find its way through the water, and a well-constructed canoe is said to fly of its own accord when its crew is threatened.

Rakshasahs Evil spirits of Hindu India. They are dedicated to war against mankind, haunting cemeteries and devouring the bodies of the newly dead. Rakshasahs serve Kurea, the god of riches, and guard a huge cache of gold and pearls which swarms with poisonous vipers. Many stories are told of foolish mortals who have attempted to rob the Rakshasahs, and whose bones now crumble amongst that glittering treasure.

The spirits may assume any shape at will, with the males often appearing to have the body of a man and the head of a bull. Rakshasahs are hideous to behold, with bloated bellies, tangled hair and backward-pointing hands. They possess enormous strength, which increases during the night and reaches its peak at midnight. Other talents include the ability to grow heads and arms again as promptly as they are cut off, to cause leprosy and to call the dead to arise from their graves and form a grisly army. The female rakshasahs can be quite beautiful, however, and have been known to seduce holy men with their wiles, only to attack and eat them.

Raven In Arabia the raven was called Abu Zajir (Father of Omens), while ancient Teutonic legend has it that the raven was not a mortal bird; rather, it was an extension of the god Odin's memory and toured the world to report on happenings. Men have continued to regard the raven as an all-seeing, supernatural bird, with remarkable gifts of prophecy. Similarly, the Irish use the phrase 'raven's knowledge' to describe any person's ability to foresee the future. More gloomily, the raven is invariably a portent of death or destruction. Gay, in his *Pastorals*, wrote of:

> The boding raven on her cottage sat
> And with hoarse croaking warned us of our fate.

And Christopher Marlowe, in *The Jew of Malta* (1633), concurred with:

> Like the sad-presaging raven that tolls
> The sick man's passport in her hollow beak
> And, in the shadow of the silent night
> Doth shake contagion from her sable wing.

Reculver Babies One of the saddest GHOST stories comes from Reculver, in the south of England, and concerns a Roman fort built on an ancient sacred site of the Druids. On stormy nights the heart-rending sobbing of babies can be heard on the wind, and this is inevitably an omen of death for any child within earshot. When archaeologists excavated the fort they found several babies' skeletons, presumably the remains of some primitive sacrifice.

Redcap A particularly horrid GOBLIN who lives in ruined fortresses and towers along the Scottish border, where many battles have been fought. The bloodier and more murderous the battle, the better, for he likes to re-dye his cap in human blood. W. Henderson, in his *Folklore of the Northern Counties*, describes Redcap as follows:

> . . . with long, prominent teeth, skinny fingers armed with talons, like eagles', large eyes of a fiery-red colour, grisly hair streaming down over his shoulders, iron boots, a pikestaff in his hand and an old red cap on his head.

Nor is it safe to loiter around such places alone, for Redcap will be delighted to kill, so as to top up his supplies of blood. He will, however, vanish with a howl of dismay when scripture is recited or a crucifix is shown.

Redcaps were less dangerous elsewhere. In Holland, for instance, they are mild-mannered BROWNIES who either keep trysts with GHOSTS of ancient families in the ruins of castles, or come to work in farm kitchens.

Remora An enormous fish, reported to be companion to the Biblical sea-monster, the LEVIATHAN. It was believed to be reasonably gentle in its attitude towards men, and would actually help a distressed sailing vessel by surfacing beneath it and ferrying it to shore. The Remora was, however, quick to anger, and would swallow the whole ship and everyone upon it if one of the crew had the temerity to shoot or harpoon it. During Columbus' time, the Remora was reported as creating a vacuum of air around a ship, protecting it from storms which raged nearby.

Revenant The name given to any person who reappears from the dead after a long absence. Unlike GHOSTS, which usually appear quite soon after death and often have a specific mission or task to accomplish, a revenant may not come forth for several centuries and is unlikely to cause any trouble when it does. Revenants are most usually described as dressed in period costume and retracing the steps they took just before they died.

Rhea At once the sister and wife of CRONUS, Rhea appeared on earth as a mortal vestal virgin who was raped by the arrogant MARS. She was later given the epithet 'The Mighty Mother', and equated with CYBELE, the Mother of the Gods in Asia Minor. Cultists worshipped her with frenzied rituals which were based on her earthly experiences.

Roane The old Gaelic word for 'seal', also used to describe a gentle race of mer-people who live off the shores of the Scottish Highlands as well as in the Orkneys and Shetlands in underwater places of pearl-shell. They have to don a seal or fish skin to swim through the water, but will cast them off when they come ashore to dance in the light of a full moon.

There are many tales of how fishermen will steal one of these skins, thus forcing the roane to become his wife. With their knowledge of medicine and midwifery, their fertility and gentle nature, roanes make excellent wives although their yearning for the sea means they will return to it as soon as they regain their skins.

Roaring Bull of Bagbury A very wicked man lived at Bagbury Farm in England and when he died, instead of reappearing as a GHOST of himself, his neighbours reported a rambunctious-natured giant bull. This bull hurled itself through fences, roaring so loudly that barns collapsed and other animals died of fright. One of its more unpleasant habits was to lurk under the town bridge, roaring loudly when a pregnant woman walked overhead in the malicious hope she would miscarry. At last the villagers, fed up with the beast's noise and destructive nature, called for twelve parsons to subdue it. This they did, conjuring him down until he fitted into a tin snuff-box, which the people of Bagbury tossed into the sea.

Roc An enormous white bird, also known as the 'rukh' and 'ruc'. It was sighted above both Greece and China, but usually made its home on the Island of Madagascar. So strong, it was said to truss elephants in its talons before flying to great heights in order to drop the beast and feed on its flesh at leisure. Sometimes thought to be a gigantic eagle, the Italian voyager Marco Polo described it as having:

> a wingspan of thirty paces [90 ft.] and
> each feather's quill twelve paces long . . .

The roc is best known from *Tales of the Arabian Nights*, wherein Sinbad used the bird as transport from Madagascar to Baghdad, by tying himself to its claws using cloth from his turban. His men were foolish in their treatment of this bird, however; they broke a roc's egg 'equal to 148 hens' eggs' in size, and ate it, only to be bombarded with rocks flung at them by the angry parent birds.

Romulus and Remus The outcome of MARS's rape of RHEA was the birth of twin brothers, Romulus and Remus. The pair were set adrift in a basket, being found and raised by a she-wolf. When they grew to manhood they founded the city of Rome. Strife was engendered between the two brothers and Remus was slain, Rome being named in Romulus' honour. Romulus demonstrated a preference for low life, inviting criminals and murderers to live in his city; one of his more notorious acts was to organise the wholesale capture of the Sabine women in order to furnish his citizens with wives. However, he was successful in building a fine city and establishing a mighty army, so the gods rewarded him by naming him as the god Quirinius.

Rumpelstiltskin This popular tale of a passionate DWARF who is bested by a mortal appears in the folklore of many lands: in Scotland he is Whuppity Stoorie; in Austria, Kruzimugeli; in France, Robiquet; in Russia, Kinkach Martinko; and in Iceland, Gilitrutt. Best known of all is the version of the Brothers Grimm, wherein a miller's daughter tries to impress the king through her claims to be able to spin straw into gold. The dwarf does this for her, on the condition that she gives him her first-born son. The monarch marries her, and a year later she gives birth to the child. When Rumpelstiltskin returns to claim the child, she grieves so bitterly that he promises to relent if she can but guess his name within three days. With only one day left, one of the queen's pages passing through the forest comes upon the dwarf dancing around his fire, singing:

> Little dreams my dainty Dame
> That Rumpelstiltskin is my name!

The queen thus saves her child and the dwarf kills himself in a rage, splitting in half as he stamps upon the floor.

Rusalki In Europe, these are spirits of girls who have drowned in waterways, and their personalities differ from country to country. In Russia, rusalki appear as wrinkled old harridans floating on the surface of the river, with bloated faces and bodies like corpses. These horrid creatures reach up to the banks and snatch livestock or an idling child, take them down to the riverbed's bottom and then torture them. Rusalki who haunt the German Danube, however, are usually seen swimming gracefully with the current, or lolling amidst branches overhanging the water; they are invariably lovely and sing most sweetly as they comb their hair with long white fingers. Remember, though, their motives are as vicious as their Russian cousins', and they delight in trapping passers-by and drowning them.

If rusalki are foiled in their murderous plotting by a potential victim having the prudence to wear an amulet containing wormwood, they will tumble irritably in the water, damage mills and dams, tear at nearby trees and toss fish on the banks to die. Once a year, on Midsummer's Eve, they will leave the water and walk the shore in search of prey. Their only constructive contribution to the mortal world is that, wherever their feet fall, bright blue flowers will spring up.

S

Sakarabru The African natives of Guinea and Senegambia build miniature huts at the entrances of their villages, for this is where the God of Darkness, Sakarabru, lives. Quite terrible to behold, Sakarabru has large bloodshot eyes, long legs and feet that point both ways. He is usually naked, his skin being thickly covered in tattoos, and he has a fearsome mouth of large, pointed teeth. The natives say that 'Sakarabru's smile brings life, though his frown means death', by which they mean he is a fair god. He will wander the villages at night, but will only crush a man in his horrid jaws as just retribution for a misdeed.

Salamander A sort of lizard which, unlike its modern counterpart, was thought to be able to live in fire. In fact, the extreme frigidity of its body was thought to extinguish all but the very hottest fire. Swift wrote:

> Further, we are by Pliny told
> This serpent is extremely cold;
> So cold that, put it in the fire,
> 'Twill make the very flames expire.

Thought venemous, salamanders had the body of a cat, webbed wings and a serpent's tail. They were used by medieval alchemists in their spells to turn lead into gold, the creatures being used to control the temperatures of the flames. Salamanders were said to delight in flames and could be found on mountain-sides as part of a volcanic eruption of lava, or just spontaneously appear in a very hot fire. Their skin was believed to be made of asbestos. The salamander was much used in heraldry as a symbol of endurance and courage; the word was also used to describe anything red or fiery, so Shakespeare's

Falstaff humorously described Bardolph's ruddy nose as 'a burning lamp' (from *Henry IV*).

Saturn The Roman god of agriculture and vineyards. Saturn was originally an Italian king of great antiquity who came to be identified with the Greek CRONUS. His wife was Ops and they were the parents of JUPITER, who eventually ousted his father from power. The planet Saturn is named after him, as also is Saturday. A great festival was held in Saturn's honour in mid-December, called Saturnalia. This was marked by much revelry and distinguished by masters serving their slaves. During this festival, businesses and schools were closed, no war could be waged, nor any criminal brought to trial. People gave each other lighted candles, and children slapped each other with evergreen boughs to signify the continuance of life through winter — many Christmas customs are the dim relics of Saturnalia.

Satyrs Lusty creatures from the court of DIONYSIUS, the god of wine. They had human bodies and faces, with the legs and horns of a goat, and they haunted island glades often kidnapping mortal women to attend their orgiastic feasts. Most popularly depicted playing on reed pipes and cutting a caper through vineyards, satyrs are sometimes quite rowdy. The best-known is their leader, PAN, who is the curly headed god of pasture, and his troupe will dance and play as they help herd sheep. However, if they become overly drunk, satyrs will frighten travellers with their maniacal laughter, chase NYMPHS and scatter animals. An indication of their precocity may be seen in a collection of satyrs' names: Simon (Snubnose), Posthon (Prick), Hybris (Insolence), Komos (Revelry).

Screaming Skulls Skulls were regarded as 'seats of the soul' and the source of all psychic power, so they were often kept indoors or bricked up in walls as a protective charm. This could be related to foundation sacrifice, or to the ancient custom of head-hunting. However, some ghosts clung tenaciously to their mortal remains, refusing to leave the body and/or house where they had been happy during their lives. The best-known manifestation of this is 'screaming skulls'. These appallingly active and noisy skulls shriek and pursue the surviving family member who dares to remove them from their chosen spot in a house. A tale is told of the screaming skull of Bettiscombe Manor, which once belonged to a negro slave who had asked his master to return his bones to his native land for burial. The man disregarded the slave's wish and buried the skull on the property. Hideous screams tormented the family and many misfortunes befell them, until the skull was unearthed and placed on a Bible in the library.

Sebek In ancient Egypt the River Nile was guarded by this crocodile-headed god. His attendants could be seen as the crocodiles who basked lazily by the water's edge, monitoring the comings and goings of man. Sebek had rubies for eyes and, along with the help of other gods, defeated Set, the God of Chaos. From then on, he was able to control the tides which had hitherto ravaged the countryside causing drought and flood alternately.

Sedna The Eskimo goddess of the sea and sea-creatures. Also known as 'The Mother of the Sea', her epithet is 'The Eating Place', a reference to the ocean providing the key source of food for these tribes. Folklore has it that Sedna was once a disobedient little girl, and her exasperated father flung her out of his canoe as punishment. She clung to the sides of the boat but her father was ruthless and chopped off her grasping fingers and thumbs. As each digit fell into the icy water, it turned into shoals of whales, seals or fish, thus populating the sea. The fingerless Sedna sank to the bottom of the ocean, where she became Queen of the Underworld. In view of her father's actions, other fishermen are ill-advised to travel too far into her domain, for she still nurses her wounds with some bitterness.

Sekhmet The fire goddess of Egypt, mother of Imhotep and wife of PTATH. So fierce-natured was she that she was given charge of warfare and battles. Sekhmet was usually depicted with a lioness' head bearing a solar disc, and clenched human fists. Her bloodthirsty cry was translated as 'When I slay men, my heart rejoices'.

Selkies English sea-fairies closely related to the ROANE found further north. Like them, female selkies — or seal people — have beautiful liquid brown eyes and a mild nature. They wear sleek hides to enable them to travel easily through the water, though they have to emerge regularly to breathe. Selkies were thought to be a remnant of a race of humans driven into the sea for some crime. This explains why they periodically shed their skins and come ashore, in the guise of lovely maidens. Should the skin be stolen, however, the selkie is forced to remain. If she weds a mortal, children of the union will have small horns between their fingers and be gifted with medical knowledge. Unlike the roane, selkies have a quite violent nature and will raise storms and upturn fishing boats, in a bid for revenge if a school of seals has been slaughtered for their skins in that vicinity.

Sesha *see* ANANTA

Seven Whistlers In the north of England people referred to a group of seven wild geese passing overhead as a portent of death. Before anyone understood the night-flying habits of migratory birds it was thought that their eerie whistling call to one another was a summons to spirits of the newly dead. Wordsworth likened these geese to the GABRIEL HOUNDS:

> He the seven birds hath seen that never part,
> Seen the Seven Whistlers on their nightly rounds,
> And counted them! And often times will start,
> For overhead are sweeping Gabriel's Hounds,
> Doomed with their impious lord the flying hart
> To chase forever on aerial grounds.

Shadhavar A miraculous creature featured in Persian mythology.

Rather like an antelope in appearance it was an aggressive predator. The shadhavar had strange, hollow antlers, each nub of bone being an orifice, so when the beast held its head into a breeze, musical notes would issue. This music was so sweet and plaintive that other animals would stop to listen and be lulled to sleep — only to be attacked and eaten by the shadhavar.

Shaman The 'medicine man' of the North American Indian tribes. Educated in sorcery as well as the use of charms, stones, trees and herbal plants, the shaman could communicate with spirits and petition them on the tribe's behalf. For example, a shaman could be charged with ensuring a good harvest, respite from a disease, or to bring about success in battle. Typically, a shaman would seek his knowledge in the shapes that formed in smoke from sacred fires, or during a solitary pilgrimage amongst the nature-spirits of mountain lakes. However, a shaman was generally thought to be born endowed with supernatural powers which could not be learned by any ordinary mortal. A potential shaman could be identified at birth by certain marks or moles on his body; for instance, a baby born with a full set of teeth was thought especially gifted.

Many shaman were wise and kind, such as the great Hiawatha who envisaged unity amongst all the warring tribes. He ended his days on earth by paddling across the sky to Heaven in a magic canoe. Not all shaman used their powers for good purposes, however; there was an evil guild, known as the Midewiwin, much feared for their curses and ability to invoke the restless dead.

Shamir Sometimes described as an insect or as a wormlike creature, the Shamir appears in Hebrew legend and was reputedly able to chew through stone. It was made by God on the sixth day of Creation, and was employed by Solomon to cut blocks of stone for his temple. The Shamir was thought invulnerable and, rather like a SALAMANDER, to thrive on fire. Apparently God sent the Great Flood to drown the Shamir, who was becoming too powerful.

Shellycoat A mischievous Scottish BOGIE who haunts fresh-water streams. Festooned with garlands of weed and shells which clatter when he moves, the shellycoat enjoys playing pranks on travellers. A favourite trick involves creating a din on the river bank by crying for help and shaking all his shells, like castanets. A bewildered mortal will often stumble down to see if he can be of help, only to be shoved into the muddy shallows by a laughing shellycoat for his pains.

Shen In China, ancestral spirits are much venerated and welcomed into the house. They are known as 'shen' and may be contacted via divination with a split bamboo cane, rather like a divining rod. The medium holds this rod over a tray of white sand, and as characters are traced they are interpreted. Shen quite frequently appear to their family descendants, especially to warn the heir of any potential trouble or enemy.

Shin Unlike the beneficent SHEN, the shin are evil Chinese GHOSTS. There are in excess of sixty different types and each appears on an allotted day within a sixty-day cycle. The Chinese leave gifts of egg buns and red-paper prayers outside their doors at night, addressed to the 'honourable homeless ghost', in an attempt to make them leave the house in peace. If the shin are not appeased, they will appear to the household and terrify the family, servants and animals. They most often take the form of a shapeless grey mist with a horrific grinning face and, strangely, no chin.

Shiva (Siva) The Indian god of asceticism, as well as a leader of demons, he was known by several contradictory epithets; variously The Destroyer, The Howler and The Roarer, and The Terrible One or The Gracious One. Shiva is usually portrayed as fair-skinned or smeared with white ashes, and has four arms, four faces and three eyes. This third eye, in the centre of his forehead, is sometimes represented by three horizontal lines, a mark favoured by his devotees.

Together with BRAHMA and VISHNU, Shiva forms the Vedic

Triad of the Brahmin religion. He once spent most of his time in solitary meditations high in the Himalayas, having deserted his exquisite dancer-wife, Parvati, in their marriage bed. A flower-shaft arrow from KAMA, the messenger of love, shook Shiva from his lethargy and he came before Parvati to woo her with his dancing. From then on, Shiva was most often portrayed in this mode, with one leg raised and the other standing on a tiny demon who represents ignorance. Shiva represents all aspects of power, creative as well as destructive. He is therefore attended by two key symbols; the drum (speech and revelation) and fire (resolution).

Shojo Japanese sea-GHOSTS, usually the spirits of drowned sailors. Rarely evil-intentioned or ill-omened, shojo appear to make the most of their watery lot and will sing and dance most boisterously. They are characterised by bright red hair and green faces. Popular folklore has it that they love to drink sake and may be enticed to shore if they see mortal sailors enjoying some.

Sidhe Pronounced 'shee', the general name for nobility amongst Scottish and Irish fairies said to have descended from the Irish aristocrats, the TUATHA DE DANAAN. Sidhe are extremely tall and beautiful, so much so that mortals are forbidden to gaze at them. Their touch can be pernicious, sending a man mad, and their poison-tipped arrows cause instant death, as will the sight of their queen, Maeve. So beautiful is she with her white silk mantle, blue eyes and long, soft hair that men die from wonder at the sight.

The Sidhe live quite Spartan lives, caring for their animals, drinking whiskey and baking bread each day. They are very talented, coaxing marvellous airs from bagpipes, fiddle and flute. Though they appreciate generosity, and are grateful for gifts of whiskey and potatoes, it is best to leave such tributes a fair distance from their dwelling places, for sidhe have been known to kidnap mortals and keep them as slaves. Even if they are released, such folk are never the same again, becoming either madmen or prophets with great gifts of healing.

Silky A female version of a BROWNIE. Helpful and willing to undertake many household chores, they are dainty little sprites who dress in rustling grey or white silk dresses, and will chide lazy servants. They were usually found to be GHOSTS of women who had lived nearby, and often their appearance heralded a message or signal from the other world, most usually of a happy nature; for example, the whereabouts of treasure or documents. Once this was communicated, the silky would cease her hauntings. When their work was done they would sometimes sit in trees, their skirts rustling in the breeze, and for amusement would startle horses or whisper to passers-by.

Simurgh A wonderful bird of Persian mythology, also known as the Seemurgh. Its jewelled feathers were especially prized trophies, for the touch of just one could heal many ailments. The simurgh could speak and understand all languages, and it held complete knowledge of the past, present and future. Thus it became the familiar consort of royalty, both as a protector and an oracle. An old tale tells of a prince being born who was abandoned because he was an albino and considered cursed. However, the babe was found and cared for by a simurgh in its mountain nest. As an adult, the lad returned to his people, adorned only with a gleaming cape made of the simurgh's feathers, which protected him until he had safely reached the palace. He was able to claim his birthright, and the wisdom and bravery taught him by the great bird made him a splendid ruler.

Siren A dangerous creature who took the form of a beautiful woman with the legs and talons of a bird. In Greek the name means 'the entangler', referring to their sweet voice, so seductive no man could resist them. A medieval bestiary describes a siren thus:

> Lives in the sea, it sings at the approach of a storm and weeps in fine weather, such is its nature. It has the make of a woman down

> to the waist and the feet of a falcon and the tail of a fish. . . . Then it sings loud and clear and if the steersman who navigates the sea hears it, he forgets his ship and immediately falls asleep.

Scholars claim there were three main sirens — Leucosia, Ligeia and Parthenope, who played the lyre, flute and sang, respectively. They were typically depicted posing on rocks and singing to an approaching ship. The sailors would lose their minds, jump overboard and swim towards the sirens, who would, ghoulishly, eat them. Spenser in *The Faerie Queene* wrote of 'false melodies' played during Sir Guyon's 'perilous passage' through sirens' haunts, as follows:

> But the upper half of their hue retained still
> And their sweet skill in wonted melody;
> Which ever after they abused to ill
> To allure weak travellers, whom gotten they did kill.

Due to their association with death, sirens were often carved on memorial stones erected to dead seamen. The sirens were not, however, universally successful. Odysseus stoppered his men's ears with wax as they passed the sirens' haunt, and Jason distracted his Argonauts by asking Orpheus to play a beautiful air upon his flute. Furious at their failure, the sirens flung themselves into the water, becoming the black rocks off the Isle of Capri, known as the Sirenusae.

Skrimsl A mild-mannered sea-serpent, sightings of Skrimsl and his descendants have been recorded off the Scandinavian coastline since the early fourteenth century. This beast is described as having the head of a seal, a long neck and a humped back, and large paddles or fins. Seeing Skrimsl from a fishing vessel is a happy omen, for it only surfaces when the weather is mild and warm.

Sluagh *see* HOST

Sphinx A mythological creature of ancient Egypt and Greece, the sphinx has the breasts of a woman, the body of a lion and the wings of an eagle. Sometimes she was depicted with the head of a ram or falcon, though more often her face was that of a handsome woman wearing an asp in the centre of her forehead. Sphinxes were renowned for their wisdom and for their perverse habit of asking a victim a riddle before killing him via their preferred method of suffocation in their great wings (the Egyptian name for sphinx means 'the choker'). This love of riddles and perplexity has led the word 'sphinx' to be used to describe anyone or thing that is enigmatic. Spenser in *The Faerie Queene* wrote of:

> That monster whom the Theban knight
> Made kill herself for very heart's despite
> That he had read her riddle, which no wight
> Could ever loose, but suffered deadly doole.

Here, he was referring to the best known Grecian sphinx, the one who was sent to the people of Thebes by HERA to punish them for their drunkenness. This sphinx asked Oedipus:

> What goes on four feet, on two feet, and three
> But the more feet it goes on the weaker it be?

Oedipus correctly answered 'man' and was able to save the Theban people for the sphinx killed herself in a furious agony of embarrassment.

Spook A word used almost exclusively in America, and in recent times by popular cartoonists. The word itself is Afrikaner in origin, from the Spokeveld or 'spook country' area of South Africa. It was also used by American white settlers when studying Red Indian spiritual traditions. Today it is most often used to describe a GHOST or a spirit taking control of a living person's mind and body. This is often to their advantage, and many stories are told of men who apparently overnight assume the intelligence, willpower or business acumen of a recently deceased relative, and who go on to enjoy great success.

Spriggans Known as 'korred' in Spain, spriggans are native to Cornwall in south-western England. They are extremely ugly little creatures with red eyes, who act as slaves to noble fairies and guardians of hidden treasure. Although very small, they can alter their size at will and are thought to be the GHOSTS of once-powerful giants who carried massive stone dolmens on their backs. Spriggans are prophets and magicians, but their bitter nature has meant they are better known for their skills in kidnapping children, destroying buildings and causing foul weather. They will rarely harm a human being, gaining perverse enjoyment, rather, from simply being irritating. The story told by Robert Hunt in *Popular Romances of the West of England* describes the spriggans' revenge upon an old miner who had sought to pilfer their cache of gold. The greedy fellow was flung to the ground and pinched unmercifully, awakening to find himself clammy with dew and pinioned to the grass with thousands of cobwebs.

Spunkies In Somerset, south-western England, spunkies are believed to be the souls of unbaptised children, doomed to wander the countryside until Judgement Day. As with WILL O'THE WISP their presence is signalled by curious lights, thought to be the glow from candle-flames they carry to find their way at night. They may be malicious, often being blamed for upset boats or travellers being led astray from the road, and their presence is most feared on Midsummer's Eve for, as Ruth Tongue writes, 'this is the night on which spunkies go to church to meet the newly dead' (from *Forgotten Folk Tales of the English Counties*).

Squire of Swinsty In Hampshire, southern England, a tale of human iniquity many centuries old is still current. During the ghastly Great Plague in the seventeenth century when, according to chroniclers, a third of the country perished, man's inhumanity to man was often well demonstrated. One such example is the ghostly Squire of Swinsty, who may be seen at night kneeling by a stream, frantically laundering a huge pile of gold coins which are all tarnished and bloodstained. It is said that when the plague was at its height, the horrid man went to

London, broke into the boarded-up houses with the red crosses (sign of plague within) daubed on their doors, and robbed the sick and dying. He was unscathed by the disease and returned to Hampshire, where he built Swinsty Hall with his ill-gotten gains and lived out his mortal life in comfort, although he was condemned to this everlasting penance by the stream.

Stymphalian Birds Three nasty predators who feasted on the flesh of marooned sailors and were to be found in swampland near Lake Stymphalis in ancient Greece. They were huge and black, and so wide was their wingspan that when they flew in united formation their shadow blocked out the sun. The Stymphalian birds were able to shoot their iron-tipped feathers from their wings like a hail of arrows, making them a formidable enemy. HERCULES was able to defeat the three birds by deafening them so they flew about dazed, becoming themselves easy targets.

Sylphs According to medieval belief, the delicate, slender ELEMENTAL spirits of the air. They were so named by the Cabalists, from the Greek word *silphe* (a butterfly or moth), which aptly described these fluttering creatures. According to Paracelsus, sylphs, along with earth-dwelling GNOMES, marine NYMPHS and fire-born SALAMANDERS, represented one of the four earthly elements. The word 'sylvan' is derived from 'sylph', for they were thought to frequent dim forest dells.

Alexander Pope believed that any coquette became a sylph when she died, with the task of entertaining the spirits of young men who had been chaste during their mortal life. In *The Rape of the Lock* (1712) he writes:

> Whoever, fair and chaste,
> Rejects mankind,
> Is by some sylph embraced.

T

Tane The god of light and of the forest in both Maori and Polynesian mythology. He is one of the four sons of the sky father, Rangi, and the earth mother, Papa. These two so loved each other that they remained locked in an embrace and their children were trapped beneath their thighs, unable to be free. Tane put his shoulder against his mother and his feet to his father and pushed them apart, and the universe tumbled into its present arrangement between the two. Ever since, the sky god periodically bedews the world with his tears of sorrow at being separated from his wife.

Tane's brothers were Tawhiri, god of storms and winds; Tangaroa, god of fishes and reptiles; and the violent Tu-of-the-angry-face, who was the god of war. Tangaroa fought with Tane for enticing lizards into his forests, and Tane retaliated by showing Tu-of-the-angry-face how to make hooks and nets and thus capture Tangaroa's fish. Tangaroa's resultant curse introduced death to the world.

Tane was also patron of craftsmen, especially boat builders, and his aid was often petitioned by islanders as protection against Tangaroa, who sometimes took the form of a 'tailed god', or giant squid, and preyed upon fishermen. As the god of light, Tane was represented by the sun, and man's path through life is thought to move westward, along 'Tane's way'.

Tarans In Scotland, the name given to the pathetic little spirits of babies who have died before baptism. According to J.M. McPherson's *Primitive Beliefs from the North-East of Scotland*:

> The little spectres . . . were often seen flitting among the woods and secret places, bewailing in soft voices their hard fate.

These waifs were doomed to wander until Judgement Day. They could only be saved if a mortal could be persuaded to douse them with holy water and give them a name, saying 'I baptise thee in the name of the Father, Son and Holy Ghost' as they did so. This happened only rarely, for it was widely believed that conversing with any GHOST brought misfortune and death. An exception was the taran of Whittinghame in Scotland, known colloquially as 'Short Hoggers', an affectionate name bestowed upon it one night by a passing drunkard. Now that it has a name the taran does not bother the village, having gone to its rest.

Tash The Irish term for GHOST, used generically to describe all spectral beings and occurrences; also known as 'thevshi'. Many ghost stories, sightings and spiritual experiences hail from Ireland, probably due to the great antiquity of the land and its strongly emotional history. For instance, a goodly percentage of tash sightings are headless warriors and women mourning for those who have died a violent death. The keening BANSHEE is the best known type of tash.

Tawaret A gentle denizen of Egypt's divine menagerie, Tawaret (or Tauret) was the goddess who presided over affairs of women, especially pregnancy and childbirth. Most often depicted with the head of a hippopotamus, human arms and breasts and a torch to ward off night-demons, Tawaret was thought to bestow this beast's gentle and relaxed demeanour upon her subjects, along with its strength and calm. Her capacity as protector extended to all people in this world and the next, with her image being carved upon babies' cribs and mummies' headrests alike.

Tengu A race of winged GNOME-like creatures who lived in medieval Japan. They had red hair, piercing black eyes and glittering wings, like those of a humming-bird, and lived in a palace shrouded with mist on Mount Kurama. Intense, aggressive and intelligent, the Tengu were also quite silent, for they communicated solely via thought-power. They were said to take charge of the education of the emperor-elect at least a year prior to his assuming power, schooling him in battle skills and intellectual pursuits. With access to the past, present and future worlds, the Tengu were able to impart universal knowledge of mankind to the man born to lead them.

Terrible Monster A creature, known only by this name, which terrorised Jerusalem in the early eighteenth century. It was almost fifty-foot long, and described as having the head of a lion, elephant's ears and an eagle's beak and talons. Further, it could kill with the venom from its scorpion's tail and was able to resist any attackers, being completely covered with a type of chain-mail seemingly made from mother-of-pearl shell. A strange and virulent beast, local folklore claimed it was born from the blood of murder victims and was trying to avenge itself by killing any citizens who strayed nearby. It was eventually killed itself when a quick-witted fellow threw his spear down its throat, the Terrible Monster's only vulnerable point.

Tezcatlipoca The Aztec god of war. His name meant, literally, 'Smoking Mirror', which referred to the shiny black obsidian used by the Aztec priests to divine the future. He was the tutelary god of warriors and avenged misdeeds. Of terrifying powers and appearance, one of his epithets was 'The Omnipotent'. He had a bear's face and a man's body, albeit with only one leg, a souvenir of his escape from the Underworld when the great iron gates slammed shut on him. Tezcatlipoca carried a huge bronze shield in which were reflected all men's activities. He would often use this shield to play malicious tricks on mortals, blinding and confusing them.

Most importantly, though, Tezcatlipoca was a bitter rival to QUETZLCOATL, whom he irrationally blamed for his own deformity. His mischievous pranks grew in momentum; he seduced women, turned brothers against each other in war, and taught men to covet and steal gold. The people attempted to assuage him with bloodthirsty ritual sacrifices, where men and women had their hearts ripped from their breasts and offered, still beating, to the all-powerful deity. Even this was not sufficient, and Tezcatlipoca's ultimate act of destruction was to introduce the Spanish conquistadores to South America. Originally welcomed as the reborn Quetzlcoatl, these men ultimately brought about the downfall of the Aztec civilisation.

Thor According to Norse mythology, the god of war and thunder. He presided over justice, flinging thunderbolts forged with his magic hammer Mjolnir to earth, to deal with iniquity. Thor was charged by his father ODIN, with keeping order and harmony in the universe. He was powerful and much respected for his omnipotence, as recorded by Adam of Bremen in 1200AD:

> Thor, the mightiest [statue] of the three stands in the centre of the building, with Wodan and Fricco on his right and left. Thor, they say, holds the dominion of the air. He rules over thunder and lightning, winds and rain, clear weather and fertility . . . when plague or famine threatens, sacrifice is offered to him . . .

His wife was Sif, goddess of love, and they lived in his palace Thrudvangr where he received the souls of brave warriors who had fallen in battle. Thor was red-headed, symbolising lightning and the power of fire. He rode in an iron chariot drawn by two goats, and wore a heavy leather belt which doubled his power, and iron gloves which made him invincible. During Ragnarok, the altercation which destroyed the Norse gods, Thor slew the Midgard snake, only to be slain himself by Thiassi, the god of winter.

Thoth The ancient Egyptian god of learning, writing, arithmetic and astronomy. Thought to have ruled Egypt for over 3000 years before being deified, he was responsible for inventing hieroglyphics and for teaching men alchemy, including the transformation of base metals into gold.

He was usually depicted with the head of an ibis or a baboon.

Thoth was an able politician and a great magician, two of his feats having been to negotiate disputes between the gods and to have taught ISIS how to raise OSIRIS from the dead. Thoth was privy to the secret passage of the dead to the Underworld, and thus the Greeks identified him with HERMES.

Thunderbirds Birds always played an important part in American Indian mythology. The leader of the thunderbirds was Wahkeon, and the flapping of his great wings was said to be heard as thunder. Lightning, poetically translated by Spence from the Dakota dialect as 'like the sparks which the buffalo scatters when he scours over a stormy plain' (from *The Myths of the North American Indians*), occurred when Wahkeon's eyes flashed. On his back the leader of the thunderbirds carried a lake, and as he swept overhead the water would spill to the ground below as rain. He was constantly battling with Unktahe, the water god, and the seasons were thought to change with their argument. Some tribes believed Wahkeon to be a great ancestral spirit; all were in awe of him for his powers to control irrigation and, therefore, harvest.

Tiamat In ancient Mesopotamian myth, the universal earth mother took the form of a DRAGON named Tiamat, who lived in the bottomless sea from whence came all life. She was evil-natured and delighted in creating chaos around herself, using the raging winds, burning rain and quicksands at her disposal to confuse. Tiamat's wanton ways were finally challenged by the god of magic, MARDUK. He slew the she-dragon and fashioned heaven and earth from her corpse. However, the chaos and evil in her nature were assumed by the inhabitants of this new world — mankind.

Titania According to Shakespeare's *A Midsummer Night's Dream*, she was the wife of OBERON, King of the Fairies. He describes her as having more regal grace than the rather bawdy MAB, possibly because the belief in Shakespeare's age was that fairies were the same as classical NYMPHS, the attendants of DIANA. In his *Metamorphoses*, Ovid refers to the Queen of the Fairies as being Diana herself.

Tokolosh The South African version of a POLTERGEIST, a strange and sullen spirit who lives beside streams and throws stones into the water on still nights. He is rarely found indoors, preferring to frighten lone travellers on the road. Tokolosh's favourite trick is to leap upon a small animal or bird and strangle it — the panicked cry will unnerve any passer-by. Eric Rosenthal in *They Walk by Night* describes a tokolosh as being:

> . . . not much bigger than a baboon, but is minus the tail, and is perfectly black with a quantity of black hair on his body. He has hands and feet like an ordinary mortal, but is never heard to speak. He shuns the daylight . . . and his deeds are cruel.

Tower of London The list of haunted houses and castles the world over is long indeed. However, among the most famous would be the Tower of London, the centuries-old fortress and prison which has witnessed thousands of imprisonments and executions. Among the more illustrious GHOSTS who have been seen to wander the grounds — especially the grassy sward where the executioner's block once stood — are Anne Boleyn (second wife of Henry VIII), Edward and Richard Plantagenet (the Boy Princes), Catherine Howard, Lady Salisbury, Oliver Cromwell, the Duke of Norfolk, the Earl of Essex, the Earls of Balmerino and Kilmarnock, Lord Lovat and Sir Thomas More. The best known is that of Anne Boleyn; she reportedly walks in the chapel, resplendent in the silk damask gown, scarlet petticoat and pearl headdress she wore to the scaffold — and with her head tucked underneath her arm.

Triton Originally a Greek sea god, son of NEPTUNE, with a human head and the body of a fish. He was depicted by many poets as blowing a huge conch-shell, thus creating the roaring sound of the sea. Wordsworth said he could 'hear old Triton blow his wreathed horn' during a storm at sea, while Spenser in *The Faerie Queene* wrote:

Triton, his trumpet shrill before them blew
For goodly triumph and great jolliment
That made the rocks to roar as they were rent.

The name went on to be used to describe a race of rather rough and wanton mermen (*see* MERMAID). These Tritons were usually seen covered in mussels and seaweed, and when they assumed legs and went ashore they behaved worse than drunken sailors on a spree. Tritons could be identified even in their earthly state by their webbed fingers and strong smell, though their vandalistic behaviour as they lurched around coastal villages usually gave them away first. Back in the water, they were most popularly depicted as escorting water nymphs, or NEREIDS, as they romped through the surf on the backs of dolphins.

Troll A creature of Northern mythology, variously described as either giant or of dwarfed stature. Like SPRIGGANS trolls are responsible for guarding fairy treasure and can change their shape greatly; in fact, according to an old Danish ballad 'Eline of Villenskor', they may sometimes be barely visible:

Out then spake the tiny Troll
No bigger than an Emmet [ant] he.

Most usually described as being stumpy, misshapen and hunch-backed, with red hair, dark breeches and a red cap, they live in hills or mounds and are inclined to steal human babies, leaving CHANGELINGS in their place. Also known as Hill People, trolls shy away from banging noises, supposedly due to the fact that THOR was wont to chase them, flinging his hammer after them to make them run. A glimpse of one is believed to endow a woman with fertility and good fortune, a fortuitous night for sightings being St John's Night, 28th July.

Trows DWARVES found living under hillsides in the Orkney Islands, quite similar to Scandinavian TROLLS. Sometimes gigantic and many-headed, they are very sensitive to light and will be turned to stone if exposed to the sun. There are land-trows and sea-trows, both being disliked, in the main, for their ability to cause children's illnesses. 'Trow tak thee' is a phrase still used by mothers in these parts when they are displeased with their children. Trows love to dance a strange, lop-sided dance called the Henking, and play music on their fiddles on clear nights. Jessie Saxby in *Shetland Traditional Lore* describes the sound as 'peculiarly wild and sweet [with] a lilt of Gaelic as well as Icelandic tunes'. In ancient times they were referred to as 'drows', and believed like dwarves to be gifted artificers in iron and precious metals. In *The Pirate* (1821) Sir Walter Scott wrote:

> . . . I hung about thy neck that gifted chain, which all in our isles know was wrought by no earthly artist, but by the Drows in the secret recesses of their caverns . . .

True Thomas The story of True Thomas and the Queen of Elfland was based on the experiences of the thirteenth-century poet, Thomas the Rhymer. As he lay on a grassy bank he was visited by:

> . . . a ladie gay [with]
> Skirt of the grass-green silk
> Her mantle of the velvet fine.
> At ilka tett of her horse's mane
> Hung fifty silver bells and nine . . .

She was the Queen of Elfland, and trapping Thomas with a kiss, bade him come with her across deserts and rivers of blood to the gardens of Elfland. There he made to pick fruit with her, but she warned him that 'a' the plagues that are in Hell light on the fruit of this countrie'. After serving the Queen for seven years, Thomas returned to the world of mortals where he became famous as a prophet who could not lie. Most noted of his predictions was of the death of Alexander III, recorded in the *Scoticronicon* of Fordun in 1430. Some say that Thomas went back to Elfland and lives there still as poet and advisor to his Queen.

Tsao Wang The amiable Chinese god of domestic fire, also known as Tsao Chun. Usually portrayed as a kindly, plump gentleman surrounded by children, his temple is a small niche close by the cooking stove. From here he keeps a weather eye on the household inhabitants, and takes particular interest in their eating habits. Any person who takes more than his fair share will feel Tsao Wang's finger prodding him in the back, and the fiery flush of guilt in his cheeks.

Tuatha de Danaan Majestic Irish fairies, immortal folk who were born of the goddess Dana. In traditional lore they were said to have come from heaven and to be endowed with many gifts of science and craftsmanship, particularly filigree metal work. For instance, the Cauldron of Dagda, a mighty vessel of beaten and engraved brass which could feed an army and still remain full to the brim, was fashioned by the elder knights of the Tuatha de Danaan.

A brave race of gigantic warriors, they were eventually defeated by the Milesians, and drawing a veil of invisibility across themselves retreated to palaces beneath the ocean or under the Hollow Hills. The Tuatha de Danaan are thought to be eternally young and fair — however, with the coming of Christianity they dwindled in size and substance, moving further towards the spiritual world of the SIDHE, where their activities are visible only to the wise or pure at heart.

Tylweth Teg The master race of Welsh ELVES, also known as the Fair Family. Their blonde hair was the result of inter-marriage with the GWRAGGEDD ANNWN water fairies. The entrances to their palaces are invariably reached underwater, with secret passages concealed in caves and under river banks. As with visiting any fairy domain, mortals must beware the distorted passage of time in the land of Tylweth Teg, when one day actually spans one hundred years. They are generous in bestowing gifts upon people they like, though these may well disappear or become worthless on returning to the everyday world. Their greatest vice is stealing golden-haired babies and young girls.

A well known Welsh story tells of a blonde seamstress, Eilan, who was kidnapped by the Tylweth Teg and seduced by their king. A mortal midwife, summoned to help with the birth of their baby, saw a beautiful queen lying in a sumptuous chamber until she inadvertently rubbed her eye with some magic ointment. With this eye, she suddenly saw the queen was none other than Eilan and the room was really a bare, cold cave. When next the midwife went to market she saw Eilan and greeted her — the fairy king by her side asked with which eye she could see them, and when the woman naively answered, he blinded her with a bulrush.

Typhon The son of TARTARUS and GAEA, the earth mother, Typhon was the spirit of the hurricane in Greek mythology. Horrible to behold, he had the head and torso of a man, but from the thighs downwards was a mass of over one hundred poisonous, coiled snakes. Typhon also had glowing red eyes which never shut, and each fingertip was a snake's head. With a snake's treachery Typhon managed to overcome and savagely maul ZEUS, stripping him of his muscles and leaving him to die. However, Zeus was rescued and he imprisoned Typhon beneath Mount Aetna, where he continues to spit occasional flames in indignation.

Chinese culture named the hot, whirling wind which causes storms 'tai-fun', or 'typhoon', paralleling Typhon's habit of wreaking hurricanes on the other side of the world. James Thomson in his poem *Summer* wrote of:

> . . . the circling Typhon, whirled from point to point
> Exhausting all the rage of all the sky.

Tyr Variously described as a sky god or god of war, Tyr was formed from droplets of sweat shed by the giant YMIR. He was associated with the light of heaven and carried a golden spear which jointly symbolised the dispensation of justice and the outbreak of war. Tyr had only one hand, the other having been bitten off by the evil wolf FENRIR; at Ragnarok, the Day of Judgement, Tyr was to kill and be killed by Fenrir's cousin Garm, the hound-guardian of Hell. Our word 'Tuesday' is an adaptation of Tyr's Day, so named by the Romans who, in turn, equated him with MARS, their god of war.

U

Umi Bozu A most ill-omened spirit which appears to Japanese fishermen should they be in danger from bad weather or an attack by pirates. Thought to have originally been a priest who drowned at sea, Umi Bozu usually appears to have a priest's shaven head and to be praying. Its torso is variously reported as being cloud-like and grey, or long and serpentine like a sea-snake's.

Umkovu A quite horrible beast of African lore, the Umkovu is raised from the bones of a newly dead person by the tribe's witchdoctor to assist in gruesome rites. Most often, it appears with the body of a giant red-eyed spider, which spits venom at its victims. It will emit piercing screams which paralyse all living things and, spinning itself around at great speed, can create blinding dust-storms.

Undine A species of beautiful water NYMPH which haunt several European waters; also known as Ondine. According to folklore, they were created without souls and are usually thought to be the spirits of tragic young women who committed suicide due to a shattered romance. Only by making love to a mortal man can these sad GHOSTS find rest. Though they do not harbour harmful intentions towards such a fellow, he will probably drown as a result of their encounter, for he will try to follow her when she returns to her watery grave.

Men who aspire to be fine musicians will often attempt to meet an undine, for they are renowned for creating lovely, alluring melodies with their harps, strung with enchanted split reeds. Such students would be wise to tie a string about their waists and tie it to a tree on the bank before wading out to the

Undine's rock to listen and learn, thus ensuring they will be able to get back.

Unicorn In the fourth century, Ctesias described these 'certain wild asses' as having 'white bodies, dark red heads, dark blue eyes and a horn on the forehead which is about a foot and a half in length'. Pliny went on to say a unicorn had a horse's body, a deer's head, the feet of an elephant, a boar's tusks and a yard-long horn. However, the most usual view of the unicorn is that of a graceful and beautiful beast of the Middle Ages. Usually depicted as a pretty and proud white horse, its mane and tail were woven with field flowers and it bore a magical whorled horn in the centre of its forehead. This horn was much sought after, for it would change colour when it came into contact with poison. One used as a drinking vessel was kept at Windsor Castle in the sixteenth century and it was valued at £10,000 even then.

According to legend, the unicorn could be captured only by a virgin seated alone under a tree. Upon seeing the maid, the unicorn would become tame and sit at her feet. There, sadly, huntsmen would be able to attack it and the beast would sing a piteously sweet song as it died. Apart from man, the unicorn's only mortal enemy was the lion, with whom they fought for dominion over the wilderness. This animosity is referred to by Spenser in *The Faerie Queene*:

> Like as a lyon whose imperiall powre
> A proud rebellious unicorne defyes.

In some tales the lion represented the sun and the unicorn the moon; in others the unicorn was considered an allegory of Jesus Christ, who willingly entered a virgin's womb and whose single horn was taken to represent the doctrine of a single God. Emblematic of innocence and purity, many writers have waxed poetic about the unicorn. A German ballad contains the lines:

> The unicorn is noble
> God keeps him sage and high

Upon a narrow steep path
Climbing to the sky.

Yeats referred to it as 'a noble beast, a most religious beast [which] dances in the sun'. Loveliest of all is Peter Beagle's tribute:

> . . . her neck was long and slender, making her head seem smaller than it was, and the mane that fell almost to the middle of her back was soft as dandelion fluff and as fine as cirrus. She had pointed ears and thin legs and the long horn above her eyes shone and shivered with its own sea-shell light even in the deepest midnight. She had killed dragons with it and healed a king whose poisoned wound would not close and knocked down ripe chestnuts for bear cubs.
>
> DE VAVRA *Unicorns I Have Known*

The unicorn featured strongly in heraldry, symbolising strength and purity. James I adopted the proud symbol as representing Scotland, a fact referred to by Ariosto:

> Yon lion placed two unicorns between
> That rampant with a silver sword is seen
> Is for the King of Scotland's banner known.
>
> DE VAVRA *Unicorns I Have Known*

In China the unicorn was known as Ki-Lin and was a beast of the gods, rarely seen amongst men. One appeared once before the woman who was pregnant with Confucius to advise her of her good fortune; however, when she foolishly tried to bind the unicorn with silk it disappeared.

Unkulunku The name means 'chief' and refers to the supreme god of Zulu mythology. His epithets include 'The Irresistible', 'He Who Bends Down Even Majesties' and 'He Who Roars So Loud All Nations Are Struck With Terror', the latter referring to his habit of cracking a mighty whip across the sky when angered.

Unkulunku was originally an androgynous being which split into the first man and woman and shared the same name. From them sprang the first human beings. The creator of all life on earth, Unkulunku was also responsible for bringing death to the world. He was said to have sent a lizard and a chameleon to earth to act as his messengers in this regard; the lizard, with his message 'All mankind must die', reached people before the lazy chameleon, who loitered on the way. When the chameleon finally arrived, with his message that eternal life was also possible, people were not prepared to believe him.

Unseelie Court Unlike the Seelie Court which comprises benign fairies, the Unseelie Court of Scotland is made up of evil fairies and malevolent beasts. DUERGARDS, HAGS, MUCHALAVEE, REDCAPS and blood-thirsty water BOGIES are all members of this Unseelie Court, along with the HOST, the latter being the GHOSTS of mortals who have been buried in unconsecrated ground. This unpleasant tribe will take to the skies on stormy nights, swooping on victims foolish enough to be out. These hapless souls are forced to join in the Unseelie Court's wicked activities, hunting or killing other men and beasts with poison and elf-shot.

Urisk A rough, solitary Scottish fairy resembling a SATYR, being half human and half goat; also known as Uruisg. He was very lucky to have around the house, and with his great strength was well equipped to undertake heavy farm work. A rather wistful fairy, he loiters round lonely pools at night and seeks to befriend any stray travellers, who, of course, are terrified by his peculiar appearance.

Uroo A great water-serpent of Aboriginal mythology. Its twisting and turning beneath the earth's surface resulted in the formation of subterranean caves and waterways many miles long. Originally he was believed to have shunned daylight, for his body had no protection against the sun. One day, he came to the surface and mistakenly began to chase the sun, believing it to be a golden kangaroo. However, he could not bear the exposure to the light and he died, leaving only enormous bones and fossils behind to testify to his existence.

Utburd From the Norse, a vengeful infant GHOST rather like the Eskimo ANGIAK. Most often a child who had been left to die because the family could not feed it, or its mother was unwed, the tiny corpses burned for revenge. An Utburd would gather strength for years after its mother's death and would prey upon solitary travellers; sometimes a victim would be warned by the Utburd's cry, or a glimpse of a white owl, which was one of the ghost's favourite guises. Escape was unlikely, though, for the Utburd would marshall its furious energies and grow to the size of a small house, thus completely overcoming its prey.

Utukku The ancient Assyrians were much in awe of Utukku, the name they gave to envious or vengeful spirits. With tremendous powers to terrorise and destroy, Utukku preyed upon the living, and their hauntings were more feared than death itself. One of the main forms was 'alu', a horrid PHANTOM of a leprous man with an arm and a leg missing. If he brushed against a victim or managed to clutch at them, that person would also be stricken with the disease. Another was 'ekimmu' who, rather like the Celtic BANSHEE, appeared outside a home to signal an impending death within by fearful wailing and crying.

Uzume A lusty goddess of Japanese mythology, Uzume was formally referred to as Guardian of the Mysteries of the Sacred Mount of Kagu. She was depicted in flimsy gowns of bamboo grass, gathered on this sacred mountain, held on only by a slender collar and sash. Noted for her obscene dancing, Uzume usually shed any coverings as she twisted and swayed for the amusement of the gods. She was most often present at celebratory banquets or weddings, and it was her merry performance which enticed the sun-goddess AMA-TERASU to emerge from her hiding place, thus restoring light and warmth to the world. The cockerel is sacred to Uzume, and is always heard heralding the goddess' dawn appearance.

V

Valkyries Twelve bold goddesses of Norse mythology. The personal attendants of ODIN and FREYA, they were also known as 'Choosers of the Slain' for they were thought to observe battles, choose which warriors had to fall, and bear them after death to Valhalla. There they waited upon these heroes and served them endless mead and ale from bone cups, or entertained them with music, poetry and tournaments. Despite their awe-inspiring appearance, with horned helmets and breastplates, the Valkyries presented a truly beautiful sight as they galloped overhead on their winged steeds. The three main Valkyries were named Mista, Sangrida and Hilda, and they all had flashing blue eyes and long, fair plaits.

Vampire A blood-sucking creature from the eerie world of the undead. The vampire would lie as a corpse during the day, arising at night to feast upon the blood of an unsuspecting victim, preferably an unsuspecting virgin. It thus was able to replenish its own immortality, and as the victim waned and died he became another vampire in turn. The original role models for vampirism included Prince Vlad of Transylvania, and the Countess Elizabeth Bathory, who elected to bathe in virgins' blood to retain her skin's beauty.

Vampires were most frequently portrayed as having bats' wings and wolves' paws, with a menacing human face distinguished by sharp white teeth, pointed ears and foul breath. They could also assume the form of a flea or a spider, the better to attack sleepers in the back or neck. Vampires could be repelled by a bramble or hawthorn hedge, and would flee from holy water or a crucifix. They would not pass over a threshold where mustard-seed had been spread, nor were they partial to garlic. Detailed instructions are offered in old tomes as to how to dispose of this noxious creature, a stake through the heart being the most efficient.

Vegetable Lamb The sad story of this quaint little beast was told by sailors returning from exploring islands in the Caspian Sea. They described a small, many-budded shrub called the 'basometz' or 'woolly lamb' by the Tartars. When the buds ripened and opened a small woolly lamb was to be seen, and often a shrub would be bobbing and weaving, with several dozen of the creatures wriggling away. For as long as the lambs could graze on foliage within their reach all remained well. However, inevitably they would exhaust their food supply and, unable to move because their umbilical cord was grafted to the stem, they died and withered away. The fleeces of the Vegetable Lamb were picked by native women and kept as pillow stuffing.

Viracocha The supreme Mayan god, a sun god who created the first man and woman, a storm god and a god of water. He was also referred to as Universal Father and as 'The Beginning Of All Things'. Popular legend claims he lived in Lake Titicaca. From there he arose and carved the sun, moon and stars from marble, before setting them in the firmament. Displeased with his first attempts at creating mankind, Viracocha destroyed the world with a deluge before trying again.

Viracocha was known to wander occasionally amongst the people, checking their behaviour and offering advice on how to pray and how to tend crops. As he was likely to appear in the guise of a beggar, the Indians took care to treat all vagabonds charitably. Viracocha returned to Lake Titicaca from where he continues to shoot forth lightning bolts to warn of danger, and to shed tears which appear as hail.

Virikas Small, unpleasant GHOSTS found in India. Never more than eighteen inches tall, they are distinguished by their flaming red colour and horribly pointed, bloodstained teeth. Rather like

VAMPIRES, virikas gibber excitedly outside a house where a family member is about to die. They may only be repelled by a shaycana (medicine man), though they will sometimes leave a family in peace if a small shrine is erected in their honour and daily gifts of flowers and spices are burned as offerings.

Vishnu Along with BRAHMA and SHIVA he forms the divine triad of Hinduism in India; also known as The Preserver. He is the god of light and one of his epithets is 'He Who Pervades', referring to the way light infiltrates every part of the universe. Vishnu is married to LAKSHMI and is usually depicted as a handsome youth with dark blue skin and four arms. In his four hands he holds a conch shell, a discus, a club and a lotus. With Lakshmi he usually travels about the earth on the golden-winged GARUDA, though he appears on earth during regular incarnations, one of which was as Krishna.

Vodayany Water IMPS prevalent in Russia, also known as Vodyanioi. They dwell at the bottom of millponds and lakes in palaces decorated with plunder from shipwrecks. These palaces are illuminated by magic crystals which burn with a green light, and the glow from these can be glimpsed in the depths of the water on a still night. When the millwheel in a lake turns, the vodayany can be heard threshing and snarling as their waterways are disturbed. Their palaces are staffed with human souls who became slaves of the vodayany when they were drowned. Those most likely to meet such a fate are said to be people who bathe after dark without wearing a crucifix around their neck. In the past, Russian villagers have tried to appease the vodayany by offering a lamb or horse as a sacrifice, but they remain fond of snatching unwary passers-by, often taking the form of a floating log.

Vodayany are singularly ugly, with long green hair, red eyes and bloated faces. The men have beards which change colour as the moon moves through its phases. Their skin is spongy and moist, with the pallor of a corpse. When they sit on the shore, they always leave a small puddle of water behind. Vodayany age as the moon proceeds through its cycle, becoming young, vigorous and hungry with the new moon.

Vritra In Indian Hindu mythology, Vritra was a god of water and lived in clouds which shielded the sun. Hence his usual epithet was 'The Obstructor' or 'The Encloser', referring to his damp embrace. Sometimes portrayed as a DRAGON or as a snake, Vritra was extremely jealous of the other gods, who were more beautiful and intelligent than he. Aided by the storm demons he attempted to overthrow them by damming all the rivers, only to be successfully challenged by Indra, the great dragon-slayer. Indra and Vritra reached a truce whereby neither man nor god was allowed to make a retaliatory attack upon Vritra using metal, or any forged material. Vritra thought he was safe, until Indra destroyed him with thunderbolts and a cloud of poisoned sea-foam.

W

Waff In Yorkshire, northern England, the name for a person's ghostly double, or WRAITH. It is most often an omen of death, being seen only by the doomed mortal twin or a close friend. The only way to avert the effect of a waff is to scream or laugh loudly in its face, then say:

> What's thou doin' here?
> What's thou doin' here?
> Thou's after no good, I'll go bail!
> Get thy ways yom with thee!
> Get thy ways yom!
>
> TRADITIONAL

As with FETCHES and DOPPELGANGERS this spell will cause the waff to melt away, embarrassed by its inability to terrify its victim.

Water Leaper Best known in Wales, where it is called Llamhigyn y Dwr, this ugly creature preyed upon both men and animals. Eye-witnesses have described it as a giant grey toad with a serpent's tail and bat's wings. It also had two needle-sharp venomous fangs, rather like a VAMPIRE's. The Water Leaper was wont to jump from the shallows and fly at a sheep which had strayed by, bite it and drag the dazed creature back to the depths, where it would feast on the carcass at leisure. Its presence would be heralded by an unearthly scream, and the only part of its prey left untouched would be the fleece, found downstream several days later. A sole fisherman who took his dinghy out at twilight on a deserted lake was likely to suffer the same fate, with only his indigestible hat and boots reappearing the next day.

Water Wraith A quite formidable demon found in Scottish lochs and braes, the water wraith always dresses in green, dragging a train of damp weeds behind her. With her withered skin and scowling expression, she is sure to unnerve any witnessing her emerging from the shallows, and she is likely to order any spying on her to enter the water, too. These creatures usually appear to those on their way home from having a few drinks at the pub.

Wayland Smith An ELF who lived in a cave, or crombech, in Berkshire in England. Sir Walter Scott reported his popularity with the local people as an excellent blacksmith:

> Here lived a supernatural smith, who would shoe a traveller's horse for a 'consideration'. His fee was sixpence, and if more was offered, he was offended.
>
> *Kenilworth*

Wendigo Giant GHOSTS of Indian legend, also known as Windigo, and said to frequent the Great Lakes district of northern Canada. There, they lived in the forest and preyed upon human beings, especially hunters who had strayed from their usual hunting grounds. Wendigo had an insatiable appetite for human flesh, despite being extremely thin. Their hearts could be seen through their transparent ribcages, made of ice, and their twisted mouths were like freezing caverns, issuing a sound like the lonely whistling of the wind. Vicious by nature they would torment their victim with this mournful sound until he ran, demented, straight towards a precipice or tree, where the wendigo was lying in wait.

The Indians had a horror of cannibalism and it is said that the legend of the wendigo dates from times of famine when starving tribesmen preyed upon each other. Those who survived were thought to have entered a pact with evil spirits of the forest who empowered them to kill their victims. One of the first indications of possession by a wendigo was for the victim to vomit, and if this did not stop with the SHAMAN's ministerings the person was considered dangerous.

Werewolf Perhaps the origins of lycanthropy — people turning into beasts by night, then back again at dawn — were rooted in pagan Greek rituals and beliefs. Herodotus described sorcerers who assumed the form of wolves, and Pliny related that the eldest son of the Antaeus family was transformed into a wolf for nine years. In popular legend, a werewolf was dangerous and vicious in its bestial form, massacring livestock and devouring infants. During the day, however, it was most likely an inoffensive villager.

The werewolf's tail was particularly valued by the Romans as a love charm, for they believed the recipient would change during the full moon, as did the werewolf. It was well-nigh impossible to capture a werewolf by night, for they were extremely fleet of foot and their skin was bullet-proof. They were more often identified during the day by a wound sustained the previous evening. An example came from Africa, where it was once reported that a hyena wearing gold earrings was shot as it attacked the village, and the next day a woman was found to be severely wounded in the hip.

White Ladies A type of ghostly fairy found frequently in castles and old houses in England and France. They also haunt waterways and are often seen by fords and bridges, where they will ask a passer-by to dance. If they are treated with courtesy, all will be well; but if the fellow churlishly refuses them, they will throw him into a briar patch, or into the water below.

White Ladies are strikingly beautiful. One legend has it that the lovely Queen Guenevere was originally a white phantom, or 'Gwenhwyvar'. Other scholars claim it was once the sad custom to sacrifice pretty young girls by waterways to appease the river spirits, and that White Ladies are their wistful GHOSTS. In his *Hierarchie*, William of Auvergne (1248) spoke of them thus:

> One kind of these the Italians 'fata' name;
> The French calle 'fee'; we 'sybils'; and the same
> Others 'White Dames'; and of those that them have seen
> 'Night Ladies' some, of which Habundia's queen.

Throughout Europe, White Ladies are also thought to be the ghosts of women who were murdered or ill-treated in life. An example is found in the White Lady of Hohenzollern, in Germany, which is widely believed to be the ghost of Princess Bertha of Rosenberg. During her lifetime she was cruelly treated by her family, and her husband was murdered, as was she. She now returns, dressed in white with a white widow's coif, and sits watch by ailing children. If she plucks at the keys hanging from her waist, the patient will fail; though if sweet soup and carp are given to the poor in her name, she will spare the child.

Whowie In the Dreamtime, Australian Aborigines ascribed the losses of livestock or children to marauding whowies. Also known as yowies, these were fearsome huge creatures of the night, with a body like an ant and the head of a giant lizard. The whowie's mouth was large enough to swallow a grown man with a single gulp and it had a long, thick tail, like a goanna's, which was powerful enough to fell trees in its wake. Being ungainly, it could only strike under cover of night, spending its days slumbering deep in caves underground. The Aborigines eventually rid themselves of whowies by smoking them out of their caves by day, when the creatures were cumbersome and sleepy and could be attacked with spears and fireballs.

Wichtlein A German word which comes from the Saxon *unsele wiht* (uncanny creature); also known as wichtlin or wights. Chaucer in *The Canterbury Tales* used the term thus:

> I crouche thee from elves and fro wightes . . .

These house spirits are most often to be found in Germany where they live behind walls and under the floors of houses. Like their cousins the KOBOLDS, they will knock or tap three times to communicate with mortals; most commonly, such a signal indicates the death of the head of the household. Usually amiable and industrious, wichtlein are, however, fearsomely ugly. They have been known to fall in love with young mortal girls, especially pretty maidservants, and to appear before them to declare their affection. Inevitably the girl has been horrified by her would-be suitor's appearance and has screamed — the offended wichtlein has then ransacked the house, tugging at children's hair, mixing sugar and salt together and filling the garden with puddles.

Wichtlein also live beneath mounds or tree-stumps in the garden, and they will frighten away tramps and other unwanted visitors. They are, however, frightened of water and will avoid streams or creeks and hide when it is raining. This is because, with the coming of Christianity, misinformed zealots doused kindly wichtlein with holy water to make them disappear. Similarly a mast-head, anchor or other ship's artefact will repel wichtlein if displayed prominently near a house.

Wilde Beste Described in medieval bestiaries as a creature rather like a large, curly-haired spaniel, with the head of a lion, the wilde beste was ferocious in protecting her offspring. These she carried clinging to the fur on her back, shielded by her long feathery tail. Travellers told that the wilde beste would eat her babies herself, rather than allow them to be captured and taken back to civilisation.

Will O'The Wisp The curious ghostly light resembling a flame, flickering in remote or marshy areas, is traditionally referred to as *Ignis Fatuus* (a fatuous or foolish fire). Witness this comment from Shakespeare's *Henry IV, Pt I*:

> When thou ran'st up Gadshill in the night to catch my horse, if I did not think thou hadst been an ignis fatuus on a ball of wild fire, there's no purchase in money.

Throughout Europe these ghostly lights are also known as JACK O'LANTERN, fairy fire and corpse candles, or corpse lights. Often they were thought to be the spirits of people who died in the marshes where they appeared, and to bring death to any who followed them. The Germans thought they were glowing candles carried by martyrs, and the Finns called it LIEKKIO, or 'little flaming one', referring to the GHOSTS of innocent children who became lost in the woods. Milton called it 'Friar's Lantern' and other sources say the lights are lamp-carrying BOGIES on their way to frighten bad children. However, the most common explanation found in the British Isles is that it is the flame-carrying spirit of a blacksmith. In life, this smith had been named Will and had led such a debauched life on earth that he was condemned to spend eternity wandering the chilly twilight. The Devil offered Will some burning coals from the fires of Hell to warm his hands, on the proviso he lure lonely travellers to their demise in swamps, or by cliffs.

Wiyot The Red Indian denizens of California claimed this was the god who fathered all men. He ruled supreme in the heavens until he was challenged by the evil trickster god, Coyote. Coyote stirred discontent amongst Wiyot's subjects, so the mighty sky-god swept his hand southwards from the existing land beneath him, as far as he could see. Thus was the great land mass of North and South America created, and the first tribes were able to scatter over the continent and escape Coyote's mischief-making. Unfortunately, many men were attracted by Coyote and chose to run along the earth and burrow in the ground as he did, and learn cunning, sly behaviour, rather than emulate the all-seeing wisdom of the sky-god.

Wotan The ancient European god of battle, also known as the master of Fury and The Wild Huntsman. A violent god who trafficks in bloodsports and battle, he was thought to thunder across the skies with his spectral hounds in search of human souls to capture. Wotan appeared before trouble or skirmishes, taking the form of a wild north wind which swept across the land. He would also be present at the battlefield and took delight in plunging his sword into the first casualty. When peace came, Wotan would be bored and fretful and would be found plaguing livestock or herding wild deer and horses over ravines to amuse himself. In Germany he was called Woden, and his name is still commemorated in our 'Wednesday', or Woden's Day. A cruel god, he expected copious sacrifices; thus, in his *Die*

Walkure Wagner described trees by battlefields as being hung with animal hides, and the cloaks of those slain as tributes to Woden. (*See also* ODIN).

Wraith According to superstition in the Scottish Highlands, the appearance of a spectre to a person shortly about to die. Wraiths are said to appear at a distance, and to be an exact likeness of the victim. One of the most noteworthy stories was that of poet Percy Bysshe Shelley; he claimed to have seen his own wraith before stepping into a dinghy to be ferried across the Bay of Spezia in Italy. The boat did indeed capsize and the poet was drowned that day. As with FETCHES and doubles, popular theory accounting for wraiths is that they are, in fact, the soul of the person about to die. Folklore has long held that this soul must be allowed to escape from the mortal remains, and not be trapped in death, else it will be unable to rest.

Wulver A quaint and quite benevolent Scottish beast, whose fearsome appearance belies his mild nature. With the body of a stocky human, the wulver has a wolf's head and brown fur on its arms and legs. It does not share the wolf's predatory habits, preferring to sun itself on a river bank and idly catch fish for its dinner. It has even been known to leave fish on the doorstep of a poor or needy family. In her *Shetland Traditional Lore* Jessie Saxby tells us that:

> [The wulver's] home was a cave dug out of a steep knowe, half way up a hill. He didn't molest folk if folk didn't molest him. He was fond of fishing and had a small rock in the deep water, which is known to this day as the 'Wulver's Stone'.

Y

Yale *see* EALE

Yallery Brown An evil-natured fairy discovered by a Lincolnshire farmer named Tom Tiver. The fairy was lying half-buried beneath a stone, all tangled up in its long golden hair and beard. When freed, the fairy promised to help Tom in his work, provided he was never thanked for doing so. The farm prospered as a result, although its very success caused the downfall of the neighbour's business. When Tom saw this, he went to Yallery Brown, and in asking him to cease working so hard, inadvertently thanked him. Yallery Brown immediately became indignant and dangerous, wreaking havoc upon Tom's farm as he sang:

> Work as thou will
> Thou'lt never do well;
> Work as thou mayst
> Thou'lt never gain grist;
> For harm and mischance and Yallery Brown
> Thou's let out thyself from under the stone.

BRIGGS *The Fairies in Tradition and Literature*

Yara A disagreeable GHOST found in eastern Russia. Like her counterparts the LORELEI, she is thought to be the vengeful spirit of a maiden murdered by her sweetheart. Since then, she has preyed upon other young men, luring them to the water's edge in an attempt to drown them. It is thought possible to avert Yara's spell by carrying a small shell, into which the lad's mortal sweetheart has sung a love-song. The shell will hold the tender melody and, should the young man be tempted by Yara's song, he should hold the shell to his ear so as to hear his sweetheart's voice, instead.

Yena A hideous GHOST who lives in African tombs and preys upon the newly dead, ripping at shrouds, plundering jewels and tearing flesh. It is thought to have given rise to the name for a wild dog, 'hyena', and this beast's horrible howling usually precedes the ghost's appearance. The yena can assume many different shapes, often seeming to be a woman with claws, a mane and pointed ears. In any guise, the yena possesses eyes made of granite, and if a mortal steals one he will be able to foretell the future. The only thing which will deter a yena is a barking dog, but even this is fallible for it can hypnotise any animal with its stony eyes and thus render it powerless.

Yen-lo-wang The Chinese god of the dead, also known as Yen-wang. He presided over the Buddhist hell, a grim place named Yellow Springs. There, he decided when and how mortals would die and what fate awaited their souls in the afterlife. Yen-lo-wang was a formidable and pitiless judge, for, according to Buddhist ethos, a wheel of rebirth meant eternal punishment was impossible as the victim would eventually be reincarnated, and thus released from his punishment. To compensate, Yen-lo-wang would ensure that any such punishments were truly horrible.

Yeti The Sherpa natives of the Himalayas named this creature 'Yeh-teh' (a rocky place), for the yeti is believed to hibernate much of the year in remote areas. Also known as the Abominable Snowman, this is a large creature with reddish fur, a pointed head and a surprisingly shrill cry. Explorers, notably Sir Edmund Hillary, found and photographed the beast's footprints. These were large and five-toed and, judging by the depth of the tracks, indicated that the yeti was a substantial weight and at least six-foot tall. Thought to be quite shy and non-aggressive, yeti would not attack unless frightened, preferring to run away. In very cold weather, yeti have been heard further down the hillside near the villages, foraging for left-over food. Some experts say the yeti is a type of enormous bear which walks on its hind legs; another school of thought likens the beast to the Sasquatch, or big-footed ape-human of North America.

Ymir The father of all gods and men in Norse mythology. An enormous giant who arose, alone, from the melted ice and steam of primeval chaos, he was suckled by four milky streams which flowed from the cow Audhumla. While he slept, a man and a woman grew out of his arm and sons from his feet. These became the evil Frost Giants, whose steaming breath in turn eventually begat the gods ODIN, Vili and Ve, who slew Ymir after a tremendous battle. These three tossed Ymir's carcass into an enormous abyss, from whence it was used as raw material for the formation of the earth; his blood became the salty seas, his bones the mountains, his teeth the rocks, his skull the heavens, and his hair and beard every sort of plant and tree. The first mortal man and woman were, according to some sources, created from maggots feeding upon his flesh, though others say these insects metamorphosed to become the first fairies, or nature spirits.

Yumboes Enchanting fairies of African mythology who are said to frequent the Pap Mountains. Less than two-foot high, they have pearly skin and silver hair, and they dance and feast by moonlight. Thomas Keightley in his *Fairy Mythology* wrote:

> When evening's shades o'er the Goree's Isle extend
> The nimble Yumboes from the Paps descend,
> Slyly approach the natives' huts and steal
> With secret hand the powdered cous-cous meal.

Z

Zeus The supreme deity of Greek mythology, Zeus was the usurping son of the Titans CRONUS and RHEA. The Greek epic poet Hesiod, eighth century BC, wrote in his *Theogony* that Zeus was:

> ... wise in counsel, father of gods and man, under whose thunder the broad earth quivers ...

He was reared in a secret cave on Crete and suckled by a she-goat so as to avoid the wrath of his father, who had eaten all his siblings. On maturity, he overthrew his father and, with his wife HERA, was enthroned upon Olympus to rule the other deities. A composite figure, he was variously the sun god, rain god, and god of thunder. Fidelity was not Zeus' strong point and he had many liaisons with both mortals and other goddesses, and appeared in many guises to father children. For example, with Danae he was a golden shower of rain; with Leda, a swan; with Alcmene, he appeared as her husband; and with Europa, he took the form of a bull.

Zeus was held in high regard by the Greeks, who staged the Olympic Games in his honour and invoked his presence at all other important occasions, including weddings and legal judgements, though his temper was feared. Zeus was generally depicted as a lusty, bearded man in full maturity, lounging against the clouds and clasping a handful of lightning bolts which he flung to earth if displeased. The Roman god whose nature paralleled Zeus' was JUPITER, though Zeus also appeared in his own right at the centre of the Orphic cult, and was described as:

> ... the foundation of the earth and the starry sky ... male and

immortal woman . . . the beginner of all things, the god within the dazzling light.

Ziz An enormous bird, revered by the ancient Hebrews. Rather like the ROC in appearance, it had a great beak like an albatross and, when its feet were on the ground, its head grazed the clouds. God was said to have created Ziz on the fifth day and to have charged him to use his wings to shelter and shade the earth when needed. Although the bird's nature was mild, its very presence threatened the earth, for each time an egg hatched the pieces of falling shell would flatten forests and cities. For this reason, God encouraged Ziz to fly high above the earth; the huge bird's wings may be seen each evening as they slowly move to cover the sun, and its cry may be heard as the whistling wind.

Bibliography

Arrowsmith, N. and G. Moorse. *A Field Guide to the Little People* Macmillan, London, 1977.

Aubrey, J. *Miscellanies* 5th edn, Reeves & Turner, London, 1890.

Brewer, Revd E.C. *Dictionary of Phrase and Fable* Cassell, London, 1981.

Briggs, K.M. *The Fairies in Tradition and Literature* Routledge & Kegan Paul, London, 1967.

Briggs, K.M. *Abbey Lubbers, Banshees and Boggarts* Kestrel Books, 1979.

Campbell, J.F. *Popular Tales of the West Highlands* Vol.IV, ed. A. Gardner, Paisley & London, 1890.

Cotterrell, A. *A Dictionary of World Mythology* Perigee Books, New York, 1979.

de Vavra, R. *Unicorns I Have Known* William Morrow & Co., New York, 1983.

Dickinson, P. *The Flight of the Dragons* Harper & Row, New York, 1979.

Duffy, M. *The Erotic World of Faery* Hodder & Stoughton, London, 1972.

Evans, B. *Dictionary of Mythology* Franklin Watts, London, 1970l.

Haining, P. *A Dictionary of Ghosts* Robert Hale, London, 1982.

Henderson, W. *Folklore of the Northern Counties* Folklore Society, London, 1879.

Hope, M. *Practical Celtic Magic* The Aquarian Press, Wellingborough UK, 1987.

Hoult, J. *Dragons — Their History and Symbolism* Gothic Image, Somerset UK, 1987.

Hunt, R. *Popular Romances of the West of England* Chatto & Windus, London, 1923.

Huxley, F. *The Dragon* Thames & Hudson, London, 1979.

Kirk, R. *The Secret Commonwealth of Elves, Fauns and Fairies* 1691; republished Mackay, Stirling, Scotland, 1933.

Lloyd Jones, H. *Mythical Beasts* Duckworth & Co., London, 1980.

Lurker, M. *Dictionary of Gods, Goddesses, Devils and Demons* Routledge & Kegan Paul, London, 1984.

McPherson, J.M. *Primitive Beliefs in the North East of Scotland* Longmans, London, 1929.

Maple, E. *Supernatural England* Robert Hale, London, 1977.

Newall, V. ed. *The Witch Figure* Routledge & Kegan Paul, London, 1973.

Page M. and R. Ingpen. *Out of This World* Weldon Publishing, Sydney, Australia, 1986.

Parker, D. and J. *The Immortals* Barrie & Jenkins, London, 1976.

Ramsay Smith, W. *Myths of the Australian Aborigines* Geo. G. Harrap, London, 1977.

Readers Digest Association Ltd. *Folklore, Myths and Legends of Britain* London, 1977.

Rovin, J. *The Fantasy Almanac* E.P. Dutton, New York, 1979.

Sawyers M. and W. Reusswig. *The Book of the Far East* Odhams Press, London, 1970.

Saxby, J.M.E. *Shetland Traditional Lore* Norwood Editions, 1974.

Sikes, W. *British Goblins* Sampson Low, London, 1880.

Spence, L. *The Myths of the North American Indians* Geo. G. Harrap, London, 1914.

Spence, L. *The Outlines of Mythology* Watts & Co., London, 1944.

Spence, L. *British Fairy Origins* Watts & Co., London, 1946.

Spencer Robinson, H. *The Encyclopedia of Myths and Legends of All Nations* Kaye & Ward, London, 1962.

Teale, S. *Giants* Rufus Publications, London, 1979.

Time Life Books. *The Enchanted World* Sydney, Australia, 1985.

Tongue, R. *Somerset County Folklore* Vol.VIII, ed. K.M. Briggs. Folklore Society County Publications, London, 1965.

Tongue, R. *Forgotten Folk Tales of the English Counties* Routledge & Kegan Paul, London, 1970.

Vinycomb, J. *Fictitious and Symbolic Creatures in Art* Gale Research Co., Detroit, 1969.

White, C. *A History of Irish Fairies* The Mercier Press, Dublin, 1976.

Wilde, Lady. *Ancient Legends, Mystic Charms and Superstitions of Ireland* Ward & Downey, London, 1887.